The Irony of Heidegger

Continuum Studies in Continental Philosophy
Series Editor: James Fieser, University of Tennessee at Martin, USA

Continuum Studies in Continental Philosophy is a major monograph series from Continuum. The series features first-class scholarly research monographs across the field of Continental philosophy. Each work makes a major contribution to the field of philosophical research.

Adorno's Concept of Life, Alastair Morgan
Badiou and Derrida, Antonio Calcagno
Badiou, Balibar, Ranciere, Nicholas Hewlett
Deconstruction and Democracy, Alex Thomson
Deleuze and Guattari's Philosophy of History, Jay Lampert
Deleuze and the Meaning of Life, Claire Colebrook
Deleuze and the Unconscious, Christian Kerslake
Derrida and Disinterest, Sean Gaston
Encountering Derrida, edited by Simon Morgan-Wortham and Allison Weiner
Foucault's Heidegger, Timothy Rayner
Heidegger and the Place of Ethics, Michael Lewis
Heidegger Beyond Deconstruction, Michael Lewis
Heidegger's Contributions to Philosophy, Jason Powell
Husserl's Phenomenology, Kevin Hermberg
The Irony of Heidegger, Andrew Haas
Levinas and Camus, Tal Sessler
Merleau-Ponty's Phenomenology, Kirk M. Besmer
The Philosophy of Exaggeration, Alexander Garcia Düttmann
Sartre's Ethics of Engagement, T. Storm Heter
Sartre's Phenomenology, David Reisman
Ricoeur and Lacan, Karl Simms
Who's Afraid of Deleuze and Guattari? Gregg Lambert

The Irony of Heidegger
An Essay

Andrew Haas

continuum

Continuum International Publishing Group
The Tower Building   80 Maiden Lane
11 York Road   Suite 704
London SE1 7NX   New York NY 10038

www.continuumbooks.com

First published 2007

British Library Cataloguing-in-Publication Data
A catalogue record for this book is available from the British Library.

ISBN-10: HB: 0-8264-9796-9
ISBN-13: HB: 978-0-8264-9796-3

Library of Congress Cataloguing-in-Publication Data
Haas, Andrew.
   The irony of Heidegger: an essay/Andrew Haas.
     p. cm.
   Includes bibliographical references.
   ISBN-13: 978-0-8264-9796-3 (HB)
   ISBN-10: 0-8264-9796-9 9HB)
   1. Heidegger, Martin, 1889–1976. 2. Fallacies (Logic) 3. Heidegger, Martin, 1889–1976.
Sein und Zeit. 4. Ontology. 5. Space and time. I. Title.
   B3279.H49H233 2007
   13–dc22
                              2007020193

Typeset by BookEns Ltd, Royston, Herts.
Printed and bound in Great Britain by Biddles Ltd, King's Lynn, Norfolk

Contents

Acknowledgements   vii

Abbreviations   ix

Apologia   xi

Introduction   1

1 Sham of authenticity   5

2 *Ta megala panta episphalē*   47

3 Only such art is under consideration here   70

4 Still far from pondering the essence of action   103

5 In a lofty sense ambiguous   142

6 Only a god can still save us   159

Post-scriptum   167

Bibliography   169

Index   175

Acknowledgements

Portions of this text were originally presented as a course in the School of Philosophy at the University of New South Wales, Sydney. Other portions were formulated into a paper proposal for the meetings of the American Society for Phenomenology and Existential Philosophy, otherwise known as SPEP, but never presented. Sections were finally presented at Monash University in Melbourne, at the Australian Society for Continental Philosophy in Sydney, at Bonn University and at Bochum University. Versions of chapters also appeared as articles in *Dialektik* and in *Philosophy, Art, History, Future*.

Research support came in the form of a travel grant from the Humanities Research Program, a Europe Fellowship, and the kind permission to take one semester's leave-without-pay, all from the University of New South Wales, Sydney. Additional institutional support was provided by the University of Bonn.

I am especially indebted to my students at UNSW and members of the Heidegger reading group of the Sydney School. I must also thank: Leander Scholz and Thomas Schneider for the essential *Diskussionen*. And Sarah Campbell of Continuum Publishing, not only for publishing this work in hardback, but for insisting I cut the original to 90,000 words, thereby avoiding verbosity. Special thanks also goes to Helen Lambert for her suggestions, encouragement and continual critique.

Abbreviations

BT	M. Heidegger, *Being and Time*, SUNY Press, 1996; *Sein und Zeit*, Niemeyer, 1993.
BOT	F. Nietzsche, *Birth of Tragedy*, Vintage Books, 1967.
BW	*Basic Writings*, Harper and Row, 1977.
CPR	I. Kant, *Critique of Pure Reason*, St. Martin's Press, 1965.
EH	J.-P. Sartre, *L'Existentialisme est un humanisme*, Gallimard, 1996.
FD	M. Heidegger, *Die Frage nach dem Ding*, Niemeyer, 1962.
GA (plus volume number)	M. Heidegger, *Gesamtausgabe*, Klostermann.
HOP	H.-G. Gadamer, 'Martin Heidegger's One Path', *Reading Heidegger from the Start*, SUNY Press, 1994.
HW	M. Heidegger, *Holzwege*, Klostermann, 1950.
IM	M. Heidegger, *Introduction to Metaphysics*, Yale University Press, 2000; *Einführung in die Metaphysik*, Niemeyer, 1987.
KPM	M. Heidegger, *Kant and the Problem of Metaphysics*, Indiana University Press, 1997.
KSA	F. Nietzsche, *Kritische Studienausgabe*, de Gruyter, 1980.
LH	M. Heidegger, 'Letter on Humanism', *Basic Writings*, Harper and Row, 1977; *Über den Humanismus*, Klostermann, 1991.
NHG	M. Schapiro, 'A Note on Heidegger and van Gogh', *Theory and Philosophy of Art*, Braziller, 1994.
NhP	W. Heisenberg, 'Das Naturbild der heutigen Physik', *Jahrbuch 1953*, Max-Planck-Gesellschaft, 1954.
PLT	M. Heidegger, 'Origin of the Work of Art', *Poetry, Language, Thought*, Harper and Row, 1971.
PM	M. Heidegger, *Pathmarks*, Cambridge University Press, 1998; *Wegmarken*, GA9, Klostermann, 1967.
PP	W. Heisenberg, *Physics and Philosophy*, Harper and Row, 1958.
QCT	M. Heidegger, *The Question Concerning Technology and Other Essays*, Harper & Row, 1977; 'Die Frage nach der Technik', *Die Technik und die Kehre*, Neske, 1991.
RR	M. Heidegger, '*Die Selbstbehauptung der deutschen Universität*', Klostermann, 1983; 'The Self-Assertion of the German University', *Review of Metaphysics*, 38, 1985.

TP	J. Derrida, *The Truth in Painting*, University of Chicago Press, 1987; *La vérité en peinture*, Flammerion, 1978.
UKR	M. Heidegger, *Der Ursprung des Kunstwerkes*, Reclam, 1960.
WCT	M. Heidegger, *What is Called Thinking?*, Harper & Row, 1968; *Was heißt denken?*, Niemeyer, 1984.
WN	M. Heidegger, 'The Word of Nietzsche: "God Is Dead"', *The Question Concerning Technology and Other Essays*, Harper & Row, 1977; 'Nietzsches Wort, "Gott ist tot"', *Holzwege*, Klostermann, 1950.
ZS	M. Heidegger; *Zollikonen Seminane*, Klostermann, 1987.

Apologia

For the book that follows, I am of course solely responsible, and I offer it for what it is worth. If I intended to prove that Heidegger is being ironic, I probably have not quite succeeded. And some have come to the conclusion that this work, however interesting, is dead wrong. The readers who are willing to settle for interesting, may therefore find here something suitable.

If I had intended however, to demonstrate that Heidegger is not being ironic, but serious, it may be that I have equally failed – although perhaps no one can accuse me of that which they accuse him. And the *ressentiment* that some readers feel against Heidegger, I hope will not be used against me.

Still, I wanted to write this book neither as a dismissal nor as a simple defence, and I have tried not to pass judgement, although here again some insisted that I take sides – and I am probably guilty of failing to do so clearly enough for them, although there is certainly some value in clarifying the charges before carrying out the sentence.

Nevertheless, I make no claim to have invented these charges, nor to have been the first to raise them against philosophy or a particular philosopher; and whether Heidegger escapes or not, does nothing to ameliorate the threat.

If certain readers therefore find my reading of Heidegger a mere curiosity, if some find my examination of his case somewhat biased, or my arguments not quite convincing, and if they therefore fail to acknowledge the threat of irony, the fault lies surely not with Heidegger, but with me.

For this I offer an *apologia*, and I can only repeat that I have here just tried to raise the possible threat of irony to the point where it no longer simply escapes notice, at least to the extent this is possible.

dio dē pas anēr spoudaios tōn ontōn spoudaiōn peri pollou dei mē grapsas pote en anthrōpois eis phthonon kai aporian katabalei. Heni dē ek toutōn dei gignōskein logō, hotan idē tis tou suggrammata gegrammena eite en nomois nomothetou eite en allois tisin hatt' oun, hōs ouk ēn toutō tauta spoudaiotata, eiper est' autos spoudaios, keitai de pou en chōra tē kallistē tōn toutou; ei de ontōs autō taut' espoudasmena en grammasin etethē, 'ex ara dē toi epeita', theoi men ou, brotoi de 'phrenas ōlesan autoi'.

For this reason no serious man will ever think of writing about serious realities for the general public so as to make them a prey to envy and perplexity. In a word, it is an inevitable conclusion from this that when anyone sees anywhere the written work of anyone, whether that of a lawgiver in his laws or whatever it may be in some other form, the subject treated cannot have been his most serious concern – that is, if he is himself a serious man. His most serious interests have their abode somewhere in the noblest region of the field of his activity. If, however, he really was seriously concerned with these matters and put them in writing, 'then surely' not the gods, but mortals 'have utterly blasted his wits'.

(Plato, *Epistolē*, VII, 344c1-d2)

Yet do we today, have an answer to the question of what we mean by 'serious' and 'not serious'? Do we have an adequate response to the threat of irony? Not at all. Thus it is perhaps fitting that we raise anew *the question of seriousness, and the threat of irony*. The aim in the following work is the defence of philosophy against this threat; to raise the question seriously once again, and to do so concretely in the case of Martin Heidegger (1889–1976).

But the reasons for making this the aim, the means that such an undertaking presupposes, the value of its accomplishment, the openness required, and the path that leads to its success, call for some introductory remarks.

Introduction

The threat has today been forgotten – not due to other threats, but because the charge of irony is perhaps no longer levelled seriously. Our time seems to prefer accusations such as dogmatism, pseudo-science, politically incorrect, mere literature, hogwash, bullshit or frankly nonsense. Yet this does not mean that the problem of irony has been resolved; on the contrary, it seems to wait in the wings until we have finished with our philosophies – then it goes to work.

Yet irony was not always met with forgetting; the Greeks took it seriously. Heidegger translates Plato's *Letter VII*: 'Certainly, therefore, no serious man would ever write about serious things and thereby deliver his discoveries to the envy and misunderstanding of men ... In a word, this means that if someone sees ... something made public by a person, be it laws or other matters ... it can be taken for granted that what the person in question made public was not for him anything serious ... if indeed he is a serious man ... on the contrary, what most properly concerns him, what is most proper to him, resides in the most beautiful place, i.e., in the soul itself ... And if in fact a person exposes in writing what is for him ... the most decisive ... then it was not the gods, but men, who have deprived him of his understanding.'[1]

But is such caution necessary today? For public envy can be mitigated by modesty, and aporia resolved in open discussion. And neither speech nor writing are at issue here, but seriousness. And either we make serious discoveries public, or keep them to ourselves – it seems that simple. But at the moment that seriousness is raised to the level of a question, the question of the seriousness of the serious, we find ourselves confronted with the problem of maintaining the seriousness of the question. If you command me to 'Be serious!', I wonder if you are not joking.

It is perhaps time then for the threat of irony to be taken seriously once again. And this becomes more serious when we are not certain that the threat is serious – then we appear paranoid, suspicious, sceptical, untrustworthy, weak-willed, irrational or lacking in seriousness at least. And it may therefore be necessary to raise anew the issue of irony, for those who think they know but do not, and refuse to hear otherwise, for those who do not know because they cannot know, but insist they know. The goal of this undertaking however, would not be just to do away with irony, as if this could be accomplished by being serious; it would mean recognizing the threat for what it is, attempting to grasp the uncertainty of its essence, or its essence as uncertainty.

An example is needed – both as exemplary, and in order to make an example of someone – an example from our time, the time when irony has been forgotten, and when our forgetting can therefore be exploited. And the example must come not from those who already see themselves as ironic, or explicitly employ irony in their writing (like Plato); nor those simulators and dissimulators of thought like Nietzsche, who readily take up the mask; nor from those who claim that philosophy is at an end, dead or dying; nor from those dogmatic positivists who maintain that the world is governed by empirical science and its universal laws, or formal logic; nor from those superficial sceptics who insist that relativism is true. Rather the example must be the most serious of philosophers.

Perhaps no one fits the bill better than Heidegger. As K. H. Bohrer writes: 'Heidegger's philosophy would be the extreme high-point of the *seriousness* of being and of Dasein that was announced by Fichte and Hegel, but sharpened around the high-point of ontological and historical argument.'[2] Indeed, today no one seems to doubt that Heidegger is one of the most serious thinkers of the twentieth century, if not the most serious. No wonder then that Heideggerians spend their efforts in serious engagement with his philosophical work, for the most part attempting either to explicate the text or disprove his theses once and for all. And no one yet seems willing to entertain the suggestion that Heidegger, or at least his texts, might not be so earnest.

It is therefore time to take the seriousness of Heidegger seriously. And that means not only seriously, but just as much the possibility that his seriousness could be its opposite, not serious at all, a feign or pretense to seriousness – and that we have missed it all along. But if the seriousness of Heidegger's work is at issue, it could be for at least two complementary and co-possible reasons. On the one hand, if Heidegger is assumed to be a serious philosopher, earnest to the highest degree, no possibility that the seriousness is less than serious, no wink or nod, humourless and without satire, self-parody or irony – for as Schlegel knew: irony is no joking matter – if Heidegger is perfectly serious, it is because philosophy itself is serious business. Heidegger's seriousness would be the confirmation that this is authentic philosophy, earnest thought not idle talk, the real thing not some kind of fake, truth itself not falsity, deception, *pseudos*. And Heidegger constitutes the clearest confirmation that, as Benjamin notes, 'the most European of all accomplishments, *that more or less discernible irony* with which the life of the individual asserts the right to run its course independently of the community into which it is cast, has completely deserted the Germans'.[3] Then Heidegger's work is a condemnation of irony on par with Hegel's: 'Irony is a playing with everything; to this subjectivity nothing is any longer serious; it makes the serious, but only to destroy it once again, and can transform everything into appearance. All noble or divine truth dissipates in nothingness (universality); all seriousness is simultaneously only a joke.'[4]

On the other hand, if Heidegger's own seriousness is taken seriously; it is in danger of becoming a joke, just as his philosophical pose threatens to become its opposite at the very moment that it 'poses as philosophical'. Once we insist we are not joking, the funnier the joke – so the Thracian maid might be right to laugh at Thales, although perhaps not simply for star-gazing;[5] just as by repeating that we are serious philosophers, we open ourselves up to the charge of not being serious at all. Then if Heidegger is not ironic, he is ironic; the more the work insists on avoiding irony, the more it opens up to it.

Two opposing yet compossible readings therefore become necessary: one that takes seriousness seriously, following philosophical rigour as rigorously as possible; the other that demonstrates how this rigour breaks down, fails to accomplish the goals it sets, opens itself up to an ironic reading, 'the perverse reading of Heidegger'[6] that leads us back to the question with which we began – but a double interpretation then of this failure as well: one that succeeds in saying what it means and meaning what it says; the other demonstrating that no success is possible, that if we do not know, it is because we cannot know, and cannot even know that we cannot know. Thus an esoteric and exoteric reading, public and private, open and secret: one that shows how the thought proposed could seriously be accomplished, that (as Heidegger insists in the *Beiträge*) gives the appearance, *den Anschein*, of a 'scholarly contribution' to the 'progress of philosophy' (Heidegger's quote marks);[7] another that demonstrates that and how, *daß und wie*, it could not be accomplished at all – and that takes this failure itself as both a success and a failure. But these readings themselves, these alternating interpretations, 'each becoming by turns the alibi of the other',[8] will themselves be subject to the same criticisms they propose: they both succeed and fail, and the truth of both then may lie in their double-interpretation, their *alētheic*-truth, which may be Heidegger's point.

But what would be the value of demonstrating that these texts could be read as ironic? Indeed, if Heidegger and Heideggerians weren't so serious, so serious about philosophy, and about seriousness, all this might be superfluous. But the effects of an introduction or reintroduction of the actuality or possibility of irony into the work of philosophy should not be underestimated – and what if, from the fundamental ontology of the Being of beings, through the question of the origin of the work of art and the essence of technology, the response to fascism and the call for humanism, to the thought of a world where only a god can save us – what if all this were not so serious? And what if the feign to philosophical seriousness was merely a ploy? If thinking and writing themselves were always threatened by irony, seriously or not?

A series of questions then, questions that can neither be immediately answered nor ignored, questions that may be compressed in such a way as to produce a critical mass, air of doubt, explosion of implications, implosion of the text. But here in the Preface, without adequate preparation, we should perhaps recall Hyppolite's words: 'Don't take a preface seriously. The preface announces a project and a project is nothing until it is realized.'[9] Then because no preface or introduction or *apologia* would be sufficient, or because preparations are themselves never preparatory, these questions are not just questions, but statements, misdirection, attack – at the same time as they seek the truth that philosophy claims for itself, and are therefore questions that were perhaps never designed to be answered, especially if we fail to respond to their questionability. With respect to Heidegger's texts therefore, these questions cannot be answered, at least not in any convincing way, without the investigation of the work that follows.

Notes

1   M. Heidegger, *Plato's Sophist*, Indiana University, 1997, 240/346.

2   K.H. Bohrer, '*Heideggers Philosophie wäre dann die äußerste Zuspitzung eines Seins- und Daseins-Ernstes, der sich bei Fichte und Hegel ankündigte, nunmehr aber verschärft um die Zuspitzung des ontologischen und historischen Arguments*' ('Heideggers Ernstfall', *Sprachen der Ironie, Sprachen des Ernstes*, Suhrkamp, 2000, 367; my translation and emphasis).

3   W. Benjamin, 'One-Way Street', (1928), *Selected Writings*, Vol. 1, Harvard University, 1996, 453, my emphasis.

4   G.W.F. Hegel, '*Die Ironie ist das Spiel mit allem; dieser Sujektivität ist es mit nichts mehr Ernst, sie macht Ernst, vernichtet ihn aber wieder und kann alles in Schein verwandeln. Alle hohe und göttliche Wahrheit löst sich in Nichtigkeit (Gemeinheit) auf; aller Ernst ist zugleich nur Scherz*' (*Vorlesungen über die Geschichte der Philosophie I*, Vol. 18, Suhrkamp, 1971, 460, my translation).

5   Plato, *Theatetus*, 174a; *FD*, 2; see also J. Taminiaux, *La fille de Thrace et le penseur professionel*, Payot, 1992.

6   J. Derrida, *Of Spirit*, University of Chicago, 1989, 134; *De l'esprit*, Galilée, 1987, 153n.

7   GA65, 3.

8   Derrida continues: 'In saying this myself right now, in cautioning you that I can by turns or simultaneously play on the two turns or turns of phrase, I withdraw into the secret of irony, be it irony in general or the particular rhetorical figure called irony. But here is yet one more turn, and it is political: is it not also democracy that gives the right to irony in the public space?' (*Rogues*, Stanford University, 2005, 91–2).

9   J. Hyppolite, 'The Structure of Philosophic Language According to the "Preface" to Hegel's *Phenomenology of Mind*,' in *The Languages of Criticism and the Sciences of Man*, Johns Hopkins, 1970. Thanks to James Griffith for reminding me of this comment.

1

Sham of authenticity

1.1

Page one of *Being and Time*, the opening page, a page that comes not from Heidegger, but from Plato, from the *Sophist* (244a6-8). Heidegger cites: '*dēlon gar hōs humeis men tauta (ti pote boulesthe sēmainein hopotan on phtheggēsthe) palai gignōskete, hēmeis de pro tou men ōometha, nun d' ēporēkamen*'. And then, as one might expect, he does not simply refer to Schleiermacher's translation: 'Now clearly because we have no clue, you thereby make even us quite embarrassed with respect then to what you want to indicate when you say being. For obviously you've long known it, and although we believed that we knew it before, we now stand clueless.'[1] Rather he translates the passage himself. 'For manifestly you have long been aware of what you mean when you use the expression "being." We, however, who used to think we understood it, have now become perplexed.'[2] It is also however, possible to translate quite differently: 'Well, then, since we are in a state of perplexity, you go ahead and make them evident to us adequately, whatever you want to indicate whenever you utter "that which is". It's plain that you have been familiar with this for a long time, and we used to believe it of ourselves before, but now we are in a state of perplexity.'[3]

Already then, the first line of Heidegger's text is enmeshed in a series of translations and translation problems. In fact, it seems that almost all the themes of *Being and Time* are present in the quote, the problem of making clear or manifest, *dēlon*, of expressing or speaking, *phtheggēsthe*, and its difference from meaning or wanting to mean, *boulesthe sēmainein*, that which you knew, *gignōskete*, know or do not know, although you thought you knew, thought that we could know, *ōometha* – for we are now perplexed, at a loss or in a state of aporia and immobility, *ēporēkamen* – problems of the being, *to on*, of things themselves, and of the stranger, *xenos*, or other, of ourselves and that which is not ourselves. And because these words are spoken by the character of the Stranger, a fact that must not go unnoticed in an analysis of Plato or Heidegger, these words take on an altogether singular meaning. The task here however, is not to work through the philological details in order to determine which translation is more true to the original, or which language is best able to produce a proper likeness or image of the Greek; but to come to grips with the scene of translation that opens *Being and Time*, the 'task of the translator',[4] and with Heidegger's choice of translation, *Über-setzung*, putting-over, transportation or transformation, movement or change – for this is the preparatory theme or first question of the text even before singling out the question of the meaning of being that is held up in lieu of the question of translation. Indeed, the problem of translation with which Heidegger begins marks everything that follows – so 'tell me what you make of translation, and I will tell you who you are'.[5]

Yet before beginning an analysis of either the passage from the *Sophist*, its place in *Being and Time*, or any of the themes therein, could one not rightly object? For does the quote from Plato not simply serve as an epigraph, a letter prior to the letter or image in front of the image? Is the fact that the quote comes from Plato not really irrelevant to any understanding of Heidegger? Does it not merely serve as a mark of that which *Being and Time* is not? Is the quote not a reminder of that which has been forgotten and hence must be reawakened through the work to come? Or is the quote not simply expendable, an appendage to the text, like a third hand or prosthetic that could be removed without scar or residue? For is the reference to the *Sophist* not really decoration, not to be confused with serious philosophy, and the analysis and argument that follow?

In fact, Heidegger insists on just the opposite. Two years after *Being and Time* – in *Kant and the Problem of Metaphysics*, a text that, in an extraordinary show of consistency remains largely unchanged for almost fifty years, through four editions from 1927 to 1973 – Heidegger maintains that this is not mere decoration, not extrinsic to that which follows, not an appendage, not to be erased or excised or forgotten, but fundamental. Heidegger writes: 'The passage from Plato's *Sophist* that opens the study [*Being and Time*] serves *not as decoration*, but as an indication that in ancient metaphysics the gigantomachy over the being of beings had broken out.'[6] So the quote is not decoration, but an indication that the war of the giants, among which Heidegger might even situate himself, has begun. *Being and Time*, along with Plato's *Sophist*, is to find its place in metaphysics, on that which Kant called the 'battlefield of these endless controversies'.[7] The indicative status however, of the passage from the *Sophist* that opens the study is not enough to contain the fire that it ignites. If the opening of the study, an investigation supposedly limited to the 'question of the meaning of being'[8] and the 'concrete working-out of the question of the sense of "being"',[9] that is, its 'interpretation of time as the possible horizon for any understanding whatsoever of being'[10] – if the opening is not decoration, then the door to the Stranger, philosophy's other, sophistry, irony, has been opened.

How then can we read the passage that opens *Being and Time*? How can we begin to approach the 'beginning' before the beginning of the text? The

'Introduction' or ~~Introduction~~ (exed out) or **Introduction** (the shadow, ghost or double) before the Introduction, preparation before the preparation, 'origin' before the origin? How can we assess the challenge or threat that the *Sophist* poses to *Being and Time*, and perhaps to Heidegger's work as a whole? How can we authenticate its birth certificate, *Geburtsbriefe*? What would be the effect of placing *Being and Time* under the sign of the *Sophist* from which it takes its theme? Does Heidegger not risk a massive confusion? Must we not demand whether it is possible or desirable or inevitable to resist the threat of mistaken identity? In other words, once the very possibility of sophistry has been raised, can we ever be certain that everything that follows is itself not sophistical? Or like Socrates' ironic claim to know that he does not know, can we even be certain of our uncertainty? For if Heidegger chooses to begin with the question of the meaning of being in the *Sophist*, and thus with sophistry itself, does he do so because he knows a sophist from a philosopher or statesman or madman? Or does he know that he does not know? So if the *Sophist* marks *Being and Time*, is it not essential to distinguish the sophist from the philosopher, the ironic from the serious – not just for Plato, but for Heidegger?

1.2

In fact, Plato's *Sophist* contains a technical definition, or definitions, a diaeresis of the sophist's work as an acquisitive, *ktātikai*, and productive art, *poiātikai*.[11] On the one hand, the acquisitive sophist (supposedly like the angler who secretly hunts living animals that swim in the water, taking them by force, by a blow during the day from below – although there is a difference between hunting fish and humans, between hunting, mathematics and philosophy), hunts tame, land animals, that is, wealthy young men, privately for money, by offering the semblance of education;[12] or acquires by exchanging or selling the knowledge of virtue as food for the soul; or by eristics or pugnacious fighting through words and controversy in private discussion and disputation, that is, argument in order to make money, or by purifying the soul, unblocking the way to understanding. Here the sophist and Socrates agree: 'When a person supposes that he knows, and does not know; this appears to be the great source of all the errors of the intellect.'[13] On the other hand, the sophist is a producer, a creator or *dēmiourgikē*. As the Stranger concludes: 'The art of contradiction making, descending from an insincere kind of conceited mimicry, of the semblance-making breed, derived from image making, distinguished as a portion, not divine but human, of production, that presents a shadow play of words – such are the blood and lineage which can, with perfect truth, be assigned to the authentic sophist.'[14] Indeed, the real sophist creates a fake image of truth, a semblance of wisdom, a reputation and apparent knowledge of every science, but not the truth – for he is a wizard and imitator of real things, a magical mimeticist, who makes a likeness of everything, a simulation or copy that conforms to the proportions and colour of the original in every way.[15]

The diaeresis however, hardly resolves the issue – for sophists can appear as philosophers, just as philosophers (the genuine, not the sham) can appear as sophists, give the impression or create the image that they are that which they are not, produce a semblance of philosophy, a *phantasma*. And the diaeresis is supposed to enumerate the sophist's multiple forms, but 'if we can produce different enumerations of the elements in a unique form, then the form cannot present us with a definite look.'[16] If the Stranger's hunt of the sophist then, far from capturing its prey, demonstrates that diaeresis cannot do so, no wonder the results are contradictory: the sophist does and does not take fees; produces and does not produce his own goods; is both tame and wild – for the sophist can look like a member of any family, and we cannot discover his true family, if he has one, if we are unable to distinguish between 'being' a member of a family and 'looking like' a member of a family.[17] And if we cannot distinguish between being and not-being, much less between looks, if the look looks like that which it is not, then the game of sophist-hunting may already be over, even before it begins.

If the dialogue however, seems unable to capture the sophist, is it the failure of method, or a critique? A demonstration of the limits of diaeresis for philosophy? And if we cannot define sophistry, how can we differentiate between the sophist and the philosopher? How could we know that we had in fact caught the sophist, if he assumes all forms? Or what if the 'blood and lineage' of the authentic sophist is also that of the authentic philosopher? Would sophistry not threaten everywhere? And if no one could prove they are not a sophist, could anyone demonstrate that they were one?

The impossibility of catching the sophist through diaeresis however, could also show that the method is inappropriate for distinguishing between philosophy and sophistry, likeness and semblance, seriousness and irony, and between existence and non-existence, motion and rest, sameness and difference, forms that are constantly blending or bleeding into one another, partaking and participating in one another, being translated, *koinōnia* or *methexis*: being is one, unity, namely being, and not change or rest, other than them, but being, which means that it is a unity, and not changing, but the same; unity is, thus being, and is itself, the same, other than change; change is one, but not changing, at rest, in order to be that which it is, and also changing in order to be change, which means not that which it is, but other than itself. And knowing that diaeresis cannot catch the sophist, philosophy turns to dialectic in order to grasp the original principles or forms of things, as well as that of sophistry, whereby it can then be differentiated from philosophy. As the Stranger insists: nothing, not even an evil demon, could make it so that the originals are not. And the blending of forms, like the copy or fake and the icon or phantasm, is possible on the basis of originals – for not knowing the originals, the forms, the sophist cannot become a philosopher.[18]

But 'there is a fundamental defect in the Stranger's strategy. Even if he should succeed in "persuading" us of the truth of his doctrine of forms, he would remain open to the charge that he is the most powerful of sophists.'[19] No wonder then that the Stranger falls into difficulty when considering that which is not, *to mē on*. Here the response to Parmenides' injunction forbidding thinking that non-being is, *einai mē eonta*, resorts to the form of otherness.[20] Clearly 'that which is not' cannot be approached by a discourse of calculation, enumeration, mathematical formulation – for then we fall into self-contradiction – and expressions of non-being are 'unpronounceable, inexpressible, without *logos*, and discursively unthinkable'.[21] Yet nor can non-being be seen – for it has no 'look' that could be or be one, that could blend with the forms of being, unity, sameness. Rather, 'that which is not' can only be grasped dialectically, in relation to the other forms – for it is not the opposite of being, nor is it a form itself, but 'other than being,' just as the sophist is other than the philosopher, as falsity is other than truth.

It is to the forms therefore, and their other, that we must turn in order to grasp the sophist – although the Stranger is no 'friend of the forms' – to the original ontological letters of the eidetic alphabet.[22] Here being and unity, rest and change, are to be seen in the looks of things. Just as the look of a thing is and is not the thing itself, just as the representation is and is not that which is present, or as a translation is and is not that which it translates, as a copy is and is not a copy and an original, an original copy and therefore not a copy at all, so too each form is and is not every other one. And the sophist too is, is one and many, at rest and in change, a combination of forms, *sumplokē eidōn* – otherwise the sophist could not even be sophistical. Then if the forms look contradictory among themselves, they would be so in relation to beings; and even things themselves, *to pragma auto*, insofar as they share or participate in the forms, are translations of forms, have forms in common, would seem contradictory as well. Yet if the Stranger's terminology with respect to the forms seems or looks self-contradictory, it may simply be because we have not grasped the forms themselves; although this does not mean that the hunt for sophistry's non-being is over – even if the doctrine of the forms remains intact, something that has not yet been proven, but presupposed. As the Stranger maintains: if we can find the other of being, that which is not, we will have found the sophist.

Otherness then brings the problem of the forms to a head. While change is other than otherness, sameness, rest, and even being; otherness is itself, and other than itself, other than otherness, *heteron tou heterou*. Otherness is both the relation of itself and another, and of others, other forms from each other. But if every form must be other than every other form, otherness cannot be a form – for it is far more the *dynamis* of forms, like the force of law, the power to be other than each other, and that is to be themselves. In this way, otherness is more original than the original eidetic alphabet, more original than the origin; it is supposed to be other than itself, but never is, never is other than otherness – for if it were other than itself, it would still be other. The other lies at the root of the Stranger's doctrine of the forms – for unlike the being that is, otherness must be itself and not itself, even in order to be itself. Thus otherness is essentially contradictory: on the one hand, it is itself insofar as it shares in being, and is a form like being insofar as it provides for the difference between forms, and thereby for their sameness, their identity with self; on the other hand, it is not itself, not a form insofar as it deforms itself, but must always also share in otherness, must be other than itself, not otherness.

Have we then found the sophist? Is sophistry that which holds up self-contradiction, like the otherness of the other, as truth? Or is otherness essential to the forms, its essential other, just as sophistry is essential to philosophy? Must the philosopher not always also be a sophist?

Then if the Stranger has come to accuse the philosopher Socrates of sophistry, it may be that he knows of what he speaks. For if otherness problematizes the doctrine of the forms, it seems designed to shift our understanding of truth – as *orthos* or *alētheia* or some other such truth – away from that which is traditionally associated with Platonism, and to demonstrate ironically that even the Socratic position of knowing that we do not know, of knowing the impossibility of any attempt to represent the forms, may not succeed. When faced with the impossible, as with otherness, or with that which is not, we seem at a loss. And irony may be the most appropriate response: if sophistry thinks the impossibility of thought, if it consistently formalizes the inconsistency of forms; it may be just the kind of 'wisdom' through which Socrates knows that he does not know, if that is wisdom at all.

Perhaps then neither diaeresis nor dialectic can catch the sophist. And whether the sophist maintains the doctrine of the forms or not, it seems that we might miss him – for he is always other than himself, dissimulating, even to the point of dissimulating dissimulation, both verifying and falsifying falsity and truth. In this way, the original principles are no longer original: the very possibility of the form of otherness means that every presentation is the representation of a presentation, every original an image, look, copy of an original, every reality a phantasm of the real, every immediate intuition of the truth already mediated. The forms therefore, do not escape the threat of simulation, and we can never be certain that what looks like a form – insofar as it has a 'look' at all – is or is not a form. A false look – like an inaccurate image of a thing, a distorted *logos*, ratio or proportion of a being – can always be more 'accurate' than a true one; but if the false is true, the true is not true at all, only another way of looking. And a sophist-sighting could always mislead – not just because it takes on a multiplicity of forms, but because it always looks like philosophy. So although the look of the sophist is not the sophist, the look must be the look *of* the sophist, must look *like* the sophist, which is to say it must look like the philosopher, not the sophist, if it is to belong to the sophist, if it is to be the look of the sophist. Here the representation both is and is not the presentation; the image of the sophist is the same but not identical to the sophist. On the one hand, if phantasms and icons, copies and representations, semblance and resemblance, are only possible on the basis of some original, we should be able to differentiate the authentic philosopher and the real sophist; on the other hand, if the sophist really looks like the philosopher, and the philosopher like the sophist, it is because they are indistinguishable. As the Stranger insists: the philosopher is as difficult to find as the sophist, albeit for another reason – while the latter hides in shadow, runs into the darkening of 'that which is not', and is obscured from sight by the lack of light; the former, hiding under the blinding light of noon, is hard to discern because of the brilliance of the ideas' place.[23] Staring into the pitch of night, or the fire of day, is just as difficult, if not impossible. But even if some other method were invented to see or know the sophist, or the specific difference between sophistry and philosophy, like that between seriousness and irony, some kind of intellectual intuition whereby we should be able to grasp the essence or concept itself, we still could never confirm that what we hoped we had seen or thought, we had in fact seen and thought. We would have to resort once again to looks or intuitions (grasped in an *Augenblick*, to that which insofar as it can deceive does so) for confirmation that the sight of the original is not a copy. And the making of false images can only be condemned, if we can differentiate them from the true ones; just as the counterfeiter can only be attacked, if we can distinguish the original from the fake. But the sophist maintains that forms, ontological originals, pure eidetic elements, are merely something in which we believe, useful, a kind of noble lie, functioning in a web, *sumplokē*, of meaning, although only as true or false as fantasies. The 'real world' of forms can become an illusion, originals can become copies, nature artificial – because they were illusions and copies and artifacts all along.

But if the sophist has masked as a philosopher, if both originals and copies look like originals, and look like each other, and therefore like copies, if false copies and phantasms, look like real copies and icons, if the simulation of knowledge looks like knowledge; must we not acknowledge the essential confusion, blending or gallimaufry of presentation and representation as the condition of the possibility of philosophy and sophistry alike? Would not indistinguishability, or rather uncertainty with respect to difference – not distinction or identification, nor difference or indifference, nor their difference – would this not ironically be the 'wisdom' or ~~wisdom~~ to which the Stranger points?

A sophist then would be not just one who shows how to make the weaker argument the stronger, nor simply reduces considerations of things themselves to those of form, calculation, enumeration; nor merely one occupation among many, a teacher of rhetoric who looks like he knows but does not know; nor just a phantasm of the philosopher, an inaccurate image of the wise, a distorter of genuine ideas, original principles or forms; the sophist would be the one who, lacking any positive doctrine or axiomatic system of thought, knows that he does not know – not because he is ignorant and in need of education like the *Meno*'s slave, but because he remains uncertain with respect to knowledge, knowing that one cannot 'know thyself' or others, that action only happens under the condition of uncertainty, that public speeches can never be known to correspond to private thoughts, that we cannot share the other's pain, that truth is only possible in the region where falsity is not only possible, but necessary, and that philosophy only happens with sophistry, the other that is itself, under the constant necessity of their confusion, uncertainty, the essential threat of synchysis. The sophist's truth then is Socratic: he knows that he does not know because he cannot know, that the possibility of wisdom lies in the impossibility of knowledge, that philosophy can never disassociate itself from sophistry.

Have we have then caught our prey? Maybe. Nothing proves it – but nothing proves the contrary either. And we remain uncertain as to the definition, *logos*, image, *eidos*, icon or phantasm of sophistry. How then could we, like the Stranger, accuse Socrates of sophistry? With what right could we try, or try again, to judge Socrates? And how could we convict him for something like sophistry, if we cannot even be sure what it is and that he did it? If sophists are the kinds of animals that always escape – and even this escapes, remains unnoticed, or at least unnoticed as unnoticed, or noticed, because the unnoticed would be noticed, not noticed, or even un-unnoticed, that is, never to be noticed, that which could never be noticed as noticed or unnoticed – well then how could we punish them? Is sophistry not the kind of problem that remains (and always must remain) a problem, not to be solved, but precisely therefore essential? An essential uncertainty? Then can the problem of the sophist be made problematic? And is that not the problem?

Is this perhaps why Heidegger places the *Sophist* before *Being and Time*? Can we now trust that the philosopher's text is not sophistical? That the Stranger, Socrates, even Heidegger, is not a sophist? For does Heidegger not thereby level the Stranger's charge as much at Socrates as at himself? An attempt at auto-immunization? The origin of *Being and Time*? Irony prior to all seriousness? *Scherz* before *Ernst*? Would the lack of jokes convince us? To determine Heidegger's guilt or innocence? Would we be forced then to read Heidegger 'as if' he were a sophist – or a philosopher – maybe even both? If the text remains open to the charge, is it not because he too has worn every disguise: philosopher, statesman, sophist, madman? Could we then be certain that he is not dissimulating? That he is telling the truth once he lied – or even if he had not yet lied, but could do so? Could we be certain that he is not now lying? Was the trust ever pure, or was its purity far more a lie? And if so, does 'wisdom' not consist in trusting the lie, only under the condition of lying? Or in trusting that we are lying? For we can only trust if we have already been betrayed, and a trust purified of the lie, a condition in which we could not be lied to, is one in which we cannot trust.

Indeed, the Stranger's irony cannot be resolved into seriousness or irony; it is no longer univocal, does not mean saying one thing in order to mean another, and is neither simply the 'noble dissimulation of one's worth, of one's superiority ... of one's wisdom', nor 'expressing on a "wise" subject such thoughts (e.g., generally accepted thoughts) as are less wise than one's own thoughts or refraining from expressing any thoughts regarding a "wise" subject on the ground that one does not have knowledge regarding it and therefore can only raise questions but cannot give answers'.[24] Rather the essence of irony lies in uncertainty, the inability to certify whether the Stranger is being ironic, the epistemic uncertainty of truth, the ontological uncertainty of being itself. And if it were possible to take away this uncertainty, the force of irony would be undercut; it would be powerless to destabilize power – it wouldn't even be ironic.

1.3

But back to *Being and Time*, to the beginning of Heidegger's text, to the Introduction, to the question that repeats again everything that follows – or rather back to the rumour or reputation, *Ruf*, always insufficient for proof,[25] ('not because the necessary proofs are lacking, but because the desire for proofs and the demands for proofs are not appropriate to the subject matter here') the opinion or suspicion, *doxa*, the interpretation or reading that is beginning to build-up evidence. Back to the question of the meaning of being, and the serious work of interpreting and questioning Heidegger – for we are supposed to 'say what we mean and mean what we say' – that is the ethics of reading and writing, the call to honesty, the demand for clarity, truth as certainty, imposed or self-imposed upon the sciences; although we may begin to wonder if it is ever possible for a question to be just a question, not an answer or answers, accusation or charge, allurement and pretence, arrow and barb – for once irony has entered into questioning, the call for an ethical reading of Heidegger (and who would call for an unethical one?) may become questionable. So back to 'the question of the question',[26] the question that Heidegger perhaps never properly raises, the question of the questionability of questioning, that is, its uncertainty. And back to the question 'Why question in the first place?', of the essence and existence of questioning that which is questioned, the things themselves. And this question seems beyond ethics and ontology and *erotics* – for that which is questionable in questioning is nothing questionable; it is one of utility, efficacy, strategy. The question: 'Why this question and not another?' becomes: 'Why this weapon?' or 'Why this answer?'

It is not simply as a retreat therefore, nor out of ignorance, that Heidegger raises the question: 'Do we in our time have an answer to the question of what we really mean by the word "being"?'[27] But here, 'the content of the question reacts upon the questioning itself.'[28] The question of the meaning of being is marked by the recoil of the question, the return of that which is asked (as if in the middle-voice) to the one who asks; and although we do not know what we mean by being, it must already be, and be available, in some way, like the question even if as unknown – in order for us to even pose the question of its meaning. The question here however, does not mean that *Being and Time* will answer the question of the meaning of being; the opposite, that the text will demonstrate that the answer is impossible, that we can never answer the question of what we really mean by the word 'being'. In this case, the question is a feign, a simulation of interest, an intentional (perhaps noble) lie or a lie of intentionality, designed to strike at those who think that they know when they do not know, who think that they know the answer to the question, or who think that at least they can or will eventually know it, who think that an answer is possible or necessary, when it may be somehow impossible. And for this reason, Heidegger too answers in the negative – he does not give an answer, perhaps cannot give one, but only writes: *keineswegs*, 'not at all'.[29] Does *Being and Time* then show itself as not an answer to the question of the meaning of being, but as a demonstration of impossibility, of the unanswerable questionability of the question?

And what is the question? What is the question to which Heidegger answers that we have no answer? On the one hand, it is obviously the question of being; on the other, it is the question of the 'meaning' of being – and that is why the question of being is never alone, never a simple or univocal question: the question of the question in *Being and Time* is always also the meaning of meaning. And if it is impossible to answer the question of the meaning of *being*, it is perhaps because it is impossible to answer the question of the *meaning* of being. In other words, the question of the meaning of meaning is the question of the meaning of being – for the meaning of the being of things themselves is itself meaning. And this is why Heidegger seeks to 'raise anew *the question of the meaning of being*',[30] to 'reawaken an understanding for the *meaning* of this question',[31] or 'to work out the question of the *meaning* of *being*'.[32]

If the question however of the meaning of being in *Being and Time* cannot be answered, or at least if Heidegger does not or cannot provide an answer, not because of some slip in rigour or lack of resolve, but because an answer is perhaps impossible; it may be because the question of the meaning of meaning, of *Sinn*, cannot be answered. If we have no answer to what we mean by being, it is not because we cannot assign a single meaning, or multiple senses, to being, not because 'being is spoken in many ways',[33] but because being itself cannot be meant at all – for it exceeds all attempts to know it, is beyond all beings and meanings, and therefore remains questionable. Then maybe we do not in our time, or any time, have an answer to what we really mean by 'being' because we can neither say what we mean, nor mean what we say about that which transcends all meaning; and this is not a meaning, nor meaningless, but beyond meaning and meaninglessness alike. Then *Being and Time* is the concrete working out of this beyond – to the extent such a thing is possible, or impossible – the demonstration of the (unquestionable) impossibility of the question of the meaning of being.

This impossibility would then be the goal of Heidegger's 'interpretation of *time* as the possible horizon for any understanding whatsoever of being'.[34] For there is no 'answer' to the question – and no surprise that Heidegger provides none – but only an interpretation. We cannot simply know therefore the meaning of meaning or raise the question of the question, and our interpretation of being is an interpretation of our non-knowledge. If a question then, however answerable or not, is never just a question; it is because it is always already an interpretation, an interpretation before the interpretation or pre-interpretation – questioning is interpreting, as are the origin and end of interpretation.

And if time then is the horizon for the interpretation of being, it is no surprise that it is an interpretation that can never be merely achieved or accomplished; can never be completed or actualized, but remains an interpretation that can never be that which it should be, namely an interpretation – for the horizon (like the withdrawal of being itself) is always in recession. Indeed, the horizonal structure of time means that an interpretation of being in terms of time is never to be reached but not like a Kantian idea that might regulate or orient, if not constitute, a possible interpretation of being – rather, if time serves as the horizon for the interpretation of being, it is only under the condition that the interpretation itself remains uninterpreted and uninterpretable, open to interpretation and reinterpretation reached as unreachable.

Is the interpretation of being then only possible under the necessary condition of its impossibility? Isn't that what Heidegger means? Is this why Heidegger abandons *Being and Time*, never finishing the Second Half – for it could not have been successful; or more precisely, because the First Half already demonstrates the impossibility of the project, the impossibility of the question of the meaning of being? And of meaning? And half-text, cut-off, unfinished, preliminary and incomplete work, fragment, finished as un-finished or unfinishable, open and open-ended – is this not an appropriate interpretation of the question?

But then *Being and Time*, as a demonstration of the possible (that is, necessary) impossibility of raising the question of the meaning of being – this question too could be a feign, a feign upon a feign, question of the question of being. In fact, those who think they know, do not even know that they do not know – something that at least St Augustine (with respect to time), knew he could not know: 'If no one asks me, I know; if I want to explain it to someone who does ask me, I do not know.'[35] Even if we 'know' then that time is the meaning of being, we must ask 'What is time?' – not only because time is; but also because even if time is understood in terms of presence, we must ask 'What is presence?' The question of meaning shows itself as an infinite regress of meanings, meaning as infinite, and infinitely receding.[36]

And even if the meaning of being is not supposed to be time, but only understood in terms of time (as for instance, now, presence, *parousia*), does this do anything to explain the meaning of time or presence? For it would not be enough simply to appeal to the circular structure of reasoning (that Heidegger explicitly rejects although not the hermeutic circle),[37] nor to a kind of 'notable "relatedness backward or forward"',[38] that is, a filling in of that which is only sketched out in a phenomenological description designed to let the thing show itself as itself, to allow the being of being, the being that is no being at all, to show itself, to reveal the truth of itself – for this would only mean speaking as if one knows about that which one does not know. In other words, even if being means time as presence, presence means being, and this backwards and forwards is the horizon of what we mean by being and presence, namely, presence and being. Now do we have an under-standing of the meaning of being? Or do we know that we know what we already knew that we did not know? That no 'understanding' of being is even possible? In other words, does the strange or noteworthy movement of 'backwards and forwards' let us know anything more, or does it tell us that we do not know because we cannot know the meaning of being, presence or time? Or if this interpretation is supposed to be open to interpretation, infinitely open, does the questionability of the question of the meaning of being remain questionable? Or is *Being and Time* far more the closing down of the very question it seeks to open and keep open?

1.4

Regardless, Heidegger does seem to propose a positive philosophical doctrine – although this does not mean that it is impossible to maintain a double or essentially ambiguous reading of *Being and Time*: on the one hand positive, possible or necessary, consistent, if not experienceable then at least thinkable, knowing what we know because we must know; on the other, negative, impossible, contradictory, ungraspable, unthinkable, knowing that we do not know because we cannot know, questionable, open. And although we continually seek to maintain a firm foothold in the text, we may increasingly find that we have begun to slip from one reading to the other – but this does not preclude the argument that takes both quite seriously, or not, nor an attempt to grasp their uncertainty.

Take the 'definition' or 'sense' of being, for example, in the Introduction to *Being and Time* – for here we think we know the answer to the question of the meaning of being: '*Being is the transcendens pure and simple*',[39] *das transcendens schlechthin*. But what is the meaning of *transcendens*? And as Heidegger insists, being is not *the* only one: 'Within the task of deriving the "transcendentals" – that is, the characteristics-of-being that lie beyond every possible material-generic determination of a being, every *modus specialis entis*, and that are necessary attributes of every something, whatever it might be – the *verum* too should be demonstrated as such a *transcendens*.'[40] If being and truth then are both the *transcendens*, what about others suggested by the Schools: *unum* and *bonum*? Or the Stranger's *heteron tou heterou*? And is time not just as much a *transcendens*? Not to speak of that which Heidegger, at least here, leaves out, but which has qualified in the history of philosophy: unity, totality, God, substance, will, will to power, sameness, difference, otherness, etc.? And what kind of absolute is being, if it not *the* absolute? Thus the answer to the question of the meaning of being raises it to the level of a question: What is the transcendence or transcendentality of the *transcendens* pure and simple? Thus not simply a positive philosophical doctrine at all, *keineswegs*, nor a negative one; but the continual displacement of the question of the meaning of being as the truth – of infinite openness (from being as *transcendens*, temporality, horizon, beyond beings, or beyng, *Seyn*, to the event, *das Ereignis*).[41]

Heidegger nevertheless insists that ontology must respond to the question of the meaning of being: '*All ontology, no matter how rich and tightly knit a system of categories it has at its disposal, remains fundamentally blind and perverts its innermost intent if it has not previously clarified the meaning of being sufficiently and grasped this clarification as its fundamental task.*'[42] The question then for *Being and Time*, if it is to be considered a serious 'scientific' investigation or fundamental ontology: Has Heidegger clarified the meaning of being sufficiently? Or has he demonstrated that such clarification is impossible? Or both? On the one hand, if the question of the meaning of being is to be worked out concretely, it cannot remain simply the absolute *transcendens*; on the contrary, prior to an understanding of being lies the necessity for (what Heidegger calls) a suitable explication of ourselves, of you and me as that being which understands whose being is an issue for it, of Dasein (Da-*sein*) as that 'being that we ourselves in each case are'.[43] On the other hand, 'the possibility of carrying out the analysis of Dasein [also] depends upon the prior elaboration of the question of the meaning of being in general'.[44] Along with the ontological priority of the question of being lies its ontic priority; and we are that being 'ontically distinguished by the fact that in its being this being is concerned *about* its very being'.[45] In other words, we understand our relation to being 'in some way and with some explicitness'.[46] For the '*understanding-of-being is itself a determination-of-being of Dasein*'.[47] But what if our understanding of being, of our own being, the being about which we are so concerned, is in fact no understanding at all? If what we understand is that we do not understand because we cannot understand? In this sense, the way and explicitness with which we are able to know ourselves would be a kind of non-knowledge or impossible knowledge – for if we cannot leap over our own shadows, if the mirror that we hold up to ourselves always distorts, if the being of ourselves that we seek continually slips between our fingers, then our grasp of being is what we miss. We cannot 'clarify' ourselves to ourselves, anymore than we can think ourselves thinking thought.

Nevertheless, Heidegger insists that the being to which we relate is our own existence. And we are not merely what we are, but are in relation to being. The (existentiell) understanding of ourselves is always in terms of our being's possibility (ontically) 'to be itself or not to be itself'[48] – hence the need of fundamental ontology for an existential analytic, or an interpretation of our three-fold priority over other beings in the world (ontically, ontologically and ontic-ontologically). *Being and Time* thus takes us as the primary being to be interrogated – for its goal is a 'radicalization then of an essential tendency of being that belongs to Dasein'.[49] Assuming therefore, that the question of the meaning of being has been retrieved and linked to the question of the meaning of our being, we must be able to be or not to be ourselves. But what would it mean not to be ourselves? Could we not be ourselves in our being? Or is it simply a question of not understanding ourselves as we are? A mistaken identity or confusion of ourselves with ourselves? In which we both are and are not ourselves?

Heidegger answers none of these questions here; rather, in exposing the priority of the question of the meaning of being, the possibility of a response is left in suspension – which may be his response. The question of whether we can in fact be or not be ourselves is not yet answered – if it ever could or should be answered, or if the question itself is not the answer. The retrieval of the question, of the matter at hand, the 'what is asked about' or theme, that which will be spoken about, the being, the *ti* to be interrogated, is the first step. The giving of the name of Dasein is the second. The determination of its origin as that being that is an issue for it – not simply a being among beings in the world, but that being that is insofar as it exists, that is, 'the leading of a life, which is characterized by a determination of *telos* [death, being towards death, *Sein zum Tode*], a *telos* functioning for *bios*, itself an object of *praxis* [care. *Sorge*]'[50] – is the third.

The three steps then, for raising the question of the meaning of being, seem to have been determined. But does *Being and Time* actually go through them? And do they allow us to remember or retrieve the question of the meaning of being that has today 'come into forgetting', *in Vergessenheit gekommen*?[51] Or has the question only been forgotten because we never could remember it? Because it is impossible to remember being, if it only is that which it is *qua* forgotten? Then *Being and Time* would be not the remembering of being, not the retrieval of that which has been lost or forgotten such that it would be found – for that would be not only a necessarily false account of being, but an impossible task, the remembering of that which must be forgotten, can never be remembered, the remembering of the task of remembering, under way to retrieving – so if being was remembered, if the attempt to retrieve it were successful, it would no longer be that which it was. Does *Being and Time* then, not have to be a spectacular failure, not success in failure – for the reversal of metaphysics is itself metaphysics – but an absolute failure? Failure without success? Forgetting without the possibility of remembering? The forgetting of that which must be forgotten? In this way, the forgetting of the question of being would not only be necessary, *a priori* and universal, but the forgetting of it as forgotten would be necessary as well. And this is not neglect or refusal, but just the opposite: the forgetting of the forgotten *qua* forgotten. Or is this not itself a kind of remembering or retrieval? And must the project of forgetting, even the possibility of forgetting, itself be impossible? Then did Heidegger build self-destruction into the destruction of metaphysics? Did he construct *Being and Time* such that it demonstrates the impossibility of raising the question of the meaning of being? Is the existential analytic of Dasein anything more than the latest failure of thought (under the name of metaphysics, post-metaphysics, phenomenology, etc.) to think the essence of the being that we are? That being whose being is an issue for it, that is, whose being cannot be an issue for it? Is then the announced priority of our Dasein, and its supposed concern for its being, a feign or a sign pointing elsewhere? Are we not concerned with our being, not because we need to be reminded, not because we have forgotten anything, anything that could therefore be retrieved, but because we couldn't care less?

1.5

Not only the theme or themes of *Being and Time* however, but the method as well must be worked out in terms of the question of the meaning of being. Insofar as we are the beings that do phenomenology, carry out fundamental ontology, we must first examine ourselves as a means, a way, *hodos*, of correct access to the investigation of being. But just as diaeresis proved itself to be inappropriate for catching the sophist, phenomenology may be unable to approach the being of Dasein and the being of beings. Then the text is a demonstration – and thereby perfectly Socratic, if not sophistical, in its approach to philosophy – of the limits of phenomenology for fundamental ontology and the existential analytic, when faced with the question of the meaning of being.

But Heidegger insists (having begun with our average everydayness, the way in which we remain not ourselves, *Unheimlich*, not metaphorically in the sense of uncanny, but 'not at home',[52] not homey): 'The analysis of Dasein, however, is not only incomplete but at first also preliminary. It only brings out the being of this being *without interpreting* its meaning. Its aim is rather to expose the horizon for the most primordial interpretation of being. Once we have reached that horizon the preparatory analytic of Dasein *requires repetition* on a higher, genuinely ontological basis.'[53] But does the required repetition ever happen? So is this because Heidegger simply didn't get to it? Because he didn't have the time or the desire to finish up? Or because it was unfinishable from the start? Because the required repetition would itself require a repetition, *ad infinitum*? And isn't that essential to the science of phenomenology? Or because the horizon for the most primordial interpretation can never be reached, because the horizon as receding (itself to be interpreted), presupposes being, which presupposes the horizon? Then how can the horizon of being serve as the ground of interpretation if it *is* as well? And if being is neither a genus (Aristotle) nor a predicate (Kant), but horizonal, does it make an interpretation of Dasein possible? Or far more impossible? A necessary impossibility?

Regardless, Heidegger repeats: if 'the meaning of the being of that being we call Dasein proves to be temporality. This proof must preserve itself throughout the repeated interpretation of the previously indicated structures of Dasein as modes of temporality.'[54] First 'that' Dasein is; second 'how' it temporally is. The first analytic is 'without interpretation' and aims only at an exposure or lay-free of the horizon for the interpretation; the second repeats the analytic with interpretation.

But which is a repetition of which? Are we not confused, and must we not avoid this at all costs? And are we not back in the *Sophist*'s problem of original and copy, of repetition, and repetition of the repetition? Then is the question not only *that* and *how* an interpretationless analytic of Dasein is possible, but *that* and *how* this is itself an interpretation? And then how can we repeat an interpretation of an analysis that is itself without interpretation? How could we even haul out the being of this being, the being of Dasein, of its average everydayness, without always already having the ability to identify it, point to it, grasp it as the being of Dasein? As Heidegger insists: 'Every questioning is a seeking. Every seeking takes its direction beforehand from what is sought.'[55] Some kind of pre-interpretation of the being of Dasein would be necessary even in order to bring out the being of this being. But how could we hope to have the meaning of the being of Dasein, without interpreting it, without glozing it, even before we had it? And why the repetition of repetition? Would one repetition not have been enough? Or is the repetition itself indicating some other repetition?

Still, Heidegger insists: 'with this interpretation of Dasein as temporality the answer to the guiding question about the meaning of being in general is not already given'.[56] The digression through us, through Dasein, is necessary in order to approach an answer to the question of the meaning of being. But if the goal is not achieved, if *Being and Time* never thinks being *katholou, kath' auto*, in general, universally, in and for itself, as such; then this is however, no flaw in analysis, no lack of rigour or will – although it may be the preparation of the soil, *der Boden*, for that which will not grow, for an answer that cannot be gleaned. The preparation is the end – although an end that is no 'end' at all – its own completion. And our inability to harvest the meaning of being lies not with us, but with being itself.

The digression through the existential analytic – like the Stranger's attempt to trap the sophist – in order to grasp (the ungraspable, define the indefinable, answer the unanswerable, get to the meaning of) being itself, might then be a feign. And if the analytic shows itself unable to think the being of a being, us, Dasein; it may be because it is impossible to think the meaning of being in general. No wonder then, that the same fate that befalls Dasein binds the task of working out the meaning of being in terms of temporality – for as that in terms of which being is supposed to be understood (in its modes and derivations), time too (and its determinations) remains a task 'to be worked out'. And although Heidegger argues that with temporality, 'the concrete answer to the question of being is given',[57] it is an answer that simply reposes the question: no longer 'What is the meaning of being?', but now 'What is the meaning of time?' And if *Being and Time* never conducts the 'elaboration of the *temporality of being*',[58] is it because it will not, or cannot?

1.6

Then after the ontological 'task' of the interpretation of being as such – a task that may prove Sisyphean, or messianic, to come, an unfulfilled or unfulfillable promise, or a task that is already completed once it is started, and thus no task at all, which may or may not confirm the determination of being as temporal, or its originality, not to speak of its seriousness – after this task, comes that of a destruction or '*destructuring of the history of ontology*'.[59] Here the question of determining the meaning of Dasein (and of being) becomes more difficult – for Dasein 'is determined by historicity in the ground of its being, [but] if historicity remains concealed from Dasein, and so long as it does so, the possibility of historical inquiry and discovery of history is denied it'.[60] In truth (as *a-lētheia*), if history remains a *Versagen*, a failure for us; the task of historical inquiry would be impossible. If our historicity remains concealed from us, an impossible task, and if the unconcealment of history necessarily involves its concealment, we may never be able to accomplish the destructuring of the history of ontology. Then destructuring would not be about accomplishing anything, nor about fulfilling some kind of need or lack, but about impossibility: insofar as concealing essentially belongs to the unconcealment of history, we could never simply know our history, never be able to appropriate our past or come into possession of our historical selves.

The ontic-ontological inquiry of *Being and Time* then, would be marked neither by historicity nor ahistoricity, but by a double or two-faced concealing and unconcealing history. We never fully grasp our tradition, but only make it 'more or less' explicit – and it is this tradition that deprives us of leadership, *Führung*, in questioning and choosing. So it is never just a question of choosing or not choosing, questioning or not, but rather of more and less – for the truth is that we are not the leaders of ourselves, and the goal is not to become the *Führer*, but to realize that leadership itself is impossible, or perhaps only possible *qua* impossible. With Heidegger, the myth of the leader is at an end (although this is neither to say that, like Nietzsche's God, we will not be living under its shadow for centuries to come; nor that it wasn't already over when Heidegger took over to end it).

The destructuring of the history of ontology in *Being and Time* then, will not simply loosen the sclerotic tradition of concealments, or negate and supersede all earlier attempts – for we can never disburden ourselves of our past, nor completely do away with that which our unconcealing efforts themselves repeatedly conceal – but rather will point to the origin, or display the 'birth certificate' of ontological concepts. To this end, Heidegger asks, which interpretations of being have been thematically connected with the phenomenon of time?[61] He answers: Kant is 'the first and only one'.[62]

Indeed, *Being and Time* stands under the shadow of Heidegger's interpretation of Kant, even if it appears two years later in 1929. If Aristotle inaugurates the question 'What is being?', *ti to on*, 'What is being *qua* being?', *to on hē on*; then Kant's 'Copernican revolution in thought' brings metaphysics to systematic ontology, and transcendental philosophy is no longer epistemology, but fundamental ontology. While Kant, however, may seem to have solved the problem of metaphysics, for Heidegger he merely posed the question – for in grounding metaphysics on an originally groundless ground, a non-ground or un-ground, *Ungrund*,[63] critical philosophy reveals the limit of what it can think and not think.

As Heidegger argues, Kant lays the ground of metaphysics as fundamental ontology through an analysis of human finitude in answer to the question, 'What is the human being?', insofar as it synthesizes the three questions: 'What can I know?', 'What should I do?', and 'What may I hope?' Then in order to lay the ground for metaphysics, 'Kant brings the problem of the possibility of ontology to bear upon the question: "How are a priori synthetic judgments possible?"'[64] But this question presupposes fundamental ontology. If the universality and necessity of knowledge then, cannot be found in experience, but before experience; it is because the ground of the experience of beings is nothing experiential – and that which makes ontic knowledge possible is nothing ontical, but ontological. Thus the *Critique* demonstrates how we can make *a priori* synthetic judgements *of* experience, but not *from* experience; insofar as experience is always the experience of beings, the possibility of experience lies elsewhere, prior to beings, in being.

For Heidegger then, judgements that connect subject and predicate through syllogism are about beings. And the *Critique* deduces the original ground of these syntheses, the ground of human reason in all its finitude – for we are not gods – the basis upon which we may make *a priori* claims, the right that the subject has to know objects *quid facti* and *quid juris*, *that* and *how*, *daß und wie*, that is, to transcend its own subjectivity and provide knowledge of objects, of that which it is not, of that against which it finds and defines itself. The question of synthetic *a priori* judgements then, must be brought to bear upon the question: 'How is transcendence possible?' – for objects are those beings that transcend us. Here the *Critique* is understood as the science of the truth of ontological transcendence, not solipsism, and thereby of the possibility of all ontic knowledge and any truth whatsoever. Yet what is transcendence? And how does transcendental philosophy make it possible?

For Kant, in order for finite human beings to know that which they are not, they must be in such a way that they can go beyond their own finitude – and reason is the way. The finitude of human reason however, lies in intuition: if knowledge is primarily intuition, it is not because presentation, the presence of things in themselves, but representation is the structure of human knowledge. The Copernican revolution in thought means: Kant solves the problem of the possibility, that is, the necessity and universality of *a priori* synthetic judgement with representational epistemology – for it is only under the condition that objects as representations of things in themselves present themselves to intuition that they can ever correspond to our concepts *a priori*. If human reason were not finite, if we had God's intuition, *intuitus originarius*, we would not need to have objects given to us as appearances; they would not have to present themselves, *sich vor-stellen*, as representations, *Vor-stellungen* – no introductions would be needed to sensibility, and we could intuit the manifold of beings in themselves. As Heidegger writes: 'Human intuition is not, therefore, "sensible" because its affection takes place through "sense"-organs, but the reverse: because our Dasein is finite – existing in the midst of beings that already are, beings to which it has been delivered over – therefore it must necessarily take this already-existing being in stride, that is, it must offer it the possibility of announcing itself.'[65] Humanity consists in the necessary detour through *intuitus derivativus*, whereby finite human reason submits to the law or *nomos* of representation.

Reason then, allows us to know and judge that which is given, that which we have not created, although not as it is in itself, but for us, as it appears to us, as a look, *eidos*. Knowledge is always knowledge *of* intuitions, but not always *from* intuitions; rather, pure knowledge is conceptual, and a judgement via concepts is a representation of a representation, *Vorstellung einer Vorstellung*.[66] Knowledge then, the *quid pro quo* whereby things give themselves to us as representations and we give them the opportunity to show themselves to us, not as they are, but as appearances – all this is concerned with 'that and how' things *are* as intuitions; and 'that and how' we let them *be* by means of concepts. And: 'the being "in the appearance" is the same being as the being in itself, and this alone'.[67] But not in the same way: on the one hand, things are in themselves; on the other, things are as they represent themselves. Thus for Kant: 'the thing in itself is not another object, but is rather another relation, *respectus*, of the representation of *the same object*'.[68] As Heidegger insists: 'The double characterization of the being as "thing in itself" and as "appearance" corresponds to the twofold way according to which the being can stand in relation to infinite and finite knowing: the being in the standing-forth and the same being as standing-against [*ob-jectus*].'[69] And the difference between things in themselves and as they appear is necessary, a question of *phainomenon*, not merely the way in which a thing introduces itself to different audiences at one and the same time, nor simply the perspective we take on a given being, but the face that it turns to face us; it is a demonstration of respect for the thing itself. Allowing things their look however, is not simply a passive act of good will; it is the transcendental bargain by which we gain the right to constitute objects of sensibility.

Beings then – submitting to the forms of intuition, becoming objects for us in space and time, mediated by concepts – are representations in representations for representations in order to produce representations (judgements of the understanding), that are ultimately grounded in representations (ideas) – for truth is representation, not just the representation of truth. In this sense, Kant's theory of knowledge upholds an almost zoological hierarchy:

> The genus is *representation* in general (*repraesentatio*). Subordinate to it stands representation with consciousness (*perceptio*). A *perception* which relates solely to the subject as the modification of its state is sensation (*sensatio*), an objective perception is knowledge (*cognitio*). This is either *intuition* or *concept* (*intuitus vel conceptus*). The former relates immediately to the object and is single, the latter refers to it mediately by means of a feature which several things may have in common. The concept is either *empirical* or a *pure concept*. The pure concept, insofar as it has its origin in the understanding alone (not in the pure image of sensibility), is called a *notion*. A concept formed from notions and transcending the possibility of experience is an *idea* or a concept of reason.[70]

Just as the Transcendental Aesthetic sets out the *a priori* conditions under which things and humans must *be* given or presented to us in order for them to *be* represented in intuition, the rest of the *Critique* presents a representation of the ways in which kinds of knowledge in a representative theory of knowledge must *be* in order for us to *be* able to know. Heidegger writes:

> A finite, knowing creature can only relate itself to a being which it itself is not, and which it also has not created, if this being which is already at hand can be encountered from out of itself. However, in order to be able to encounter this being as the being it is, it must already be 'recognized' generally and in advance as a being, that is, with respect to the constitution of its being. But this implies: ontological knowledge, which here is always pre-ontological, is the condition for the possibility that in general something like a being can itself stand in opposition to a finite creature.[71]

Sensibility provides the *a priori* formal conditions under which beings can be intuited; understanding, the conditions under which they can be recognized as objects of knowledge. Thus transcendental philosophy provides objectively valid knowledge, knowledge of objects, because the knowledge of beings as objects is grounded in the being of beings.

Sensation alone then, insufficient for us, must be accompanied by understanding, the faculty that allows knowledge via concepts insofar as it represents many as one: 'thoughts without content are empty, intuitions without concepts are blind'.[72] Judgement then takes place only on the basis of conceptual unity. The understanding however, does not simply provide the form of knowledge, *a priori* or *a posteriori*; it determines its content through categories – for pure concepts make the unification of each judgement first possible. Conceptual knowledge however, is not merely abstract; it is concrete insofar as the categories pertain to beings and provide pure predicative knowledge. In other words, the concepts of the understanding determine how beings must be in order to be objects of knowledge for us in the first place; they constitute objects as unified in advance according to rules. In this way, beings become that which they must be for us: intuition gives the being to be known; understanding supplies the transcendental rules by which it is known – and the ground of their connection lies in an original synthetic unity, transcendental apperception, the 'I' that is able to know, the 'I think' that brings categories to bear upon objects, that does not bring forth concepts, but 'works with them'[73] in the unity of judgement that constitutes *a priori* that which can be known.

Yet Kant insists that prior to apperception lies imagination: 'the principle of the necessary unity of pure, productive synthesis of *imagination, prior to apperception*, is the ground of the possibility of all knowledge, especially of experience'.[74] The two stems of finite human knowledge, empirical and transcendental, are rooted in imagination – and the essential difference between the A and B Deductions lies in the role of transcendental imagination: in the latter, it is absorbed by transcendental understanding; in the former, it shows what Heidegger takes to be its true function, namely to provide the original unity of synthesis, the ground of Kant's representative theory of knowledge, the power or *Kraft* on which an univocal image, *ein Bild*, of experience and thought is built, *Einbildungskraft*. Heidegger insists: 'while in the first edition all synthesis, i.e., synthesis as such, sprang forth from the power of imagination as a faculty which is not reducible to sensibility or understanding, in the second edition the understanding alone now assumes the role of origin for all synthesis'.[75] For in the B Deduction, the 'power of imagination is now just the name for empirical synthesis, i.e., for the synthesis related to intuition'.[76] And 'the transcendental power of imagination no longer functions as independent grounding faculty, mediating in an original way between sensibility and understanding in their possible unity. Rather, this intermediate faculty now falls, so to speak, between the two separate grounding sources of the mind. Its function is relegated to the under-standing.'[77] Thus: 'with reference to this most central question of the whole work [namely, metaphysics], it [the first edition] deserves a fundamental priority over the second'.[78] Indeed in the A Deduction, transcendental imagination serves as the unity of unities, the synthesis of syntheses or ground of grounds – for the synthesis of reproduction in imagination mediates between the synthesis of apprehension in intuition and the synthesis of reproduction in a concept. The power of imagination provides the condition of the possibility for sensibility to meet understanding (and ultimately reason), that is, it gives us the schematism. Intuition gives objects, understanding concepts, but imagination allows them to correspond, to be one and true – for here, truth is correspondence of object and concept.

This is why Kant insists that the 'third thing', the transcendental schema, the mediating representation, homogeneous with category and appearance, must be double, two-faced: on the one hand intellectual, on the other sensible – so a contradiction or paradox, an intelligible intuition or intuitive intellect.[79] And the schematic contradiction cannot simply be resolved or superseded by understanding – for it must remain both sensible and intelligible. Indeed as a representation, the transcendental schema can only be provided by transcendental imagination, *facultas imaginandi*, the faculty of representation, that which provides the transcendental determination of time as the 'formal *a priori* condition of all appearances whatsoever',[80] that is, of inner and outer sense, as well as that which 'as the schema of the concepts of the understanding, mediates the subsumption of the appearances under the category',[81] Indeed, 'the schema is in itself always a product of imagination'.[82]

But if 'it is schemata, not images of objects, which underlie our pure sensible concepts',[83] the essence of the schemata is time. In fact, time serves as the unity in which truth happens, objects represent themselves and correspond to concepts, show their sensible and intelligible faces; it is the condition of the possibility of synthesis, the ground that unifies the unifications of intuition and understanding. As Kant insists: all modifications of the mind are 'subject to time as that in which they must all be ordered, connected, and brought into relation'.[84] And the faculty of imagination is responsible for producing the schematism, the cause or *aitia* of time. As Heidegger reminds us: 'if the transcendental power of imagination, as the pure, forming faculty, in itself forms time – i.e., allows time to spring forth – then we cannot avoid the thesis...: the transcendental power of imagination is time'.[85] If transcendental philosophy is not simply epistemology, but metaphysics; no wonder that time is, for Heidegger, the condition of the possibility of fundamental ontology – then the *Critique of Pure Reason* is a chronontology.

Transcendental imagination however, is not only responsible for producing time; it must also show time to us as that place in which object and subject can meet. The schematism makes transcendence possible for finite human beings not only by building a single knowledge, a unity of unities, nor as Heidegger would have it, by constructing a pure image of unity, but by producing the pure look of time – for unlike its empirical counterpart, transcendental imagination is not simply the power to produce images, it is the faculty that produces pure time for a pure correspondence of pure intuition and pure understanding. In other words, time always also has its look; and the difference between beings in one and the same time is not simply one of space or mood, but of *eidos* or aspect, as the origin of the face a being presents of itself, as a thing in itself or an object, the kind of appearance of a phenomenon in time, and the aspect of a sensible or intelligible being. The paradoxical correspondence of sense and intellect always has a look – for *aspect is the other of time*,[86] and the time of truth is essentially aspectual. In this way, it is not only necessary for all knowledge whatsoever that time schematize, but that aspect does so as well.

Kant's example is illuminating: the homogeneity of time is not enough to allow an empirical being (a plate) to look like or have the identical shape/image of its transcendental ground (a geometrical circle); on the contrary, their sameness (roundness) must be both known through concepts and sensed through intuition. Time accounts for identity, but transcendental aspect accounts for difference, allows us to produce an image of a concept, to make it look like, if not be, that which it looks like. So the aspect of transcendental imagination is not itself an image, but the condition of the possibility of imaging, not merely at the same time, but with the same aspect, or not. Heidegger calls this the schema-image.[87] The transcendental schema however, is not simply the two-fold unity of time and aspect – for just as time itself is the condition of the possibility of times, so too is aspect the condition of the possibility of aspects, of how beings are in time, how they look different even at the same time, as simple or continual, complete or incomplete, sensible or intelligible. So the objects (or beings) of pure imagination, take on their aspect in time. Thus an account of time, of beings in time, of being and time, of that which is and is one in time, would remain incomplete without aspect.

A representative epistemology however, one that is just as much the representation of a method, must not only be able to *know* with respect to a pure temporal aspect – it must also be able to *represent* in pure intuition. As Kant insists: 'Now this representation of a universal procedure of imagination in providing an image for a concept, I entitle the schema of this concept.'[88] Transcendental imagination creates for a concept its own image, the pure image of the pure concept, like God's Adam, created in its own image. And it is only through the schema that pure figures in space can be the images of, for instance, triangles or circles. Kant's example: 'The concept "dog" signifies a rule according to which my imagination can universally delineate the figure of a four-footed animal, without being limited to any single determinate figure that experience provides, or any possible image that I can represent *in concreto*.'[89] By representing or tracing the constitutive and universal rule to which a multiplicity of beings must conform in order to be 'dogs', the pure image is double: 'dog' applies not only to many intuited empirical quadripedal beings, but also to the one conceptual dog that is always so, its identity across times and aspects. A transcendental image then, is precisely not a concrete shape or figure; on the contrary, it has pure aspect in pure time – for aspect is not just the look of a being that is present, nor some kind of after-image of a being that is absent; it is that which a being has whether present or absent, real or unreal. Pure aspect is *how* something must be, here and now or there and then, in order to look like or give the image of *that* which it looks like – for aspect is the transcendental other of time.

Time alone therefore, cannot provide the unity of understanding and intuition, of pure image and pure concept, *synthesis speciosa* and *synthesis intellectualis* – for the schema must be what Kant calls: 'a *monogram* of pure *a priori* imagination'.[90] Here on the one hand, time is the condition of the possibility of the mono-, *monas*, a unit, unity, *hen*, one unit; aspect on the other hand allows for the being, *on*, of the -gram, *grammē*, letter, mark, character, writing, drawing of the image. And while time determines *that* transcendental imagination serve as the ground of synthetic unity, aspect shows *how* transcendental unity is first possible, *how* the schema as *contradictio in adjecto* unifies sense and intellect. Insofar as imagination creates the image of a being, although not the being itself – we are not gods – and determines the rule according to which a thing appears to us, according to which it must be constituted as an object of knowledge, 'it is *subjectio sub aspectum*, that is, a faculty of intuitive presentation, of giving'.[91]

Heidegger therefore insists that the schema is actually only a phenomenon. And as the science of *phainomenon*, the transcendental image, pure image or appearance, phenomenology is the science of the pure aspect of unified beings (corresponding to concepts) in time. So phenomenology is the science of transcendental truth – for 'the schema is properly only the *phenomenon*, or the sensible concept of an object, in agreement with the category'.[92] The schema is that which first allows beings to represent themselves in intuition, as well as that which *a priori* permits concepts to constitute the pure form of objects, 'to bring them into one image'.[93] And if pure imagination can determine phenomenal objects in advance, prior to any experience, prior to the presence or absence of beings, and thereby make experience first possible; it is because it is not simply a matter of time, but also of aspect. Transcendental imagination is the original faculty of time and aspect, aspect's time and time's aspect, time as aspectual, aspect as temporal; and thereby the condition of the possibility of knowledge and truth, providing the unity of that which unifies, that which is synthetic in synthesis, or the very origin of synthesis, of synthetic *a priori* judgements – for it is the representing unity of representations, the pre-presenting or *Vor-stellung* of the pre-presentations of sensibility and under-standing, intuiting and knowing, the ground of empirical and transcendental knowledge of that which is one, of unified beings as they represent themselves, not in themselves. Thus the science of phenomenology is the science of the schematism, but this cannot be limited to time – for it is just as much the science of aspect, and of that which makes objects, unified beings, first possible. The *Critique of Pure Reason* is the science of aspect and time, unity and being, onto-heno-chrono-phenomenology, or just phenomenology for short.

Nevertheless, if the schema of Kant's critical phenomenology, the ground of truth as the correspondence of subject and object, remains a contradiction, intelligible and sensible, image and concept; it determines not the conditions of the possibility of knowledge, of any experience whatsoever, but of its impossibility. And the *Critique* does not resolve the schematism's contradiction; it reveals that it knows it cannot know. Kant demonstrates that displacing the problem of truth from the empirical to the transcendental, repetition in the realm of the schematism, solves nothing – on the contrary, as in Lambert, it shows the impossibility of a solution.[94] But this is no flaw or shrinking back from the abyss or non-ground of non-knowledge,[95] nor is it an ungrounding of the ground upon which critical philosophy is constructed; it is a precise taking account of the finitude of human reason, with the knowledge that we do not know, the uncertainty of certainty, the thought that thought cannot think. As Kant insists: the schematism is 'a concealed art', *eine verborgene Kunst*, one buried 'in the depths of the human soul', one whose truth nature is unlikely ever to reveal.[96]

1.7

But to return to the *what* and *how* of *Being and Time*, the *theme* and *way* – for the destructuring of ontology is not yet complete, if it ever could be. Heidegger insists that Kant remains loyal to the scholastic/Cartesian ontology, itself derived from the Greek determination of the meaning of being as presence, *ousia* as *parousia*, *Anwesenheit*; and hence, thinks time as 'the present'. In other words, 'to be' means 'to be present', not simply here, but now. Speaking, thinking or more precisely apprehending a being in its pure objectivity means presenting, making present, bringing into presence. Yet for Heidegger, this Greek onto-chronology is a double-failure: the temporality of being remains implicit, and 'time itself is taken to be one being among others'.[97] Hence the need to explicate the meaning of being, and interpret time as its horizon, not a mere being.

Yet Heidegger is quick to qualify not only the project of *Being and Time*, but the entire destructuring of ontology – for the question of the meaning of being is, like Kant's schematism, deeply concealed, *tief eingehüllt*.[98] In fact, Heidegger explicitly warns against exaggeration: 'In this field where "the matter itself is deeply veiled," any investigation will avoid overestimating its results.'[99] The amount of exactness a science provides must be appropriate to its subject matter, especially if being loves to hide – although the temptation to overestimate may be stronger when the object of investigation is masked or veiled, when 'an enclosing *shell* and a *kernel*' seem to present themselves,[100] even if this temptation may itself be the result of another overestimation or temptation. For who can say with certainty that the veil does not conceal another veil? That the depth of veiling is not infinite? Or that the act of tearing away the veil does not far more re-veil that which veiling unveiled?

Yet even further – for the warning does not stop with the essentially concealed status of the question of being (access to which should be gained through the existential analytic of Dasein), of the meaning of being, the interpretation of being in terms of time, and the meaning of time – Heidegger continues: 'For such inquiry is constantly forced to face the possibility of disclosing a still more original and more universal horizon from which it could draw the answer to the question "What does 'being' mean?"'[101] So a horizon for the horizon? But under what conditions would that be possible? A more universal universal? Or more original origin? Like some other *contradictio in adjecto*? Is this another opening of *Being and Time*? Or is the inquiry perhaps designed to fail in its announced task, the destructuring of ontology and the disclosure of the universal horizon for any understanding of being whatsoever? Is this field of disputations, the bloody 'battle-field of these *endless* controversies',[102] not the kind of feign that points elsewhere? To a perhaps unannounced task?

Regardless, having determined the *what*, Heidegger turns to the *how*, to phenomenology as the science of phenomena, 'To the things themselves!', '*Zu den Sachen selbst!*' And here the question concerns the extent to which the method is appropriate to its matter, its ability or inability to capture its prey: for if phenomenology, as Heidegger understands it, shows itself unable to grasp the meaning of being, it is perhaps in order to demonstrate the limits of the method – especially as Husserl first formulated it – and its inappropriateness, even in Heidegger's rearticulation, for thinking anything like being. Even further, at issue will be whether phenomenology can determine itself as a method in the first place for getting closer to that which is self-evident, and maintain itself in opposition to 'all free-floating constructions and accidental findings; in opposition to taking over concepts only seemingly demonstrated; in opposition to pseudo-questions which often are spread around as "problems" for generations'.[103] Can then phenomenology avoid all four (or five) of the pitfalls that present themselves in Heidegger's list? And will all the slips of method be forgiven, if *Being and Time* is able to get to being itself? Or at least succeeds in demonstrating that any attempt to do so must end in failure?

Yet even if the method is to show itself as unable to live up to the task at hand, to reveal itself as inappropriate, and if its failure is to be convincing; Heidegger must take it seriously, must give phenomenology its full force. Rather than simply take it over from Husserl therefore, Heidegger derives an even more fundamental concept of phenomenology from *phainomenon* and *logos*. But this is not an etymological derivation, even if it gives us cause to pause with Pausaneus, and philological arguments about its violence will not be sufficient.[104] We must far more assess the ability or inability of phenomenology – as Heidegger articulates it – to raise the question of the meaning of being.

First then phenomenon means: self-showing, *'what shows itself in itself,* what is manifest'.[105] And that means privatively: what *could* show itself as what it is *not* in itself, as a semblance. But this does not mean appearance – for what does not show itself, but only, like the oracle at Delphi, gives a sign, a symptom or symbol. And an appearance therefore, can be either of a referent (that which makes itself known as something that does not show itself, the question or the being, matter or thing itself), or a sign (that which does the making itself known, that which indicates something that does not show itself) – although appearance is also used to designate phenomenon as self-showing. Indeed, as Heidegger admits, the confusion is compounded – and here, the question will be to what extent, if at all, it can be avoided, that is, whether a description of phenomenon is effectively possible, or impossible – by the fact that appearance can also mean, mere appearance, what is produced, 'what comes to the fore in the nonmanifest itself, and radiates from it in such a way that what is nonmanifest is thought of as what is essentially *never* manifest'.[106] Then although we should be able to keep the meanings distinct from one another, confusion is inevitable – all showing is appearance. So the list: (1) What shows itself: self-showing, phenomenon. (2) What does not show itself: semblance. (3) What does the showing: appearance as sign. (4) What does not show itself in the showing: appearance as referent. (5) What never shows itself: appearance as production. Yet Heidegger insists that (5) must not be confused with (2): 'this not-showing which veils is not semblance'.[107] And Kant is invoked in order to clarify their difference: on the one hand, what shows itself are appearances, as in objects of empirical intuition, semblance; on the other hand, appearance as the emanation of that which conceals itself insofar as it appears. Furthermore what shows itself (1) is constitutive for appearance in the sense of what makes itself know through a self-showing (4), that is, something like the Kantian noumena or thing in itself, although Heidegger avoids the words here, that shows itself as phenomena. But does this clarify anything? Can we clearly and distinctly differentiate between these appearances and phenomena? Or have we been led down a dead end, a *Holzweg*? Has Heidegger demonstrated the constitutive role of phenomenon as self-showing for all kinds of appearance? Or has he far more made the inevitability of confusion clear?

The confusion deepens – for if phenomenon can turn into semblance, and appearance can turn into semblance, then phenomenon can turn into appearance, and vice versa. Everything can turn into – or look like, show itself as – everything else. Heidegger's example, with respect to symptoms of illness as appearances: 'Under a certain kind of light someone can look as if he were flushed. The redness that shows itself can be taken as making known the objective presence of fever; this in turn would indicate a disturbance in the organism.'[108] Or not – for the redness could also be a function of the observer, of rose coloured glasses, or an aberration in the instrument of observation (e.g., my own blood-shot eyes could mean that the other's flush is mine); or the redness could indicate a shift in the criterion, in the normal colour to which the so-called redness is compared, contrasted and condemned (in which case, red is relative to some kind of neutral skin colour, a colour that may or may not exist as black, white, red, grey – and deviance would be a means for instituting and legitimating a control: 'I am normally flushed'). In other words, the conditional character of phenomenology cannot be used as exemplary for what should be (if such a thing is possible) fundamental ontology – for it proves just the opposite. Even further, the example demonstrates the incapacity of any kind of necessary connection between sign and referent; as in language, there is no natural or necessary (but only an arbitrary) bond between word (being, *Sein*, *l'être*, *on*) and being. And the redness could be a sign of illness just as much as that of health, as in the very German motto: *Salz und Brot macht Wangen rot*, salt and bread make cheeks red. Indeed, the example is supposed to demonstrate the possibility of error, of falsity or deception, but under what conditions could we even determine that we had been wrong? Aren't we always under a certain kind of light? Is light not the condition of the possibility and impossibility of seeing red in the first place? Could we ever be sure to distinguish situations where fever was objectively present from those where it was not? Are we not dealing with the interpretation of symptoms? Symptoms of causes that are themselves symptoms? Is it not impossible to ever reach the original cause of redness – for how would we know that we were there, and not simply looking at another effect? In fact, the look of redness is just as much a look as any other. And the example shows not that a phenomenon is constitutive for appearance, not that a phenomenon can turn into a semblance – but just the reverse, namely, that appearance is constitutive for appearance, and that semblance can turn into phenomenon.

Regardless, self-showing is supposed to be the ground upon which all kinds of appearances make their appearance, the origin of the look, and cause of the symptom. Indeed everything hangs on being able to distinguish phenomenon as self-showing from other kinds of showing. We must be able to maintain the original self-showing of things prior to appearance. As Heidegger insists: 'The confusing multiplicity of "phenomena" designated by the terms phenomenon, semblance, appearance, mere appearance, can be unraveled only if the concept of phenomenon is understood from the very beginning as the self-showing in itself.'[109] Self-showing however, is still showing. Then how can self-showing-phenomena be unravelled from the confusing multiplicity of other phenomena? Or has Heidegger's analysis reached the structural limits of phenomenological method? Is confusion not only possible, but necessary, at least insofar as neither self-showing nor any other showing gets out of the phenomenological loop? In other words, if self-showing remains a showing, can it ever guarantee that what it shows is itself and not another? If self-showing shows itself as that which reveals itself as an 'appearance', but simultaneously conceals itself in the appearance? And are the quotation marks enough to avoid the confusion of 'appearance' with appearance? For if self-showing is still a showing, how could phenomena serve as the ground or origin of showing? And if, as Heidegger insists, *Being and Time* remains within 'the horizon of the Kantian problem',[110] is it because its transcendental showing remains a representational onto-epistemology? Has the representational economy not been overcome, but only pushed a step back, from the look to that look which produced the look, to that showing that produces the show? If transcendental self-showing is in itself a show?

In fact, Heidegger responds to the confusion of showing and self-showing, look and look, original and copy, presentation and representation, with 'formal indication', *formale An-zeige*.[111] Dasein's existentials are neither categories nor representations – for the facticity of human experience can only be formally indicated, pointed to or shown as, non-representable, non-showing. Singularities of individual experience, as well as the *a priori* or transcendental conditions of their possibility, of the experience of experience, the universality of universals, the formalization of forms, can only be pointed out – hence experienced as beyond all possible experience. And this kind of showing, formally indicative, is therefore prior to the abstractions of metaphysical concepts and ontology alike – it is preconceptual, preontological. Formally indicative language, the impersonal tropes in which German is supposed to specialize – it's raining, it's pouring – no longer grasps an object with some kind of conceptual or mechanical apparatus, but nevertheless allows the pretheoretical forms of life to show themselves, to be read-off in a hermeneutic description of that which shows itself. The formal indications of *Being and Time* are only supposed to point towards things themselves, inaugurating a science of pretheoretical experience, a semiotics of life, not theory but signposts, *Wegmarken*, just as the Oracle at Delphi does not speak but gives a sign. As Heidegger insists: 'This self-showing (phenomenon in the genuine, original sense) is, on the other hand, "appearance" as the emanation of something that makes itself known but *conceals* itself in the appearance.'[112]

But as Gadamer insists: 'an indication [*Anzeige*] always stays at the distance necessary for pointing something out [*Zeigen*]'.[113] Forgoing the ability to represent things themselves is not enough – for formal indication remains loyal to the logic of showing; it shows that which cannot be shown, points to, shows, *zeigen*. Indeed, formal indication is not supposed to reveal that which is concealed, only point to it; but it reveals formal indication, shows the non-showing of phenomena, as well as the way to the way of non-showing, just as it reaches unreachability, decides upon indecidability, is certain of uncertainty. And formal indication is supposed to point us in the right direction, to indicate or show the way; but it could therefore also fail to reach its target. For formal indication is supposed to point us to the possibility of experience, but before it can do so, we must be able to read, to interpret the signs, understand the indications – an entire semiotic field or system of meanings is presupposed. And formal indication is supposed to be merely formal, without material and contentless – but it always also has at least one concrete content, namely itself; the sign is always a sign of itself as well as of that which it does or does not signify. So too, formal indication of experience is itself experience, and we would need indications of indications *ad infinitum* – the science of pretheoretical experience would remain ungrounded. And formal indication is supposed to add nothing to that which it indicates, but only indicate: the origin of experience should remain unaltered in its expression, or in the expression of its inexpressibility – a being can *show* itself only under the condition that it not show *itself* – for a non-look essentially belongs to the look. As Gadamer concludes: 'the "formal indication" points us in the direction in which we are to look';[114] but then we could never verify that a formal indication never arrives at that to which it points, never touches or contaminates that which it is supposed to indicate, nor that we had been pointed in the right direction, nor that we had not simply arrived there by chance; and even adding nothing to experience, formal indication adds that it does not add. Formal indication therefore is not a way out of the logic of showing, but far more a way more deeply in – for concealing essentially belongs to and is given with revealing. As Heidegger insists: phenomenology shows, or lets be seen, something that does not show itself, something concealed, that is, 'something that essentially belongs to what initially and for the most part shows itself, indeed in such a way that it constitutes its meaning and ground'.[115] Showing has come back to haunt that which should never show itself. Yet we can never show self-showing, nor the non-self-showing or non-look, the concealment or that which conceals itself in the appearance – for this too would conceal itself, the concealment of the concealment. And if it shows itself as concealing, it would once again fall into the economy of self-showing, appearance, semblance of concealment, confusion and misrecognition – for the concealment shows itself as concealing. In this way, revealing and concealing not only serve as ways of self-showing, but of non-self-showing, of never-showing, of that which shows itself precisely as that which does not show itself. Indeed, *Being and Time* is transcendental philosophy insofar as it allows the fundamental structures of phenomena to show (and not show) themselves thematically. And the existential analytic is a transcendental analytic (or transcendental dialectic?) insofar as the constitutional modes of Dasein (not merely categories, but existentials) are brought thematically to self-showing (and non-self-showing) through phenomenology.

It is no surprise then, that when it comes time to articulate a science or *logos* of phenomenon, phenomeno-logy, *Being and Time* must remain true to the economy of showing. Here, *logos* is supposed to be understood primarily not as reason, logic, judgement, concept, definition, account or ratio, but as that which makes clear or manifest, *dēloun*, that which shows itself through language, in speech, *legein* – for it lets what shows itself to be seen from itself, *apophainesthai ta phainomena*. As letting-be-seen, *logos* is the ground upon which what-is-said can be synthesized or taken with something else that is said; it is the truth, original unconcealment or noticing (or more precisely, not-not-noticing, the un-unnoticed, *a-lēthes*), from which something can then be judged as true or false, corresponding or in accordance with a concept. Prior to speaking of something, proclaiming it to be a particular kind of being, this or that, is the perception or *aisthēsis* of its being, that it is present (as Kant's manifold is given) – and this perception is always originary. *Logos* lets phenomena be seen, lets beings be seen as self-showing.[116] And as fundamental ontology, phenomenology allows not only beings, but the being of those beings to show itself; it is the method to the concealing of things themselves, the *how* to the *what*, to beings and the being of beings: 'Phenomenology is the way of access to, and the demonstrative manner of determination of, what is to become the theme of ontology.'[117] But then the preliminary concept of phenomenology is not preliminary at all – for its preliminarity is final. And although it may not arrive at the things themselves, beings or being, phenomenology does come to itself, secures and fixes a way, determine the *logos* of phenomena – which may very well be the price it pays for being a science, or at least looking like one.

But if phenomenology only seems to remain faithful to an economy of showing, appears to determine our *logos*; can we differentiate that which is phenomenology from that which is not? If self-showing is always threatened by appearance, by a possible (or necessary?) confusion with that which it should not be, if phenomena could not avoid looking like appearances, and if appearances could become phenomena, as they could become mere appearances, if we could produce the appearance of phenomena, not merely false or pseudo-phenomena, but copies of original self-showing, if we could uncover that which was never covered and hold it up as a discovery, then would we not make the fictional world a reality? And once the threat of confusion enters into the economy of phenomenology, is not the guarantee of its originality always suspect? Could the 'birth certificate' of appearances not always be forged? Or rather, has it not always already been forged? Is its originality not itself a forgery? Then is the non-originality of the original the possibility of phenomenology itself? Must self-showing not always be an other-showing in order even to claim the status of self-showing? For if phenomena could show themselves as they are not, must they not do so? And so once Heidegger introduces concealment into the economy of (self or other) showing, can we ever be certain that he has not concealed something essential from us? Or is that not precisely the point, or the truth: if *Being and Time* reveals anything, it is only on the condition that it always also conceals? That revealing is always also a concealing? Showing always also a non-showing? Is this not a more revelatory concealment? And if phenomena can be so deceptive, is not the rest of *Being and Time* open to question? Is Heidegger then, to be trusted? Concealing as he reveals? Or perhaps quite untrustworthy? Or both, necessarily both? And is this not a more trustworthy kind of trust? If we can trust him to betray us, would not philosophy (as phenomenology or fundamental ontology, as onto-theo-epistemology or thinking) always also – and from the first page of *Being and Time* – be a question of trust? Then can we trust Heidegger only if he could betray us? And would the uncertainty of betrayal be able to make trust possible? So if he could betray us, he must betray us? Before any betrayal?

1.8

Regardless, the rest of *Being and Time* seems to take up the theme and method of its Introduction in all seriousness (although we cannot, nor perhaps must we, take up a complete explication and exhaustive analysis of Heidegger's text, and not only because there are others who have already done it, Heidegger specialists or specialists in what Heidegger calls the 'Heideggerian mode of interpretation').[118] Indeed, Heidegger is quite clear: 'The real theme is being.'[119]

The preliminary object of the investigation however, is precisely not being, but us, that with which we are all familiar, that is perhaps easier for us to see, that being whose being is an issue for it, in order to let it show itself from itself, insofar as *'the "essence" of Dasein lies in its existence'*[120] – for 'the being which this being is concerned about in its being is always my own'.[121] And if we can capture the being of this being, we can presumably do so for being itself (although this is not at all certain, not only because the relation between beings and being has not yet been clarified, and it may be simply inenubilable, not merely because the ontological difference cannot be bridged by analogy or equivocation, identity or difference or sameness, but also because the means appropriate for an analytic of Dasein may not function for being, or because the results of one investigation may not apply to the other – just as results *in vitro* don't always apply *in vivo*, just as Plato's task in the *Republic* of finding justice in the soul by searching for it in the city may be doomed to failure). The digression (through an interpretation of Dasein in terms of temporality and the explication of time as the transcendental horizon of the question of being) should raise the question of the meaning of being, or at least to determine that any attempt shows itself as essentially indefeasible.

Is there then a moment in *Being and Time's* existential analytic in which the question of the meaning of being becomes questionable? Or if there are many, then is our choice of an exemplary moment simply arbitrary? Should we choose, for instance, that moment in which Dasein, delimited initially as being-in-the-world, must be grasped in the unity of our fundamental structure (the worldliness of its world, being a self and being with others, being-in as such, to the extent that such unity can be or be grasped), that is, our existential meaning as care? Or perhaps when, after showing that we understand our being neither as an object of a particular science of the human being (anthropology, psychology, biology, ethnology – for we are not simply objects submitting to categories) nor as a subject within the history of philosophy as metaphysics that defines us as rational animal, a living being that has, possesses in its hand, language or speech, *zōon logon echon*; that takes us as a finite being, *ens finitum*, as opposed to God, *ens infinitum*;[122] but as a being that, in its being, relates to its being, to itself (if this can be shown) – for 'Dasein is the being which I myself always am', and 'mineness belongs to existing Dasein as the condition of the possibility of authenticity and inauthenticity'?[123] Or maybe the moment when mineness is not equated with authenticity, just as neither indifference, nor authenticity's negation, non-mineness, not belonging to myself, not taking myself over from or to myself, can show itself as inauthenticity (insofar as it can be distinguished from authenticity)? Or when, after arguing that the essence of my being lies in being so that I always belong to myself (no matter how I relate to myself), Heidegger asks whether I can now take responsibility for myself, if I must always belong to myself (if this is at all possible)? Or perhaps when, insofar as I am in the world, insofar as a world belongs to me and I to it, I am always in relation to the world, caringly in the world, and can therefore care more or less about this or that thing in the world – for 'to be' means primarily not 'to have' a world (to the extent they can be distinguished), but 'to be in the world', and if we have or know a world, it is only on the basis of the way we are in the world, primordially dwell with beings in the world?[124] Or perhaps at the moment in which we relate to beings in our world insofar as we use them, take them as practically ready to hand, or as merely objectively present, or not, that is, insofar as they disclose themselves and our world to us, insofar as we encounter them – but this because, as in the world, we are caring; although being in the world is not simply a function of a practical subject, but *quid pro quo*, we encounter beings in the world because they make themselves known to us, announce themselves and let themselves be appropriated as the world itself recedes into the background, serves as the horizon by virtue of which beings can meaningfully (or meaninglessly) be for us, relevant to us?[125] Or rather maybe when Heidegger formulates the being of beings in the world in their worldly character, not merely as extended and shaped objects (Descartes), but as inner-worldly beings in the primordial totality of interlocking relations significant and signifying to us (or lacking signification), that is, as belonging to a complex of useful things (the 'whereto' of *intentio*), inconspicuously familiar for Dasein's circumspective concern?[126] Or perhaps when we are thought as beings in the world because we always exist as worldly, discovering the world by bringing it near, dwelling together with (de-distanced) beings, understanding and orienting ourselves in relation to the world, letting other beings be encountered?[127] Or maybe in the moment when the 'I', unlike everyday Dasein (to the extent this difference can be maintained), is taken as a formal indication of that which reveals itself in a particular mode: being lost, not I, I myself, being-alone, being-with, here and there in the world, being a self, the they-self, one, *das 'Man'*, the irresponsible or non-responsible, the dependency and inauthenticity of nobody, 'publicness' (as opposed to 'privateness', the sphere wherein sophistry flourishes? Or do the quotation marks mark not only an inability to separate public from private, but sophistry from philosophy, the serious from its other, or from – Heidegger's marks – 'politics'),[128] being towards beings in the world as circumspectively concerned for things, leaping in for others, leaping ahead of others, mistrusting others (and what happens to being-with once the possibility of mistrust is introduced when attempting to distinguish the authentic self that grasps itself explicitly, if such a grasp is at all possible, and an inauthentic self, or Dasein dispersed and lost in the they?), being one's self as *'an existentiell modification of the they'*?[129] Or maybe where Heidegger insists that 'the ontologically decisive lies in avoiding splitting the phenomenon [of being-in] beforehand'[130] into Dasein, on the one hand, and an objectively present 'object', on the other – if that is possible at all? Or perhaps the moment in which the possibility or impossibility of Dasein being its own disclosure, its own clearing, that is, *a-lētheia*, the double or two-fold truth of itself, calls itself into question? Or when our attunement and understanding (the way we find ourselves mooded, factically thrown there as delivered over, disclosing our being-in-the-world, opening us up to ourselves), are supposed to be equiprimordially determined by discourse?[131] Or maybe in Heidegger's phenomenology of fear (of a being) as a demonstration of attunement to that of which we take care, ourselves or property or loved ones, and its essential difference from angst (to the extent the difference can be maintained, or not)? Or in the power of understanding (or not understanding ourselves and our world) of which we find ourselves (not in opposition to, nor as a modal category of objective presence, a should be or could be or will be reality; but rather, existentially, that is, as a 'primordial and ultimate positive ontological determination of Dasein'),[132] capable of disclosing our being to ourselves as a project in an authentic or inauthentic way, that is, an authenticity or inauthenticity that can be either genuine or not genuine, etc. (*ad infinitum*? – for we must here wonder to what extent the phenomenology of projective understanding demonstrates the impossibility of determining when and if a given understanding is authentic and genuine and for-the-sake-of-itself and originating-from-its-own-self and whatever else is necessary, that is, to what extent understanding, an understanding of understanding, an understanding of authenticity, of the genuine, or the for-the-sake-of-itself, is possible; especially if, as Heidegger insists, 'turning to one of these fundamental possibilities of understanding, however, does not dispense with the other')?[133] Or perhaps when *Being and Time's* interpretation that is to serve as the horizon of 'any understanding whatsoever of being',[134] an interpretation that, as

Dasein's project, is the development according to the as-structure (grounded in fore-having, fore-sight, fore-conception) of a meaning for innerworldly beings to be expressed as a statement about a something in *particular* (insofar as *logos*, like Husserlian intentionality, is always *logos tinos*)? Or perhaps should we take up the possibility (or impossibility) of our own primordial totality, the structural whole of Dasein revealed by angst as care, the unity of the totality of beings, of being and beings, as the original and continual question of *Being and Time*, the question of the meaning of being in general, with respect to the fundamental-ontological problematic (when, almost half-way through the book, the evasion of the question has finally become 'problematic', although it was so all along)? Or perhaps the moment when our angst with respect to being-in-the-world, not fear from any particular innerworldly being, but about the world as such and for being-in-the-world itself, insofar as this angst is supposed to take the possibility of understanding away from us, throw us back upon our potentiality-for-being-in-the-world, individuate us, disclose our ownmost being-in-the-world to us, our freedom to choose and grasp ourselves, the pure potentiality of ourselves, as in an existential '*solus ipse*' (Heidegger's quotation marks. But who is being quoted here? Husserl?[135] And why? Or what therefore are the quotation marks supposed to mark? An original or a result, a product of the process of abstraction or phenomenological *epochē*?)?

In fact, we might perhaps choose any of these, but let us rather pick the moment in *Being and Time* when the text articulates the difference between – and that means not negation, but relation – authenticity and inauthenticity. On the one hand, the authenticity of our being, the mode of being-our-selves, genuinely, fully, of attuned understanding, of the potential for being-free, a being-itself, being-for-its-self or being-for-the-sake-of-itself that lies in our ownmost Dasein. On the other hand, inauthenticity of Dasein's non-being, its existential mode or positive possibility of not-being-its-self – which is supposed to express no negative value judgement or disparagement whatsoever (insofar as this is possible) – as entangled with idle talk, curiosity and ambiguity, that is, as fallen prey to a tempting absorption in the world, a 'being lost in the publicness of the they'[135] or being-for-another that ends in a busy tranquilization, that alienates and closes us off to our potential authenticity, that plunges us into the groundlessness and nothingness of a concealed, normalized and revalued inauthentic everydayness. Thus authenticity and inauthenticity, *Eigentlichkeit und Uneigentlichkeit*, are possibilities of being, ways for Dasein to be, choose itself or not, assume or lose ourselves.[136]

So authenticity *or* inauthenticity, authenticity *and* inauthenticity – but there is a third; Heidegger calls it a *Vortäuschen*, a sham, fake, counterfeit. This is the inauthenticity of Dasein's non-being, torn away from authenticity and fallen in the they, that is always, *immer*, also a 'sham of authenticity'.[137] Inauthenticity displaces authenticity, changes places, simulates or feigns authenticity; in representing itself, it misrepresents itself. But if inauthenticity can look like authenticity, it can do so because they look like one another – inauthentic authenticity, like authentic inauthenticity, looks authentic. The sham of authenticity then calls to be identified, singled out and pointed to, indicated *qua* sham; we are called, authentically or not, to disentangle the authentic from the inauthentic, to differentiate and maintain the difference between authentic authenticity and inauthentic authenticity, between the authentic inauthenticity and the inauthentic inauthenticity, the sham of authentic authenticity and the real, the authentic sham of authentically inauthentic authenticity and the inauthentic.

But the task seems impossible, and the questions multiply themselves: Why must Heidegger introduce the possibility or necessity of fake authenticity, at the very moment he attempts to articulate the possibility or necessity of the real? Why does *Being and Time* insist on the threat of the sham, itself so perfect that not only is it accepted as real, but it maybe more authentic than the 'authentic'?[138] Are we not to wonder to what extent the phenomenology of projective understanding is itself feigned – for what if we could not determine when a given understanding is authentic, genuine, for-the-sake-of-itself, originating-from-its-own-self? What if an understanding of understanding, of authenticity, of the genuine, or the for-the-sake-of-itself, is not possible? And if the angst that is supposed to reveal authenticity and inauthenticity as possibilities for us in an undistorted way is itself a distortion – or a sham? What if it is impossible to maintain the difference between the authentic (being for the sake of one's self, one's ownmost, unity and totality of self) and the inauthentic (being for the sake of another, the they's, disunity and non-totalizability of self), and between their modifications? If the differences that are supposed to make a difference can – perhaps even must – be faked?

In fact, the sham threatens the authenticity of *Being and Time* throughout. Perhaps more authentic than the 'authentic', the sham corrupts the possibility of distinguishing authentic from inauthentic, real from fake, original from copy; and in this way, real and fake are ineluctably linked – for if the sham of authenticity is authentically shammed, the sham is a real sham. But if there is always a sham of authenticity, if this sham shams the very possibility of authenticity, even before authenticity and inauthenticity; the text may point to the impossibility of differentiating, understandingly or not, authenticity from inauthenticity (at least as much as, to a need or promise to differentiate). And *Being and Time* might sham the difference between real and fake, original and copy in order to indicate that – just as Dasein is always already in both 'the truth and the untruth'[139] – we are always in the authentic and the inauthentic, or alternatively to point to some other truth of authenticity and inauthenticity.

To what then does the sham of authenticity point? What is the meaning of the impossibility of understandingly distinguishing truth from untruth, original from copy, real from fake, authenticity from inauthenticity – an impossibility that simultaneously threatens the entire project of *Being and*

Time, not just its method, but also its attempt to grasp the meaning of our Dasein, to raise the question of the meaning of being (itself a sham?) and its horizon of time? What is the essence of that which threatens Heidegger's text from the moment it introduces the possibility or necessity of the *Sophist*, and the difference between irony and seriousness? Does this difference not essentially belong to irony itself, a difference that cannot be resolved, about which we can never be certain, but far more remains uncertain? So is then the uncertainty of irony, of irony and seriousness, not the very possibility of difference? Of the difference of the sham and the real, authentic and inauthentic, original and copy, and of irony and seriousness themselves? Does the sham of authenticity not point to the ironic uncertainty of this difference? And if we find this irony here in *Being and Time*, might we not also find it everywhere?

Notes

1 F. Schleiermacher, '*Da nun wir keinen Rat wissen, so macht doch ihr selbst uns recht anschaulich, was ihr denn andeuten wollt, wenn ihr Seiendes sagt. Denn offenbar wißt ihr doch dies schon lange, wir aber glaubten es vorher zwar zu wissen, jetzt aber stehen wir ratlos*' (*Sämtliche Werke*, IV, Meiner, 1958, 216; my translation). Although Heidegger praises Schleiermacher's translations, he finds him lacking in interpretive force: 'And so Schleiermacher's work on Plato, though indeed important for the history of the development of the human sciences and even unsurpassed as a translation, remains, in terms of a philosophical appropriation of Plato, beneath the demands we have to make on a philosophical interpretation' (*GA19*, 313). See M. Davis, *The Autobiography of Philosophy*, Rowman and Littlefield, 1999, 14.

2 *BT*. I have followed J. Stambaugh's translation except where noted, and with the exception of Da-sein, which I have left as Dasein.

3 S. Benardete, *The Being of the Beautiful*, University of Chicago, 1984. F.M. Cornford translates: 'We are completely puzzled, then, and you must clear up the question for us, what you do intend to signify when you use the word "real." Obviously you must be quite familiar with what you mean, whereas we, who formerly imagined we know, are now at a loss' (*Collected Dialogues of Plato*, Princeton University, 1961).

4 W. Benjamin, *Illuminations*, Schocken, 1969; 'Die Aufgabe des Übersetzers', *Gesammelte Schriften*, IV.1, Suhrkamp, 1972, 16. The parallels between Heidegger's *alētheia*, Benjamin's concept of truth as 'intensively concealed', *intensiv verborgen*, cannot be overlooked. Nevertheless, for Benjamin, in spite of 'all its philosophical packaging', Heidegger's work is basically 'only a piece of good translating work' (letter to Scholem, no. 92, ca. December 1, 1920, *The Correspondence of Walter Benjamin*,

University of Chicago, 1994, 168). Thanks to Helen Lambert for reminding me of this passage.

5 M. Heidegger, *Die Bedeutung des deinon*, *GA53*, 74. For J. Derrida, this marks a certain 'resistance to translation' of Heidegger's texts and terminology (*De l'esprit*, Galilée, 1987, 17).

6 *KPM*, 239; translation modified; my italics.

7 *CPR*, Aviii.

8 *BT*, 1.

9 *BT*, 1.

10 *BT*, 1.

11 Definition here is via diaeresis, a method perhaps suitable for mathematicians to distinguish between whole and unwhole square roots, but not for philosophy. See *Thea.* 147e5.

12 *Soph.* 223b1-7. See S. Benardete, 'Plato *Sophist* 223b1-7', *Phronesis* 5:129–39, 1960.

13 *Soph.* 229c5; cf., 224d and 226a.

14 *Soph.* 268c8-d4.

15 *Soph.* 233c10 and 235d-236c.

16 Rosen, *Plato's Sophist*, Yale University, 1983, 100; see also, Benardete, *Being of the Beautiful*, II.77.

17 *Soph.* 223c and 226a.

18 *Odyssey*, XVII.485-86. Cf. *Rep.* 381D and Benardete, *Being of the Beautiful*, II.168. On the co-implication of being and unity, see Aristotle, *Meta.*, 1003b22ff, and my forthcoming, *Unity and Aspect*.

19 Rosen, *Plato's Sophist*, 134.

20 As the Stranger insists: 'Yes, my friend, and the attempt to separate everything from every other thing not only strikes a discordant note but amounts to a crude defiance of the philosophical Muse' (*Soph.* 259e).

21 *Soph.* 232b1-7.

22 *Soph.* 253e4-254b2.

23 *Soph.* 257b6-7.

24 Strauss, *The City and Man*, University of Chicago, 1964, 51; see *Soph.* 241a2-7. Rosen, 202.

25 *ZS*, 89.

26 Derrida, *De l'esprit*, 24.

27 *BT*, 1.

28 *EM*, 4.

29 *BT*, 1.

30 *BT*, 1.

31 *BT*, 1; my italics.

32 *BT*, 1; my italics.

33 Aristotle, *Meta.* G, 1003a33.

34 *BT*, 1.

35 St. Augustine, *Confessions*, Image Books, 1960, 287.

[36] Similarly, if Descartes refused to give the meaning of human being as rational animal, then was it because he knew that it would involve him in an infinite regress of meanings. Cf., *Meditations*, I.

[37] *BT*, 7–8. Nevertheless, under the guise of retrieving the question of the meaning of being, Heidegger does resort to a kind of dismissal of questioning based on an unexplained circle (*BT*, 3): prejudices about being rooted in ancient ontology cannot be interpreted or judged until the being about which they are prejudicial is itself explained. Thus prejudices are put in suspension until the concept of being can be worked out – but if this project fails, then do the prejudices remain intact?

[38] *BT*, 8.

[39] *BT*, 38.

[40] *BT*, 14.

[41] *BT*, 38n.

[42] *DT*, 11; Heidegger's italics.

[43] *BT*, 7; *ZS*, 156–7.

[44] *BT*, 13.

[45] *BT*, 12.

[46] *BT*, 12.

[47] *BT*, 12; Heidegger's italics; translation modified.

[48] *BT*, 12.

[49] *BT*, 15.

[50] *GA19*, 244.

[51] *BT*, 2.

[52] *BT*, 16.

[53] *BT*, 17; my emphasis.

[54] *BT*, 17; translation modified.

[55] *BT*, 5.

[56] *BT*, 17.

[57] *BT*, 19.

[58] *BT*, 19.

[59] *BT*, 19.

[60] *BT*, 20.

[61] *BT*, 23.

[62] *BT*, 23.

[63] *CPR*, A697/B725.

[64] *KPM*, 13; translation modified. Originating in Aristotle, metaphysics is first philosophy, *prōtoā philosophia*, ontology, the question of the being of beings, *to on hē on*, of beings as a whole, *metaphysica generalis*. Here, being is not a being, not to be found among beings in the sensible realm; rather, it is that supersensible or intelligible being which transcends beings, and thereby makes it possible for human beings to be, and to transcend themselves, to ex-ist as transcending. And if metaphysics is the study of being, of the being of beings, if it provides ontological knowledge, then it

simultaneously determines the conditions of the possibility of ontic knowledge, of beings, of the humanity of human beings, the finitude of finite beings for a *metaphysica specialis*.

[65] *KPM*, 26, translation slightly modified.

[66] *CPR*, A68/B93.

[67] *KPM*, 31.

[68] Kant, *Opus postumum*, 653, C551; quoted in *KPM*, 33.

[69] *KPM*, 32; translation modified.

[70] *CPR*, A 320/B376–7.

[71] *KPM*, 70–1.

[72] *CPR*, A75/B51.

[73] *KPM*, 151; Heidegger's quotation marks.

[74] *CPR*, A118; my italics.

[75] *KPM*, 163.

[76] *KPM*, 164.

[77] *KPM*, 164; and 170.

[78] *KPM*, 197.

[79] *CPR*, A138/B177–8.

[80] *CPR*, A34/B50.

[81] *CPR*, A139/B178.

[82] *CPR*, A140/B179.

[83] *CPR*, A140/B180.

[84] *CPR*, A99.

[85] *KPM*, 187.

[86] Clearly, the linguistic concept of aspect is insufficient for giving an account of transcendental or metaphysical aspect, for thinking the way in which beings are and are united at one and the same time, or anytime. But a being's aspect is probably not just that which the science of metaphysics has taken as that which shows itself as itself, nor as another, like some kind of perspective or view, symptom or indication, nor an appearance of an appearance, nor that which disappears by appearing, because it is too dimly seen, nor because it is too much or many, but because in showing itself, it shows that it cannot be shown. And nor could it be merely a function of language, reason or time. Rather aspect seems to be implied by unity. A unified being then would probably not show its aspect as left or right, up and down, present or absent, relative or absolute, concealed/revealed. But if something could be united or be itself or another at one and the same time, although not in the same way, it may be because of aspect. Then the unity of a being might still have to be aspectually complete or incomplete so that it could show itself phenomenologically in any way whatsoever, could present this face or that, this perspective or that side, so that it could be before or after in this way or another, or even so that it could be something rather than nothing. See my forthcoming, *Unity and Aspect*.

87 *KPM*, 104.
88 *CPR*, A140/B179–80; translation modified.
89 *CPR*, A141/B180; translation modified.
90 *CPR*, A142/B181, my italics.
91 *KPM*, 130.
92 *CPR*, A146/B186; translation modified, my italics.
93 *CPR*, A120.
94 *CPR*, A480/B508.
95 *KPM*, 215.
96 *CPR*, B181.
97 *BT*, 26.
98 *CPR*, B121.
99 *BT*, 26.
100 *GA19*, 232.
101 *BT*, 26 7.
102 Kant, *CPR*, Aviii; my italics.
103 *BT*, 28; translation modified.
104 Plato, *Symp*. 185c.
105 *BT*, 28.
106 *BT*, 30.
107 *BT*, 30.
108 *BT*, 30–1.
109 *BT*, 31.
110 *BT*, 31. In a letter to Löwith, Heidegger writes: 'Formal indication, critique of the customary doctrine of the apriori, formalization and the like, all of that is still for me there [in *Being and Time*] even though I do not talk about them now' (T. Kisiel, *Genesis of Heidegger's Being and Time*. University of California, 1993, 19). As H.-G. Gadamer insists: 'All of us should ever be relearning that when Heidegger spoke in his early works of "formal indication," he already formulated something that holds for the whole of his thought' (*HOP*, 33).
111 *BT*, 116–7.
112 *BT*, 30.
113 *HOP*, 33.
114 *HOP*, 33.
115 *BT*, 35.
116 *BT*, 32–4.
117 *BT*, 35.
118 *EM*, 134.
119 *BT*, 67.
120 *BT*, 42.
121 *BT*, 42.
122 *BT*, §§ 10–11.
123 *BT*, 53.

[124]   *BT*, §13.
[125]   *BT*, §§14–16.
[126]   *BT*, §§17–22.
[127]   *BT*, §§23–4.
[128]   *BT*, 16.
[129]   *BT*, 130; and §§25–7.
[130]   *BT*, 132.
[131]   *BT*, §29.
[132]   *BT*, 143–4.
[133]   *BT*, 146.
[134]   *BT*, 8; Heidegger's emphasis. See *BT*, 153.
[135]   Must Heidegger not ask and answer Husserl's question: 'When I, the meditating, reduce myself to my absolute transcendental ego by phenomenological *epochē* do I not become *solus ipse*; and do I not remain that, as long as I carry on a consistent self-explication under the name of phenomenology? Should not a phenomenology that proposed to solve the problems of objective being, and to present itself actually as philosophy, be branded therefore as transcendental solipsism?' (*Cartesian Meditations*, §42; *Essential Husserl*, Indiana University, 1999, 135).
[136]   *BT*, 175.
[137]   W. Richardson argues: If Dasein 'achieves itself, it is authentic (*eigentlich*); if it fails to achieve itself, it is inauthentic (*uneigentlich*). Hence both authenticity and inauthenticity are fundamental modes of being (*Seinsmodi*) and have their basis in the fact that there-being [Dasein], as existential, is a to-be-achieved-there' (*Heidegger*, Nijhoff, 1974, 50).
[138]   *BT*, 178.
[139]   *BT*, §§35–8.
[140]   *BT*, 222.

2

Ta megala panta episphalē

2.1

1933. Infamous year. And not only because Heidegger holds the *Rector's Address*, five years after *Being and Time*, but also.[1] Still it is the year in which it seems that Heidegger's fascism, at least his politics, plays itself out; or as Celan later writes of another *Meister aus Deutschland*: '*Ein Mann wohnt im Haus der spielt mit den Schlangen der schreibt | der schreibt wenn es dunkelt nach Deutschland.*'[2] So a question – in the conditional: What would happen if it were possible, or necessary, to introduce some kind of uncertainty into Heidegger's politics, into fascism itself? Perhaps even an irony at the centre of the *Rektoratsrede*? In 1933? What then?

But of course, everyone agrees that Heidegger was a Nazi swine, a 'rather nasty piece of work – a coward and a liar pretty much from first to last'.[3] Bad man, bad philosophy.[4] And who touches the book touches the man (Whitman).[5] So either we don't read him because he was a Nazi – or we read him because he was a Nazi, which may not be so different in the end. Thus the following permutations: Heidegger and his work is fascistic;[6] he was a fascist, but his work is not; the work is fascistic, but the man was not; neither the man nor his work is fascist.[7] As Gadamer maintains: '[He] was the greatest of thinkers, but the smallest of men.'[8] Or Arendt: Heidegger's Nazism is a 'professional deformation'.[9] Or Lang: 'I myself remain in doubt about these questions: *sceptical* of any assurance that the systematic grounds for what has emerged here as his denial of the Jewish Questions can (should) make no difference to Heidegger's "larger" standing, but wary of finding in those grounds the basis for a sweeping (and as the account here has viewed them, negative) judgement; yet also unwilling to accept categorically that it has no such general implication.'[10]

1933 then, may be the year that Heidegger officially expressed his fascism – but today, although the man is dead, the address remains to be addressed. As Heidegger's son warns: this is an address 'about which many speak, some even write, without having read it'.[11] If an approach is to be possible therefore, it seems prudent to reread the address usually translated as 'The Self-Assertion of the German University'. And if Rorty is right that Heidegger is a liar pretty much from first to last, we must be careful to consider whether he has lied here as well. Indeed not only his *post facto* attempt to clarify the *Rektoratsrede* with 'Facts and Thoughts', but the address itself must be checked for lies, to the extent possible. This is not however a question of empirical confirmation, and Heidegger warns against that kind of research – for it would certainly never prove or disprove that he means what he says and says what he means, or whether he speaks not merely the correct, but the true; it is rather a question of investigating the effects of considering Heidegger a liar, ironic to the core, here as well. In other words, what if the *Rektoratsrede* is not merely a defence of the German university, German science, German mathematics, German physics, German philosophy, etc. – for even the theory of relativity and quantum physics were condemned as un-German?[12] Or what if it is a defence that is designed not to succeed, but to fail – and spectacularly so? What then?

Initially then, in the beginning – perhaps even originally – reading the text in German, we might be tempted to translate the *Rektoratsrede*, not into English, but into Greek, to retranslate the address back into the language that is supposed to have determined the fate and ground of the essence of philosophy from the beginning. And here we might suggest, taking a clue from Plato: 'The Apology [or Self-Apology] of [or for] the German University'. Indeed *Behauptung* means that the defence is successful, the assertion of oneself as innocent is accepted, an *erfolgriche Verteidigung*. But what does success mean here? Asserting the superiority of the German university above all others? Or does it mean holding one's ground – as Heidegger translates Plato: 'All greatness stands in the storm'?[13] That is, protecting the German university from politicization, preventing the Germanification or *Verdeutschung* of a science in the sense of *Wissenschaft* that reaches beyond nationalism? Or does success here far more mean failure? The demonstration that the university is not and can never be something merely German?

Indeed if Heidegger is presenting a defence of the university akin to Plato's representation of Socrates in the *Apology* – with characteristic irony – would it not be open to the same kind of reading? Not merely an apology for the German university, for the Germanification of science at the university, nor for submission to its Nazification, nor simply a defence of the university against fascism, nor just a proposal for the German university to remain true or loyal to its Greek origins, be they proto-fascist or anti-fascist, democratic or universalist, and therefore above nationalism, beyond patriotism and all other quasi-fascistic claims – none of this, but rather an argument for the essential limitations of these strategies. It may very well be possible that, ironically or not, Heidegger is speaking against, *apo-legeomai*, the German university and against fascism by speaking for it, by speaking on its behalf and by speaking the words that it speaks, articulating the will that it wills, working out the logical conclusion of a self-defence of the German university.

But this is 1933. And everything that is said may be used against you. Indeed, Heidegger's predecessor, 'Wilhelm von Möllendorf, a distinguished anatomist, was to have served as rector for the academic year 1933/34, but his political convictions (von Möllendorf was a Social Democrat) made him unacceptable to the new regime and he was forced out of office almost immediately.'[14] And not only what is said in the *Rektoratsrede*, but just as much what is unsaid – for 'Man speaks by being silent'.[15] Nor can we believe that which Heidegger writes after the war, the 'Facts and Thoughts' (1945) – for this too is suspect, not only motivated by a desire to clear his name, or by some other reason, but open to the same charges that are levelled against the *Rektoratsrede*, and just as much in need of clarification as the address that it is supposed to clarify. Surely if Heidegger's defence of the German university is questionable, the defence of the defence, then the defence of this defence is even more so – if that is what it is supposed to be – and what good would an *apologia* be if it always needed yet another *apologia*? Or is that not perhaps precisely Heidegger's point?

It seems then that a rereading of the *Rektoratsrede* has become necessary in order to determine not only the status of the address as evidence for Heidegger's fascism, but just as much to clarify the extent to which the text seems open to power, truth as power, to the deployment of irony and its uncertainty, while seeming to articulate the truth of the German university. And even here, or once again, if we are right, then we are wrong – if we are simply serious about Heidegger's irony, like being certain about uncertainty, the irony is lost; if Heidegger is not a liar, he is a liar; if he is not a fascist, he is a fascist; and if we disagree, we don't.

2.2

With the first line of Heidegger's *Rektoratsrede* however, the game is already over: 'The assumption of the rectorate is the commitment to the *spiritual* leadership of this institution of higher learning.'[16] The *Übernahme* however, is not merely an assumption or ascension to the position of rector – it is a takeover. Hence: 'The takeover of the rectorate is the commitment to the *spiritual* leadership of this institution of higher learning.' Indeed *Über-nahme*, hostile or friendly, is a military, commercial or ideological victory, the capturing of a position, successful defence via offence. Yet who has accomplished this extraordinary action? Who has taken over the German university? And captured the post of spiritual leader for this institution of higher education? Or what? Does Heidegger mean Heidegger? Has he taken over? Or philosophy? Or perhaps neither, but some other far more nefarious force? The NSPD? Has fascism a foothold in Freiburg? And is it now bound to assert itself as the essence of everything German? To defend its position as spiritual leader? And what would happen to Heidegger's address, if its goal was to work out the consequences of a fascist takeover of philosophy, of the human and natural sciences alike, under the name of essentialism or empiricism or universalism?

Certainly there is nothing in the *Rektoratsrede* to prove that the address is referring to a Nazi takeover of the university – but nor is there anything to disprove it. And although we may presume that Heidegger speaks for himself, just as we quickly take the 'I' of any text to refer to its author, we can perhaps no longer be so sure. In fact, not only the 'I' is suspect, but the 'we' as well – for who is the 'we' to whom the text refers? After the university's takeover, who is the *Führer* committed to our spiritual *Führung*? Who are 'we' who are supposed to lead and be led, follow and be followed? Does Heidegger include himself in this 'we'? Or is it reserved for the victors? For those who write the history of the German *Volk* – a history that perhaps, beginning in 1933 with the self-assertion of the German university, culminates in the Holocaust? And when Heidegger asks, 'Do we know about this spiritual mission?'[17] – does he mean that we (whoever that should be, us, the reader, or some other 'we' yet to be, yet to be determined, or never to be determined, that is, an essentially uncertain 'we', the one who says 'we', not only *wir sind ein Volk* but *wir sind das Volk*, not just 'we are *one* people', but 'we are *the* people') do or do not know? That we should or should not know? That a mission – and its possibility or impossibility has yet to be determined – has been given to us? That we accept or decline? Does he mean that secret orders have been issued to students and teachers to which we are not privy?

But Heidegger poses another very different question: although we may not yet know about the spiritual mission that forces the fate of the German people, we must know whether we are 'truly and jointly rooted in the essence of the German university?'[18] Indeed, Heidegger poses the problem of our essence as a question – not as an answer. It remains to be seen, both the essence itself, and whether it can be fixed *qua* questionable. And it also remains to be seen whether this essence has the strength to stamp us, our being, Dasein – or not – for it can only do so if and only if we will it. All this is only possible – although necessarily so. But here too, we may very well have missed the essence of the mission, and the essence of essence: although we commonly take self-governance, *Selbstverwaltung*, to be the dominant character of the university's essence, we may well remain uncertain as to its essence.[19] Thus the address does not affirm our common belief, *doxa* (because it is a mistaken prejudice?), but rather poses another question: 'However – have we considered fully what this claim to self-governance demands of us?'[20]

Regardless, if the spiritual mission is to be fulfilled, and if the essence of the German university can be willed, it must be possible for us to govern ourselves, to set our own task, determine ourselves, our own law, free, *autonomos*, and therefore able to realize the 'ought' as an 'is'. In order to govern ourselves however, we must know ourselves, know who we are. Thus Heidegger asks: '*Can* we even know this [*who we ourselves are*] without the most constant and unsparing *self-examination*?'[21] Indeed if we do not know ourselves – not because we do not now, or do not yet know ourselves, but because we cannot know ourselves – then the entire chain of command breaks down, the argument loses its force, whether Heidegger wants it to or not.

But self-governance is grounded in self-examination – and self-examination? Heidegger writes: 'Self-examination, however, only happens with the force of the *self-assertion* of the German university.'[22] Self-examination presupposes the takeover of the German university – for only then is it possible for the German university to believe that it has the power and force to accomplish the act of self-examination. The takeover of the university, its Germanification, may very well signal that philosophy is at an end, and the spiritual mission of self-governance through self-examination becomes dominant; no longer an impossible task, but one that is taken to be necessary – and this may be the beginning of sophistry or of Nazism or fascism, or at least the beginning of the end of science. Indeed if we could not determine ourselves – and that means: 'delimit what this essence is to become'[23] – we cannot govern ourselves, cannot will this essence and thereby assert ourselves.

The argument then forms a circle: the takeover of the rectorate means that 'the leaders themselves are the led',[24] by the spiritual mission rooted in the essence of the German university, and on the basis of which we will it and assert ourselves, commonly characterized as self-governance, understood as self-determination on the basis of self-knowledge and grounded in a self-examination that presupposes the power of self-assertion – and 'the self-assertion of the German university is the primordial shared will to its essence'.[25] The essence must be delimited so as to will, but delimitation presupposes will. We must know in order to act, but knowledge is already an action; just as for the Greeks, 'theory itself was to be understood as the highest realization of genuine practice'.[26] And the question of the address is not how to get out of the circle (nor simply how to get into it in the right way), but do we want the essence or not, do we will to will it, or not?

2.3

With the takeover of the rectorate however, both everything and nothing is possible. The German university has been shown the way to assert, examine and govern itself, to will its essence. But 'will we enact it and how'?[27] And these questions guide the rest of Heidegger's address – for if we do not will essence, the fault can lie with us, but also with the will to essence. On the one hand, it is possible that we fail to enact the self-assertion of the German university because we are thwarted by politics; or because it is an impossible task from the start, because we can't get the circle circulating in the right way, or because the delimitation of its essence cannot be attained, or because we lack the will. On the other hand, if we succeed in enacting the self-assertion, it may be because we succumb to politics, give up the lead to others, to the myths of those in power, or to those who would be, because we agree to be led

precisely in order to rid ourselves of freedom and responsibility, or because we
believe that freedom means submitting to the law, that responsibility means
following that which power holds up as beyond power, beyond good and evil,
transcendent or transcendental truth; or because we leave unnoticed the
impossibility of the task at hand in order to make the possible actual, actually
possible, whether its achievement remains outstanding or not, an illusion or
delusion, an ideal or regulative idea, a will to actuality; or because we fail to
notice another possibility, namely that of failure, the success of demonstrating
that the self-assertion of the German university, the delimitation of its essence
and the direction of will made possible by the takeover of the rectorate,
although never necessary, has a price. And if *theoria* is to be the highest form of
praxis, is it because in practice, the self-assertion of the German university is
fascistic? Or if an unjust law is no law at all,[28] then in an unjust time of an
untrue truth, does philosophy not have to seek untruth, love not wisdom but
stupidity, insofar as the height of justice would then lie in the submission of
injustice to its own law? So as the Athenians have received the just reputation
as the people who unjustly put Socrates to death, have the Germans not
gained the name as the *Volk* who put millions to death while willing the
essence of the German university to assert itself?

But even more questions haunt us: What if Heidegger's argument is
periagogic, designed to turn our souls around not only from leading to being
led, but from self-assertion, not to other-assertion, but to non-assertion? What
if the connection of the self-assertion of the German university through its
will-to-essence to the Greeks, turns us away from fascism rather than towards
it? Then what if the self-assertion of the German university means that it can
no longer be German? What if the disconnection of metaphysics from politics,
the gulf between the attempt – and failure – to think the totality-of-what-is
and to act with an eye to the Good, forces us to appeal to another kind of
force? What if everything depends upon will, but will itself depends upon non-
will? What then?

Regardless, the question of the address is not finished with the address – for
the writing, speaking and reading of the text are all actions, in addition to
everything else Heidegger did with and for fascism. But while we might claim
that some of Heidegger's activities in 1933 were unambiguous (and many of
these are by now well documented by historians and philosophers alike – so
we leave to others to determine, to the extent possible, why Heidegger
resigned his rectorship before it was over; or why after 1934 the Nazis turned
on him; or whether, for example, Heidegger really did ever forbid, in writing
or speech, Husserl from setting foot on the university),[29] the text of 'The Self-
Assertion of the German University' seems to resist such easy condemnation,
which is not to say that we should not condemn it, nor that it places itself
outside the polemical economy of Pro-Heideggerians and Anti-Heideggerians,
but neither does it simply submit to easy side-taking, the logic of blood or
blood-logic, with us or against us. And the facts of the Heidegger case may

resist the kind of immediate presentation or objective representation necessary to condemn the text as well – for the question of the facts are not finished with the facts. The address therefore still, or again, remains to be read.

2.4

So the takeover of the German university, its self-assertion, means willing its essence. The university's task is now understood to be the education and discipline of the leaders of the German *Volk*. The task is to be accomplished by grounding the university in science. Thus the will-to-essence is the will-to-science is the 'will to the historical, spiritual task of the German people'.[30] The connection of science with the Germans is only possible with the will-to-essence – but this is possible, Heidegger insists, if and only if we, teachers and students, expose science to its inner necessity, and if we 'stand up to [or withstand, or more precisely, resist, *standhalten*] the Germans' fate in its most extreme distress'.[31] We must both put science to the test and revolt against its Germanification. If and only if both conditions are met can the university will its essence. Indeed, it remains uncertain as to whether the task of self-assertion is possible, if we fail to expose science to its necessity, or if we – for one reason or another, because science will not let itself be exposed, because we lack the will to do so, or the means, or the opportunity – if we cannot do so, or are not equal to fate, ours or science's or the university's, if we cannot or will not be so, if we refuse, or if we cannot measure up at a time when nothing is equal or proportionate, in a world where measurement itself cannot take account of fate and its vicissitudes, if it ever could, or if we do not stand up, when fate calls out in its time of need. Indeed if and only if – and if not, the project is sunk. Thus the following permutations threaten: we may expose science to its innermost necessity, but may not be equal to fate, intentionally or by accident, whether the fault lies with us or with fate, or with both, or elsewhere; we may not expose science to its necessity, try and fail, or not try at all, but be equal to fate; we may neither be able to expose science to its innermost necessity, nor be equal to fate – a spectacular failure.

In order to expose science to its innermost necessity however, we first need to experience the essence of science. And this cannot be done negatively, that is, merely through a new concept of science whereby we contest how modern modern science is or is not; it must be done positively, that is, 'only if [condition upon condition upon condition] we again place ourselves under the power of the *beginning* of our spiritual-historical Dasein'[32] – and that means setting out from Greek philosophy and, by virtue of language, standing up in order to question and respond to beings as a whole. Yet where the choice in the exposure of science to its innermost necessity becomes necessary, the choice between a negative and a positive exposure, one that would presumably reveal that which did not belong to its innermost necessity in order to weed out the traitors in the crowd, treachery at the heart of science itself, informants posing as students of science, sophists masquerading as philosophers, or irony confused with seriousness – here the German university's self-assertion is threatened from another camp. Heidegger insists: the past decade has only provided a 'semblance of a true struggle for the essence of science'.[33] And if the struggle has been a mere *Schein*, if the semblance could go on for a decade, fooling at least some of the people some of the time; then even today, right here and now (in the present age, a place in which irony seems no longer called for), it could be continuing in its own name or in the name of another, as negative or as positive. If the semblance of a true struggle is a true semblance, it would be impossible to differentiate the fake from the real, the ironic from the serious. Indeed Heidegger's introduction of the threat of semblance into the true, or into truth – as correspondence or *alētheia* – means that everything that follows, including our equality to fate, to the Greek beginning of science, as well as the German university's self-assertion, everything could itself be mere semblance, simulation, parody, malefic masquerade.

Regardless, the task of the exposure of science to its innermost necessity means exposing it to the task of questioning beings as a whole. Whether and to what extent this task is possible (or impossible) remains to be seen – for not only is there nothing in science that makes it unconditionally necessary, so too its exposure to the task that lies in its philosophical foundation is never certain. And even if exposure seems to take place, if the question of the totality of beings seems to be raised; there is no assurance that it is, or even can be. Indeed Heidegger insists that knowledge must fail in its attempt to approach beings as a whole. The failure of science however, is supposed to be the success of philosophy; the inability to think the unity of beings creates the desire for science to become *theoria*, the highest form of *praxis*. Of course if knowledge fails, there is no guarantee that philosophy will succeed – even if philosophy's questioning is an advance over science insofar as it presumably asks the question, the one that science believes it has asked and answered, the question of the unity of beings (although the rightness of philosophy's right has yet to be determined, if it could be) – unless success means knowing that it must fail, perhaps spectacularly so. But if the original essence of science is 'the questioning holding of one's ground in the midst of the ever self-concealing totality of what is',[34] it seems that science (with or as philosophy) perseveres in spite of, or rather because of its inability to know, just as the lover of wisdom seeks but does not possess wisdom by standing fast, resisting both easy dogmatism and its faith in progress, and superficial scepticism with its cohorts of relativism, materialism, consumerism.

For Heidegger, however – in one way or another, ancient, medieval, modern – the search for the unity of beings comes to an end with Nietzsche, if it wasn't already over from the start. And if Heidegger introduces Nietzsche into the *Rektoratsrede*, it is because with *The Gay Science* ('will to power' and the teaching of 'eternal recurrence', *ewige Wiederkunft* – not eternal *Wiederkehr*, nor eternal *Wiederkommen*, nor simply *essentia/existentia*, neither coming-again, repetition of arrival, that which turns and returns, from foreign lands, a trip, from a ban or exile – for *Wiederkunft* means *parousia*, being *qua* eternal presence, which is perhaps 'the true meaning' of 'Zarathustra's teaching') science as the attempt to stand in the midst of the uncertainty of what is, comes to an end. God is dead. The god of science is dead. God as the answer to the question of the totality of beings, from the Greeks to us, is dead. And with the departure of the authoritative answer or question, God goes with it. Then the word of Heidegger on the word of Nietzsche (no longer the word of God, but God is dead), means that the question of the totality of beings cannot be answered, or even properly asked – neither by God nor by the death of God, neither by Christ nor Anti-Christ. But as Heidegger argues: 'Nietzsche holds this overturning to be the overcoming of metaphysics. But every overturning of this kind remains only a self-deluding entanglement in the same that has become unknowable.'[35] The proof of the impossibility of an answer however, is not pessimism, does not lead to nihilism, incomplete or completed, or one of its other meanings that might well complicate their reduction to a binary economy – for 'the name nihilism remains then multiple'[36] – on the contrary, it is the most joyful of thoughts: philosophy and science are free from the myth of the unity of beings, a new beginning, dawn of a new age. And Heidegger is not some kind of pseudo-pre-Socratic thinker pining away for the good old days of the Greeks – he is post-Nietzschean to the core.

When it comes time then to face its essence, the task of thinking the unity of beings, it is no surprise that science shows itself to be a failure. And thus human beings, beings among beings, albeit those featherless bipeds responsible-for or fated-to science and modern technology and fascism, standing in the midst of what is, find themselves in dire straits – for with the departure or death of God or the gods, so too goes the dream of totality; and the project of science nowadays heralded as modernity in philosophy, or unified field theory in physics, becomes untenable. In other words, if science is merely secularized religion, the substitution of one metaphysical, ontotheological, juridical, moral, or aesthetic authority for another; it simply replaces one avatar of unity with another, substitutes or infinitely displaces our desire for totality with the latest *logos*. As Heidegger warns in the *Contributions to Philosophy*: 'it is precisely the many variations of the domination of "Christian" thinking in the post- and *anti*-Christian epoch that impedes every attempt to get away from this foundation'.[37] This is the desire that culminates in totalitarianism – and it is perhaps this dream that the Germans have dreamed better than any other nation, although we might not like to leave the Soviet Union out of it, or even claim that today the Americans are doing it best, or trans-national corporations, or that historically every nation has done it, like every attempt at empire, or colonialism, like every vision of perfection, every

scheme for a purely rational government, every utopic state, from the *Republic*
to the United Nations. As Heidegger reminds us: 'Every nationalism is
metaphysically an anthropologism and as such subjectivism. Nationalism is
not overcome through mere internationalism; it is rather expanded and
elevated thereby into a system.'[38]

Regardless, if God is dead, it is no surprise that waking from the dream of the
totality of beings we find ourselves forsaken, left out in the cold without shelter,
disoriented and unable to find our way in a godless world. And Nietzsche is the
thinker of the impossibility of totality, the uncertainty of unity – henceforth,
there is no set of all sets, no idea of ideas, or original originals, no thought
thinking thought; henceforth, nothing is purely for the sake of itself, absolutely
independent, separable, objective; henceforth, there is no more belief in pure
reason, transcendental apperception, thing in itself, end in itself, pure *eidos, cogito,*
substance of substances, monad of monads, absolute reason of reasons, ground of
grounds, spirit of spirits or totality of totalities. And if Heidegger knows this, then
the task of standing in the midst of what is, like the attempt to think the being of
beings, cannot be merely a new religion, nor simply the latest dream of totality,
set up and ready for use in the self-assertion of the German university – but nor
can it be an anti-totality, the kind of anti-Platonism of which he, rightly or
wrongly, accuses Nietzsche. As Heidegger insists in 1943, ten years after the
Rektoratsrede and building upon his lectures from 1936 to 1940: everything anti-
holds fast to the essence of that against which it moves; 'Nietzsche's
countermovement against metaphysics is, as its mere inversion, an inextricable
entanglement in metaphysics'[39] – although it remains unclear as to whether
Nietzsche didn't know all this already, and whether Heidegger's movement (or
non-movement) isn't itself a countermovement.

Regardless, with Nietzsche the task given to philosophy to stand up in and
to the totality of what is shows itself as Sisyphean, or more precisely, as
structurally impossible – for a totalizing totality, like a non-totalizing one,
would be no totality at all. The task becomes one of standing up to our failure
to stand up to totality. And now we must expose ourselves to failure, to
impossibility, perhaps even to uncertainty, not the answer, nor the
answerable, but that which can never be answered – or questioned, the
truth of the un-unnoticed, the un-questionable.

2.5

The *Rektoratsrede* then insists: willing the essence of science means '*questioning,
unguarded holding of one's ground in the midst of the uncertainty of the totality of what-
is*'.[40] And whether we stand firm or not, expose and reveal ourselves or not,
whether we can resist or not, whether we will it or not, resolutely or not – the
uncertainty of unity, of the unity of beings, that in which we are supposed to
be so uncertain, itself remains uncertain (although Heidegger seems quite

certain about this uncertainty as a possibility, a necessary possibility). And at the height of the German university's attempt at self-assertion, this uncertainty shows itself as five-fold, at least: uncertainty of totality, questioning, resoluteness, exposure – and of uncertainty itself.

Uncertainty of totality. That which Heidegger calls the history of philosophy of metaphysics from Platonism to Nietzscheanism is a history of the failure of philosophy to allow the non-totality and disunity of beings to show itself as it is. Indeed the history of philosophy can appear as the history of *logos* – but this is only one history, one history of philosophy, certain of itself, and of its dominance, one to be taught and reproduced, preserved and inherited, one of super-sensory ideas, transcendent or transcendental grounds, *a priori* synthetic judgements according to mathematical or quantitative paradigms and resulting in apodictic truth, solutions all to the challenge of totality, one perhaps of which we are proud, one on which the natural and human sciences can count, and on which technology and capital can build. Another history of philosophy however, is just as possible, or rather necessary, one that lies between or beyond dogmatism and scepticism, that is neither certain of itself, nor of its uncertainty, one that is even uncertain of itself – this is the history of Parmenides' double-path, of the being and thinking of that which is and that which is not; of Heraclitus' thought of *polemos* as the creator and protector of all things, gods and humans, lords and bondsmen, justice and injustice; of Socrates' ironic (intentional?) failure to think the essence of beings as *idea*; of Aristotle's inability to approach the being *qua* being of *phusis*, as well as the limit of the categories at the smallest and greatest difference of beings; of Cartesian doubt and the limits of the *cogito*; of the Kantian limits of knowledge, the concealed art of the schematism and the merely regulative use of the ideas, especially that of freedom; of Hegelian negation, or more precisely, Spinoza's *omnis determinatio est negatio*, applied to consciousness and self-consciousness, to the end of history, Absolute Spirit, and negation itself; of the death of God in Nietzsche (thank God?) – or here in the *Rektoratsrede*, the uncertainty of the totality of beings. Indeed, in this history of philosophy, Heidegger's introduction of uncertainty into the question of the totality of what-is – that is, into the question, and ground-holding, resoluteness or will, into the exposure and totality, and into being itself – means that we cannot even be certain of our uncertainty. And the *Rektoratsrede* may be an attempt to show the effects of this introduction, the injection of uncertainty into a philosophical investigation already circumscribed by metaphysics, or a political system already taken over by fascism.

Uncertainty of the question. The task itself, the task of questioning, of exposing oneself to uncertainty, the uncertainty of the dream of the unity of beings, can appear as beyond all questioning. Indeed as Derrida insists:

before any question, then. It is precisely here that the 'question of the question' which has been dogging us since the beginning of this journey, vacillates. It vacillates at the moment when it is no longer a question ... at the moment at which we pose the ultimate question, i.e. when we interrogate (*Anfragen*) the possibility of any question, i.e., language, we must be already in the element of language. Language must already be speaking for us – it must, so to speak, be already spoken and addressed to us (*muss uns doch die Sprache selber schon zugesprochen sein*). *Anfrage* and *Nachfrage* presuppose this advance, this fore-coming address (*Zuspruch*) of language. Language is already there, in advance (*im voraus*) at the moment at which any question can arise about it. In this it exceeds the question.[41]

But of course, Heidegger knows this; he knows very well that the question of the question of the question is infinite, like peeling the phenomenological onion; there is no origin of the origin, ground of the ground, only receding groundlessness. Deconstruction is not critique therefore, but far more proof of the powerlessness of questioning to which Heidegger points. And the *Rektoratsrede* shows how the task of questioning must submit itself to questioning. If we question the questionable however, take the task to task, there is no longer any ground of grounds or original-ground, *Urgrund* – but a non-ground, *Ungrund*.[42] And the ground of questioning upon which the German university was to have asserted itself as German or not, as Ur-Greek or not, as true to its origin in Greek questioning, willing its essence, or at least seeming to do so, if not really doing so, that is, if unable or unwilling to do so – this ground shows itself as ungrounded. The question of the question is already asked and answered: if the essence of science is understood as questioning, and if – after the takeover of the rectorate – we are to will this essence; we shall necessarily fall into contradiction. And the question of the question therefore, like language itself and any other thought of ground or origin, remains questionable. Thus, the question of the essence of science, like the questioning of the German university, shows itself to be just as much answering – asking is responding; questions themselves are barbs, weapons, strategies. And questioning is not only (although always also) an attempt at self-assertion; it is attack.

Uncertainty of resoluteness. Heidegger seems certain about the task of standing firm and holding ground resolutely in the storm of uncertainty. The *Rektoratsrede* however, demonstrates not only the consequences of such a spiritual resolve towards the essence of being, but just as much the problem of constating resoluteness. On the one hand, we may hold our ground on a shifting ground, perhaps even by giving ground, here or there, in order to get it elsewhere, now or then; but if the ground is destroyed, we might just not be able to hold on. (And how could we ground a totalitarian movement on a non-ground – except perhaps through sophistry, force or violence, or claiming to have done the impossible, namely, holding ground on a non-ground, unifying that which cannot be a unity, or concealing its lack of unity, claiming to be certain of that certainty or uncertainty about which no certainty is possible?) On the other hand, we could never be certain of the certainty of our resolution, nor that we could even resolve – not only that a 'German' resolution might contain impurities (Greek, Jewish, Turkish, or otherwise), but just as much our resolve could never be confirmed. And all along, could resolution not be faked, artificial, a *converso* of resolution? Could our resolve not present or represent itself as unwavering? Could we not be shamming authentic resolution, itself as itself, while showing itself as another, either authentically or inauthentically inauthentic?

In fact, even in *Being and Time*, the possibility of resoluteness remains uncertain: just as we are always in the truth and the untruth, authenticity and inauthenticity, so too are we always already in resoluteness and irresoluteness.[43] Indeed, as taking on its own debt, and hence our being-guilty, resoluteness is supposed to contain the possibility of authentic being-towards-death – but necessarily only as anticipatory. We can takeover ourselves, our ownmost potentiality of being, our Dasein, and understand our debt or guilt – but only as being-towards-death, that is, as the nonrelational possibility of impossibility, the power to do the impossible. So on the one hand, resoluteness is certain: insofar as we are in the truth, authentic resoluteness is our capacity for keeping ourselves open to possibilities, committing ourselves and simultaneously reserving the right to withdraw, thereby remaining free – and we can be certain of being able to withdraw because of death, because we can be absolutely certain of death, that is, the omnipresent possibility of ultimate withdrawal, that through which we always take ourselves back to ourselves. On the other hand, if we are equiprimordially in untruth, then as 'a constant possibility of Dasein, irresoluteness is *also certain*'.[44] Indefinite but certain is death, and both resoluteness and irresoluteness as well. Yet how can we be certain of irresoluteness? Would we not have to be resolute? We cannot resolve not to resolve and remain unresolved; nor can we resolve to resolve – for there remains at least one resolution that we have not taken into account, and the possibility of authentic resolution opens up on an infinite regress of resolutions, each demanding a resolution of a resolution. And even if 'resoluteness is certain of itself only in a resolution',[45] who can say if we have actually made an authentic resolution? If irresoluteness is also certain, how can we be certain of resolution? How can we be certain that our resolution was not irresolute?

In the *Rektoratsrede* then, it may not be possible to be certain, not only whether it is Heidegger himself, the human being, who resolves, but just as much whether resoluteness has come to resolution. And in resolving itself, or seeming to do so, can the German university ever be certain that its resolution is its own, and not another's? Not the Nazi's or the fascist's, the economy's, history's or fate's – and who wouldn't even today, in Germany and elsewhere, want to give someone else credit, or make something else guilty, at least responsible for the will and resolution of 1933? Resolution however, with respect to being or the state or the *Volk*, is not supposed to be something that we accomplish, but something that accomplishes us; the event in which spirit finds itself primordially attuned to holding its ground in the middle of the uncertainty of the totality of what is. But in this event, has the German spirit found itself – or another? Or is spirit not always another, at least other than itself? And how could it be resolved, if it doesn't belong to itself? Even if spirit's – or our own – resolution appeared to show itself, could we be certain that it actually happened? And that nothing else – nothing else at all – happened? Then how can we be certain of the connection between resoluteness and resolution? Or is it merely a constant conjunction? Or chance? Or are both resoluteness and resolution not perhaps names and explanations of appearances? Or are they merely projections? Constructed so as to make the resolutions our own, so as to appropriate the will for spirit? And if we only know resolution by its effects, we can never be certain that we have found its cause, or if it even has one? Spirit may need resolutions to confirm its resoluteness – but this confirms nothing of the resolution itself; it remains an explanation in need of explaining. Then the event of resolution may not need spirit at all, and we may have to remain uncertain with respect to the certainty of the certainty and uncertainty of resolution, so the entire economy of resolution remains unresolved.

Uncertainty of standing our ground. We are supposed to hold our ground in an unguarded way, to expose ourselves and spirit to the uncertainty of the unity of beings. A continual refrain haunts the *Rektoratsrede* – in the conditional: 'if we will ... if we will'.[46] But even if we will it, even if spirit could be resolved, how can we be certain that we have uncovered ourselves, revealed our position, to uncertainty? In fact, showing our position may be as effective a strategy as not showing it; revealing that which is concealed may help all the more to conceal it. Indeed, as with truth and authenticity and resoluteness, we take up our guard as we drop it – for we are always guarded and unguarded, showing and not showing, revealing and concealing our resistance in the middle of the truth and untruth of beings. Even further, not only is it possible for us to fake resistance, sham exposure, drop our guard in order to be *en guarde*; but we could never be certain that we had opened ourselves up to the uncertainty of beings, exposed ourselves fully to uncertainty – for we would always hold back at least one opening, namely, that of exposure itself. Just as light is necessary for sight, there can be no sight of light itself, no pure revealing, no position without guard – or if there is, we could never take it up without simultaneously guarding it. A structural impossibility shows itself: we could never be certain that we had dropped our guard because we would have to take it back up again in order to constate our lack of guard. Thus the unguarded holding of ground, exposure of resistance, is itself resistant – and if the German university were to try and assert itself as unguardedly willing its essence, who would believe it? For once uncertainty enters into the economy of self-revelation, how could we trust that the claim to self-exposure is itself not merely the latest form of resistance?

Uncertainty of uncertainty itself. If we will the essence of science, we should be able to be certain at least of the uncertainty of beings as a whole. Indeed, as Heidegger insists with respect to modern metaphysics (as a certain kind of completion of Greek thought – if it indeed ever existed, and is not an historically necessary *a posteriori* projection at best, or mere fantasy at worst) from Descartes to Nietzsche: 'The metaphysics of the modern age begins with and has its essence in the fact that it seeks the unconditionally indubitable, the certain, certainty. It is a matter, according to the word of Descartes, of *firmum et mansurum quid stabilire*, of bringing to a stand something fixed and remaining.'[47] In other words, the desire to secure an unconditional truth, the unconditionality of the conditional, culminates in the thought of certainty – but the quest for certainty finds its latest avatar in the certainty of uncertainty. And the metaphysical arch (from Platonism to us) tightens, returning to itself via its other – then we knew that we could not know; now we are certain that we are uncertain. Indeed with the death of God (and the 'usual subterfuge' or *gewöhnlichen Ausflucht*,[48] the standard philosophemes of subject/object, form/matter, mind/body, essence/existence, ideal/real, transcendental/empirical), science attempts to show itself as standing firm, securing, fixing, holding its ground, as certain and sure of death, the guard of death, warden of the law of death – for death has been raised to the level of the law, and uncertainty is the law of the law. Now: any certainty, even the certainty of uncertainty, rather than no certainty at all. But if we can be certain of our uncertainty, we have merely found another way of accomplishing the task of metaphysics, that is, justice (*dikē, iustitia, Gerechtigkeit*), understood as securing a ground even of groundlessness, the truth not of untruth or relativism, but the justification of uncertainty, knowledge as correct representation, dealing rightly with that which is.[49] At the moment that we include ourselves however, in the questioning of what is – at this moment we are no longer so sure. Once uncertainty is raised to the level of a principle or *logos*, joins the ranks of the Good, Substance, God, Reason, Spirit, Will, Will to Power, it reacts upon itself. If the essence of science then lies in uncertainty, how can we be certain of uncertainty? And can we then be certain of the uncertainty of the self-assertion of the German university in the midst of the unity of beings? Or is the uncertainty itself just a feign, a would-be or should-be uncertainty? A snare set to trap us in the quest to assert spirit's will to essence? No longer the unconditional exercise of power, but the conditioning of the unconditioned, the certifying of uncertainty, as the establishment of justice *ex post facto*? Indeed, we cannot be uncertain about beings as a whole – without being certain, and then we would have to be uncertain about ourselves, as well as about the being of uncertainty. We cannot even be certain that we cannot be uncertain; and if uncertainty becomes uncertain, we cannot stand in the midst of the uncertainty of the totality of what is.

Five times then, at least, the *Rektoratsrede* shows itself as uncertain – even uncertain about this: uncertainty of totality, questioning, resoluteness, exposure, uncertainty. So how are we to read an address that stands and falls under the sign of its own uncertainty? An address that perhaps in 1933, like today, resists reading and speaking, and resists even its own economy of resistance? Should we accept its claim to a certain uncertainty, a claim that lies at the bottom of what could be the height of Heidegger's explicit political activity, not merely a politics against politics, nor an apolitical politics, but one that makes politics itself perhaps uncertain – can we even be certain about this uncertainty? Or is it far more a question not of that which is certain or uncertain, but neither, a question of that which never becomes certainly certain or certainly uncertain, but uncertainly uncertain, that in the midst of which there is no standing, on which we cannot hold our ground, that to which we cannot be exposed, and about which we cannot question? In other words, neither that which is certainly certain or uncertain, but rather uncertain and uncertifiably so – for the truth lies not with being certain or uncertain, nor with being both certain and uncertain; neither with certainty or uncertainty, nor in that which is or is not, in neither being nor nothing, nor becoming, in neither actuality nor potentiality; but in that which 'maybe' certain or uncertain. Indeed, it is this radical 'may-be' that lies in wait for both the political takeover of the university and its self-assertion as apolitical, at least maybe.

2.6

But doesn't Heidegger already know all this? And doesn't the rest of the *Rektoratsrede* demonstrate not only the consequences of a fascist takeover of science, but just as much the attempt to maintain it as apolitical? As an attempt to justify himself? At doing justice to what was or was not done? Who would believe it? An attempt at justice? As Nietzsche reminds us: 'the ruler establishes "justice" only afterward.'[50] As Heidegger writes, *ex post facto*:

> the address bears the title: 'The Self-Assertion of the German University.' Very few were themselves clear about what this title alone, taken by itself, meant in the year 1933, because only a few of those whom it concerned took the trouble, without prejudice, to do so clearly and without mystification, to think-through idle talk to what is said. One can freely proceed in another manner as well. One can excuse oneself from reflection and hold onto the seemingly obvious representation that here, a short time after the National Socialist takeover, a newly elected rector holds an address about the university, an address that 'supports' 'National Socialism' and that is to say proclaims the idea of the 'politicized character of science,' that crudely thought means: 'True is what is useful for the *Volk*.' From this one concludes, and indeed rightly, that this betrays the essence of the German university in its very core and actively works on its

destruction; for this reason the title should rather read: 'The Self-Decapitation of the German University.' One *can* proceed in this manner. . .[51]

But one can proceed otherwise. Maybe. One can read the address as attempting to support a science free from nationalism, politics, economics, history – but here too, one might fail to think through to what is said and unsaid.

Still if Heidegger can be misunderstood here, he can be misunderstood elsewhere; if he is a traitor to National Socialism, he can also serve as a double-agent; and if he can lie here, he can lie everywhere; if he could be taken for himself, he could be mistaken for another – or if he is someone else, we could mistake him for another in taking him for himself. Once the lie is introduced into the address, we can no longer count on the truth; once uncertainty is asserted, certainty and uncertainty become unstable. Or once the lie has the power to enter into the address, once an uncertifiable uncertainty may be potential or actual, intentional or not, active or passive, present or absent, considered or not, known or unknowable, thought or unthought, once the address might have been, be, or become, a feign, copy, ironic – once any of this is even possible, it is actual. The economy of mistrust lies at the core of trust: if I trust you and you have betrayed me, or if you could betray me, you have already betrayed me, and will continue to do so, even if you haven't, both before you have, and after, and during, or not. Thus Heidegger's 1945 explanation is no more or less suspect than if it was written before 1933.

But one can proceed otherwise. Indeed the rest of the *Rektoratsrede* confirms our suspicions – perhaps becoming even suspicious of suspicions – for the address works out the effects of willing the essence of science under the sign of certain uncertainty. On the one hand, the rector's rhetoric seems blatantly fascistic, or at least open to fascism, quasi-fascistic or opportunistically fascistic, nationalistic, patriotic, militaristic: Germany's student body is on the march; it seeks leaders, to will its essence. Academic freedom is banished as ingenuine and negative, while positive freedom is taken to lie in submission to the student law and Germany's fate. And the student body is bound up with labour service to the community, armed service to the nation, knowledge service to the spiritual mission of the German *Volk* – three services, which themselves arise out of the confrontation of the teacher's and student's will, coalesce to become *one* formative force, ready for battle.[52] On the other hand, by demonstrating the impossibility of these projects, as well as their consequences, the address could just as well serve as critique: Germany's student body would be better off acting less and thinking more, marching less to the tune of another's drummer, or their own. Leader's are themselves led – for the economy of leaders and followers, like that of ends and means, is infinite; and does not even begin to think the essence of action. Willing its essence is an uncertain, if not impossible task, with disastrous effects for the university and the nation – for belief in will, essence, certainty of certainty or uncertainty, serves the ideological interests of those in power. Replacing one law with another does not lead to freedom – for submission to the law is dogmatism under a different name, and the rhetoric of fate serves to legitimate the latest vicissitudes of power, just as it attempts to justify the university's takeover and the inauguration of a German science. (And what is not our fate? What cannot be credited *a posteriori* to fate? Can we not easily reason 'after the fact' that Oedipus must have had to kill his father and sleep with his mother? Is it not a small step from 'the Holocaust happened' to 'it was the fate of the Jewish people, and the German's were fated to complete it'? And can we not justify our desires and violences by embracing them as fate – from manifest destiny to *amor fati*?) Under these conditions, bound to the three services, the nation cannot fulfil its duty; on the contrary, it finds itself unable to do so, unable to do science, to think and act freely, a freedom that itself may be illusory, unable to defend itself, to defend its national interests, a defence that too may be used to legitimate offence. And the three-fold Gordian knot that binds Germany to one battle may be possible – or at least we may be led to believe that it is possible, not noticing its impossibility, overlooking its irony, may not accept its uncertainty, or simply ignore it – but it may not be good, in itself or in its effects. Thus, at least two readings of 'The Self-Assertion of the German University' – both possible, that is, necessary, continually reacting upon one another, that leave us unable to choose, like the ass dying in the desert, equidistant from two equally seductive piles of food.

2.7

But now, as in 1933, the *Rektoratsrede* is almost at an end. The possibility of the self-assertion of the German university seems assured. Heidegger insists: 'No one will keep us from doing this.'[53] Except maybe ourselves; perhaps we will stand in our own way, stop ourselves, retreat not from justice, but from injustice, resist the takeover of the university, the nationalization of scientific knowledge, refuse the rector's rhetoric. Maybe we have heard what is said and will not let it stand. But maybe not, maybe we still have not heard – for no one will hinder us from running through the course of history in the name of fate. And fascism remains possible, a possibility (or necessity?) for those who collude or refuse in the name of some more profound 'will to essence'. But the betrayal of fascism does not necessarily imply anti-fascism – for it too can be a feign or con, designed to propagate a more fundamental fascism in the name of universal science or the certainty of uncertainty.

The *Rektoratsrede*, therefore, insists upon the conditional: Whether (*Ob*) this happens or does not happen depends on us, on whether (*ob*, again) we will it, or whether (*ob*, third time) not. In other words, nothing the address suggests –

or leaves out, unsaid or unthought – is yet decided. On the contrary, responsibility for what happens, or does not happen, lies with us – whether we take it up or not.

Or so it seems – for in 1933, all this talk may already be mere idle rambling, the rector simply mumbling to himself, just chuntering away. Philosophers can say what they will, and the people, teachers, students, politics, can ignore it, use it, abuse it. Plato's *Republic* is just one example (albeit the example that Heidegger introduces at the very end of the *Rektoratsrede*, thereby inviting comparison and the differentiation of positions) of a philosophy ripe for abuse.

But 1933 may be too late. As Heidegger insists (his italics): the young and youngest force of the people *'has* already *decided* the matter'.[54] It is too late. Too late for us, for what we want or will, do not want or will not. With the takeover of the university, everything has been decided. The young and the youngest – not the old and oldest, nor the mean, although maybe the meanest – have decided. They have decided what we can and cannot will – for perhaps the determination of 'what' we will lies with 'who' wills (Heidegger, the Nazis, you and I?), and perhaps they are the 'we'. So they say: 'we will that our people fulfill its historical mission'.[55] In this way, they reach beyond us and our own. Or so it seems – for if the 'we' is the 'they', *das Man*, it is possible (or necessary), to the extent that it is already decided, to proceed with them in their way. But another way is also possible, although this way too may be their way – then their will shows itself as our own, a sham or fake will, an appearance or artifice, or our desire that they have already desired for us.

Heidegger finds a sign of this way, be it their way or ours, in the last line of the *Rektoratsrede*, which comes not from Heidegger at all – further complicating any attempt to certify 'who' wills, speaks, even to whom 'we' can ascribe the address. The last line of 'The Self-Assertion of the German University' is from Plato – and not only the three-fold division of labour points us here,[56] but just as much the attempt to construct an ideal state, ironic or not, desirable or not, possible or impossible, fascistic or oligarchic, as a demonstration of its perhaps inevitable failure, as a warning to philosophers and politicians, underlining the doxagraphic rhetoric of teachers and students, working out the consequences and price of fascism for the *Volk*, or as a philosophical thought-exercise, through eidetic analysis, successful or not, in order to find out that what we mean by 'justice' lies in philosophizing itself. In fact, all of this reveals the *Rektoratsrede* as a re-write of the *Republic*, just as much as an *Apologia*, a text with which those who heard Heidegger in 1933 would undoubtedly have been familiar – and it ends: *'ta...megala panta episphalē*; all that is great stands in the storm'.[57]

Or so it seems. For Jowett translates: 'All great attempts are attended with risk.'[58] And Shorey: 'For all great things are precarious.'[59] But if Heidegger provides the Greek, he invites us too to translate, to translate his Greek and Plato's; and to reread the *Republic*, to risk failing and falling in our attempt to grasp the word of Plato, a risk that may not only be fraught with danger, but one that we perhaps cannot avoid, especially in such a suspect thinker, one threatened by sophistry and irony at every turn, from the *Symposium* to the 'Seventh Letter', to Socrates' constant, perhaps feigned or artificial, ignorance. Or even more radically, by presenting the Greek, the address demands that we confirm – or deny, or at least test its mettle, perhaps as Nietzsche might have it, with a hammer – the translation. Thus the conclusion of the *Rektoratsrede* is not just a conclusion, after which we are invited to applaud the rector's rhetoric – it is a test; it is attack; war, *polemos*.

Regardless, Heidegger's translation is certainly correct – we can translate Plato in this way. But we can proceed otherwise: *episphalē* means not only 'standing in the storm', but just as much not standing, not being able to stand, being prone to fall, failure, disaster, defeat. And the *Rektoratsrede* may point us in another direction. In this case, Heidegger's slip is no slip at all, but a sign or indication that he knows that we know, that we hear the ambiguity that can be heard. Like Socrates' ironic ignorance – but doubly so, *zweideutig* at least. On the one hand, the translation underlines that what is said is not meant. Heidegger's excerpt of the Greek, perhaps against Plato's will, also reads: all that is great, *ta megala panta*, is prone to fall, *episphalē* – it does not stand in the storm, but is attended with risk, precarious, unsteady, fraught with danger, a great caducity, and not only in fascist Germany. All that is great can stumble and fall, and we may even rejoice in its demise. On the other hand, the translation demonstrates that translation is always also mistranslation: translation itself is attended with risk, precarious, prone to fall. The translation indicates not only the risk of falling, the danger of failing, the possibility of mistranslation – it points to its inevitability, the impossibility of translation, its failure and defeat. This is the trap into which we undoubtedly fall – and not only the one that Heidegger has set – for the translation is both right and wrong, and neither. And the task of the translator may be to fall into the trap. Then we too fail in our attempt to translate, especially if we do not fail, but at least we know it. We will fail, but we will translate, failing even in knowing it – for knowledge is not enough to prevent us from falling. Thus knowledge too fails to stop the fall, just as noticing fails to notice that which can never be noticed, its own failure, the fall into its own trap, and the fall of translation into its trap as well. The translation of *episphalē* as prone to fall – or standing in the storm, attended with risk, precarious – is itself prone to fall.

So all that is great falls in the storm. And perhaps so it should – for the claim to greatness is itself a failure. Then fascism's claim to the German university, whether politicized or seeking to will its Greek essence, is the root of its self-decapitation, its fall from greatness. Once the takeover has been accomplished, even an *apologia* is impossible. And in a state so fraught with uncertainty, so threatened by ambiguity, 'The Self-Assertion of the German University' may just fall into its own trap. Just maybe.

Notes

1   *RR* (May 27, 1933).

2   'A man lives in house he plays with the snakes he writes / he writes when it darkens towards Germany' (P. Celan, 'Todesfuge', *Gesammelte Gedichte*, Vol. 1, Suhrkamp, 1983, 41; my translation).

3   Rorty, 'Taking Philosophy Seriously', *New Republic* (April 11, 1988), 33.

4   For G. Ryle's assessment, see R. Bernasconi, 'Habermas and Arendt on the Philosopher's "Error"', *Graduate Faculty Philosophy Journal*, 14/15 (1991), 4.

5   Young argues that Heidegger was not a 'lifelong Nazi', and that fascism was only 'an episode' in his life and thought. Thus he attempts a de-Nazification: 'one may accept any of Heidegger's philosophy without fear of being committed to, or moved into proximity with, fascism ... one may accept any of Heidegger's philosophy, and, though Heidegger himself was far from any such commitment, preserve, without inconsistency, a commitment to orthodox liberal democracy' (*Heidegger, Philosophy, Nazism*, Cambridge University, 1997, 5).

6   Adorno, 'Letter to *Diskus*', University of Frankfurt student newspaper, January 1963.

7   Lang *Heidegger's Silence*, Cornell University, 1996, 89.

8   *Heidegger's Silence*, 86.

9   *Heidegger's Silence*, 122n18.

10 9.*Heidegger's Silence*, 97.

11 *RR*, 468/5.

12 *RR*, 483n6. See P. Lenard, *Deutsche Physik*, Lehmann, 1936–37; J. Stark, *Nationalsozialismus und Wissenschaft*, Eher, 1934; E. Brüche, '"Deutsche Physik" und die deutschen Physiker', *Physikalische Blätter*, 1947, 232–6.

13 '*Ta ... megala panta episphalē...*' (*Rep.*, 497d9).

14 See Harries in *RR*, 481n1.

15 *WCT*, 16/51.

16 *RR*, 470/9.

17 *RR*, 470/9.

18 *RR*, 470/9.

19 *RR*, 470/9.

20 *RR*, 470/9.

21 *RR*, 470/9.

22 *RR*, 471/10; translation modified.

23 *RR*, 470/10; translation modified.

24 *RR*, 9/470; translation modified.

25 *RR*, 471/10.

26 *RR*, 473/12; translation modified.

27 *RR*, 471/10.

28 T. Aquinas, *Summa Theologica*, Q. 93, Art. 3.

[29] B. Allemann, 'Martin Heidegger und die Politik,' *Merkur* 235, Kiepenheuer & Witsch, 1967, 962–76.

[30] *RR*, 471/10; translation modified.

[31] *RR*, 471/10; translation modified.

[32] *RR*, 471/11.

[33] *RR*, 471/10.

[34] *RR*, 473/12.

[35] *WN*, 75/227; translation modified. Heidegger insists: 'Even Nietzsche – whom we, in another respect, next to Hölderlin, have to thank for a resuscitation of pre-Socratic philosophy – remains stuck there, where the requestioning of fundamental questions counts, in the misinterpretations of the 19th Century. And because he takes even his fundamental metaphysical concepts of Beyng and becoming from the beginning of philosophy – but as misinterpreted – his own metaphysics drives into the dead-end [*Sackgasse*] of the teaching of the eternal recurrence.' 'Europe and German Philosophy', *New Yearbook for Phenomenology and Phenomenological Philosophy*, Noesis, 2007.

[36] *WN*, 67/220, translation modified.

[37] *GA65*, 350.

[38] *BW*, 221/32.

[39] *WN*, 61/213; translation modified.

[40] *RR*, 474/14; Heidegger's italics.

[41] J. Derrida, *De l'esprit*, Galilée, 1987; *Of Spirit*, University of Chicago, 1989, 129n5/147n1. See M. Heidegger, 'Das Wesen der Sprache', *Unterwegs zur Sprache*, Neske, 1959; and 'The Way to Language', *On the Way to Language*, Harper & Row, 1971.

[42] I. Kant, *CPR*, A697; Kemp Smith does not note the shift from the A edition to the B in his translation. See I. Kant, *Welches sind die wirklichen Fortschritte, die die Metaphysik seit Leibnitzens und Wolfs Zeiten in Deutschland gemacht hat?*, *Werke* VI, Suhrkamp, 1958, 642.

[43] *BT*, 299.

[44] *BT*, 308.

[45] *BT*, 298.

[46] *RR*, 474–5/14.

[47] *WN*, 82/234; translation modified.

[48] *CPR*, B338n.

[49] *WN*, 88–90/239–40.

[50] 'Erst der Herrschende stellt nachher "Gerechtigkeit" fest' (*KSA11*, 245).

[51] *RR*, 489–90/29–30; translation modified.

[52] *RR*, 475–9/15–19.

[53] *RR*, 479/19.

[54] *RR*, 480/19.

[55] *RR*, 480/19.

[56] Harries n9; *RR*, 476.

57   Plato, *Republic*, 497d9; *RR*, 480/19. Against Harries, we could also re-translate Heidegger as: 'all that is great stands in storm', or 'all that is great is stormy' insofar as *stehen* also means 'being'.

58   Harries n13; *RR*, 480.

59   *Collected Dialogues of Plato*, Princeton University, 1963.

3

Only such art is under consideration here

3.1

'The Origin of the Work of Art'[1] – a text as much about origin as art. Here the origin lies in what Heidegger names an 'essential ambiguity', in the *wesenhafte Zweideutigkeit* of the artwork, in the origin of the work of art, in the origin itself. No surprise then that the title is ambiguous, *zweideutig* at least – the question of the origin of the *artwork* and the *origin* of the artwork – for the lecture insists that origin, *Ursprung*, is both 'from' and 'by', that from-which and through-which, *woher und wodurch*, something like an artwork is 'what' and 'how', *was und wie*, it is. Not only double therefore, but at least four-fold: from/ by/what/how – and all the permutations or combinations at/of the origin. But if the question of 'The Origin of the Work of Art' is that of the origin of the origin, the text opens up on infinity, a *mis-en-abîme* of origins – and this question opens up three other questions.

The origin – and the lecture itself presents the issue as a puzzle that may be taken seriously enough to solve: Is art the ground of artists and artworks, or is art only possible on the basis of the actuality of works and artists? But instead of giving an answer, although we may not be justified in seeking it yet, or raising the question more profoundly, the lecture insists that however the decision falls and whatever it may be: 'this does not concern us here'.[2] Rather the question is one of essence – for the origin of the work of art lies in the essence of art, *das Wesen der Kunst*, so that art can serve as the origin of the activity of the artist and the artwork alike, as prior to both artist, *Kunstler*, and work, *Kunstwerk*. And nor does it matter that thought here moves in a circle – for the lecture insists that it is not vicious, but hermeneutic. What matters, in fact, according to Heidegger, is self-deception – for this *Selbsttäuchung* threatens the derivation of the essence of art from higher concepts (insofar as they too presuppose the very understanding of art they are supposed to find). The question becomes then, not just how to get over the threat of self-deception in the search for essence, or in raising the question of the essence of art, but what the introduction of self-deception does to the lecture. In other words, once the deception of self or other, taking one thing for another, mistaken identities and differences, once the text itself insists that self-deception is possible or necessary, could the text not deceive as well? And if we can deceive ourselves here, can we not do so everywhere?

Art – and here the lecture insists that the question remains open, either because it has no answer, or because it wants to keep us in suspense for an answer to come, sooner or later, with or without this lecture, or because the open question is the answer, or because no answer is possible, now or then – 'whether and how art is, in general',[3] that is, not only *how*, but *if* art is at all, or not, and if so then how so, and if not, why not. But 'The Origin of the Work of Art' seems to ignore the question of the 'if', or at least lets it remain in the background, and to assume that art is or prevails in some kind of work called art, that to which we give the name, rightly or wrongly, of art, as opposed to non-art, and which then gives its name to artworks and artists, although this ground of the lecture's certainty remains perhaps uncertain. But if the text cannot or does not determine *if* art is at all, presupposing it in order to concentrate on the *how*, then is it in order to point elsewhere?

And the riddle – for the lecture here begins a series of riddles, the riddle of art, the riddle that art itself is, both that it is art, whatever that may be, and that it is at all, but a row of riddles that it addresses in the 'Epilogue',[4] and that are themselves not to be solved, either because they cannot be solved, or because at the moment they are solved, they no longer are that which they should be, namely riddles, or because the answer to the riddle is itself just another riddle, or because the solution to the riddle is insolvability. But 'The Origin of the Work of Art' insists: 'the task is to see the riddle'.[5] And if the riddle cannot be seen? If in seeing the riddle *qua* riddle, it becomes riddleless? And if the origin itself is a riddle? If the origin of the work of art was a riddle all along? Or if the task of seeing the riddle is itself an infinite task – even though, or perhaps because, it is impossible, and necessarily so? If the task itself is a riddle, or riddle of a riddle?

3.2

Regardless, once the shift from the question of the origin of the work of art to its essential nature has been asserted, presupposed, hypothesized, 'The Origin of the Work of Art' is free to argue that a work of art is, first of all, a thing that shares its thingliness with other things; although if the work is art, it is because it is not merely a thing. Even if the artistry of the artwork goes beyond the thing, the work can never not be a thing as well, cannot ever simply transcend its thingliness.

What then is a thing, *ein Ding*? A being, *Seiende*, not just a collection of attributes, the *substantia* of an *accidens*, or the subject of predication; but the *hypokeimenon* in which the *sumbebēkota* are always already grounded. And here 'The Origin of the Work of Art' sees the translation of Greek to Latin – hence to German and French and English – of *hypokeimenon* understood as *substantia*, as a kind of violence or *Gewalt*, an attack or assault, *Überfall*, that can only be avoided by allowing the thingliness of the thing to immediately show itself. Once again then, translation appears at the centre of thought, and the questions multiply themselves: Is it possible to avoid the violence that translation enacts, if it is violence at all – and that has yet to be determined, not only the extent to which translation or the history of translation violates the things themselves, not to mention mortals or gods, but also whether translation deserves the name of violence, or if it should be reserved for something else, something less translatable, even untranslatable? And how is the very act of translation, violent or not, first possible? How is it possible for the thingliness of the thing to be spoken and thought in so many languages, in so many ways, in so many places and times? Must there not be something always already present in the thingliness of the thing that allows it to be translated into Greek, Latin, German, English? In other words, must the translatability or untranslatability of the thing itself not already in some sense be capable of multiple languages?

The lecture however, leaves these questions in suspense in order first to think the thingliness of the thing, to raise the question of the being of the beings known as things – for if a substance or substratum and its accidents are able to be, it is because the thing is present: 'to be' means 'to be present'. The being of a thing as a being, *Sein des Seienden*, is its presence, *Anwesenheit*. And as a thing, the work of art *is* because of being, and is present because of being's presence.[6] Yet how is it possible to perceive the thing as it is and is present? Certainly, it could be interpreted through the traditional conceptual pair of form and matter – this is the frame of art history and aesthetic theory.[7] The form/matter opposition fits natural and cultural artefacts, hence aesthetic objects, and can be displaced to a multiplicity of other conceptual schemata, rational/irrational, logical/illogical; it can be inserted into the two-fold subject/object relation, for almost nothing can resist this conceptual-mechanism, the *Begriffsmechanik* of representation or mechanical reproduction – although these structures could all be projections of grammar, of subjects and predicates, or delimitations of language. As 'The Origin of the Work of Art' however insists: 'the question which comes first and functions as the standard, proposition-structure or thing-structure remains to this hour undecided. It even remains doubtful whether in this form the question is at all decidable.'[8]

In fact, the lecture decides not to reformulate the question, but to leave it undecided, perhaps undecidable, and continues seeking the nature of things prior to their form/matter interpretation – for initially things are present as things in their thingliness, then they submit to a two-fold ordering through which they come to be and present themselves as things of use or beauty, equipment or aesthetic objects. In this way, things can be reduced to a bearer of traits, a unity of manifold-sensations, or the structure of formed material;

they can be made into tools or equipment for something, *zu etwas*, for some use and employment, *Gebrauch und Brauch*. Still we are no closer to thinking that which makes a thing into a thing – for subtracting the use-value of things through some kind of reduction, phenomenological or not, only shows us that which we have added to the thing, and this leaves us back where we were, namely, with the thing. No wonder then that we remain even further from the essence of art, if art is at all, and if we can get there, or see why we cannot – for the artwork is precisely not supposed to be a piece of equipment, although it could be used as one, nor simply a thing, although it remains grounded in thingliness.

Heidegger however, starts by insisting upon the division between equipment-things and artwork-things: art begins where equipment ends, but art lets the equipmentality of equipment come forth. A division between equipment and artwork is supposed to be possible through the law of the thing, the thing-law: determine to what extent and in what way a being is a thing, then we know whether it is art or equipment. As the lecture insists: 'Thus the piece of equipment is half thing, because characterized by thingliness, and yet it is something more; at the same time it is half artwork and yet something less, because lacking the self-sufficiency of the artwork.'[9] So equipment is between thing and artwork – but this kind of division may be misleading – for we would first have to assume that such a mechanical or calculating ordering, *verrechnende Aufreihung*, is allowed, an assumption that the artwork itself is designed to problematize. Miscalculation then, or mis-representation, threatens the lecture, at least as much as the attempt to fix the difference between the genera and species of things, between art and non-art; and this may be in order to drive towards a more accurate form of calculative reflection or mechanical diaeresis – or on the contrary, to demonstrate that raising mechanical calculation to the level of aesthetic truth-sayer, like any quantitative analysis of art, is doomed to fail. And even if the hierarchy of thing, equipment and art is not designed to quantify, but to determine the essentially qualitative differences between kinds; we may not have escaped, especially if the differences between kinds, or between art and non-art, cannot be maintained, if nature or culture continually bring forth both transitional kinds, mixed breeds, mutations, exceptions, impurities, as well as pure singularities – for qualification too may assume a certain miscalculative ordering or conceptual misrepresentating, although the lecture may show how this attempt too falls into a trap, how the difference between art and non-art, thing and equipment, cannot hold up.[10]

Then 'The Origin of the Work of Art' might provide a catalogue of wrong-headed ways of thinking the nature of art, as well as a list of (necessarily historical) ineffective means for thinking the being of the being known as art. Indeed the only way that is acceptable – and this method too may only lead us down another *Holzweg*, point in the direction of the essence of art only to show the impossibility of ever getting there – is keeping preconceptions at a distance and foregoing prejudicial notions in order, as Heidegger insists, 'to let a being be as it is'.[11] The task of thinking then, means both turning towards a being in order to think about it with respect to being, but simultaneously letting it be in itself as its own being – but if this shows itself to be impossible, if we cannot turn towards a being without turning it, and thereby not letting it be as it is, then the lecture's attempt to do so may just be the most effective way of showing it up. If the lecture names letting-be as the most difficult of tasks, *das Schwerste*, it may be not in order to get us to do the deed, but to indicate the vanity of our desire, the arrogance of our will, even here, and the inevitability of our failure – although this doesn't necessarily mean that we don't attempt to let beings be, nor that we couldn't be underway to doing so, however impossible the task may be, nor does it mean that we shouldn't seek another way to think the being of beings, or the essence of the artwork, or the necessary impossibility of the task.

When 'The Origin of the Work of Art' then comes to determining the nature of the work of art, it is no surprise that every essence it suggests, every mark of specific difference it tries to fix, fails to hold up. The mere thing is supposed to be useless and not made; equipment should be useful and made; art should be useless and made. But in order to *think* the equipmentality of equipment, the lecture selects and *uses* a work of art – so it is already at least beginning to mix modes, cross-fertilize, although apparently in the name of producing some purity, with the goal of squeezing out the pure character or essence of equipment. Indeed, the work of art is never simply equipment – although their difference might be impossible to maintain – rather art is supposed to work to reveal the thingliness of the thing and the equipmentality of equipment.

So Heidegger selects a pair of peasant or farmer shoes; but in addition, *dazu*, in order to perhaps make the visual-realization, *Veranschaulichung*, easier, he choses 'a well-known painting of van Gogh's, who painted such shoes several times'.[12] All questions however – of the thing, equipment and work, of essence, existence, being, presence, of seeing and of that which is perhaps too much to be seen – all this remains in the background, perhaps knowingly so, in order to fix that which is to be seen in the painting, namely, the essence of equipment, of the shoes as equipment for covering, protecting, ornamenting, the feet. The work of art represents something that can be made present to us as real, of certain materials in particular forms designed for specific purposes. In fact, the subject of the work is perhaps far more the utility or serviceability of shoes; it is a representation of that which is only mediately represented, that which is signified or indicated, but strictly speaking neither present nor absent – for the painting of shoes is not just a painting of shoes.

Regardless, for Heidegger, although equipment first becomes that which it is in being used, it is first in the painting that the equipmentality, *eidos*, of the equipment is supposed to show itself. Indeed, the painting has placed the shoes in a frame, a *Gestell* – although not a technological one – whether the painting is framed or not, by choosing to paint them, taking them off the feet, whether they were ever worn or not, removing them from the earth to which they belong, whether they ever touched the ground or not, tearing them out of their role as reliable, whether they were ever relied upon or not. For 'The Origin of the Work of Art', the world in which the meaning of the shoes is constituted, the context in which they are worn and cared for, is bracketed out by the frame installed by the artist, by the artist's art-world (for what is the work of art if not a kind of framing?). And the painting is a representation of the shoe-world: belonging to the earth and protected by the world, the shoes show themselves as that which they are, useful, reliable. The equipment's reliability, *Verläßlichkeit*, is its equipmentality. In our world, we rely on shoes to stand between us and the earth – and the painting is a painting of this between, this fold in which we first come to see the reliability of shoes, what equipment in truth is.[13]

For 'The Origin of the Work of Art' however, the truth of equipment is not found by examining real shoes – for there the equipmental character of equipment disappears in order to allow the equipment to function – but coming before the painting, truth shows itself, and only then, *nur dadurch*, are we supposed to be able to hear that which the work of art has to say. Indeed, only then – and if not, then not? If we do not bring ourselves before the painting, can say neither 'That's it!' nor 'Ah ha!', then does the equipmentality of equipment remain concealed? And if we do not get this truth by a description, report or observation, as the lecture insists, have we any chance of getting it in front of the painting? Perhaps 'one' could – but us? And do we really need the painting at all, the painting before us? Could we not do with a reproduction or postcard of the painting? Or a copy? Or an imagined copy? Or in fact a pair of real shoes? In or out of an art gallery or museum? And could we then maintain the difference between the shoes and the art? Or the shoes in the mind? An imaginary or conceptual framing? And what if the painting itself is not the painting, not 'the well-known painting of shoes painted several times', but a fake? A fake van Gogh? Or fake shoes? What then? In other words, what if our recognition of the truth of equipment passed by way of a misrecognition of the painting? Or misrepresentation of the shoes? What if 'the equipmentality that is first supposed to genuinely arrive at its appearance through the work and only in the work'[14] arrived somewhere else? Would this painting speak – or would it be the words of another, a copy posing as the original, a copyist standing-in for the author? And would we, the ones who heard the painting speak, could we not be hard of hearing? We who saw the painting before us, saw it with our own eyes – could we not be forgers ourselves, sophists masking as philosophers, actors faking the real, pretending to be serious or ironic, sane or mad?

3.3

'The Origin of the Work of Art' however, is not supposed to concern itself with the origin of the painting so much as that of its truth. The painting should reveal the truth of shoes, disclose their equipmentality, allow the earth and world of the shoes to appear, let the being of these beings come forth – and one can only hope, of course, that if the work is a fake, if we could determine that it is faking, that its truth is not also faked as well, although this threat too seems to remain. With the work of art then, truth comes into unconcealment, *Unverborgenheit:* the painting is the happening of truth, *alētheia*, and the fixing of this happening – not simply as *adaequatio* or correspondence of thought and thing, representation and presentation, painting of shoes and shoes themselves; rather the truth that appears in the painting is that of the universal essence of things, the *Allgemeinen Wesens der Dinge*.[15] The work of art is supposed to bring to light the essence of what it means to be and be shoes, the truth of this kind of being, of this equipment, and its being. But the painting is neither the representation of the reality of the real, *Wirklichkeit*, nor the reproduction, *Wiedergabe*, of an entity, present or absent; it is 'the reproduction of the thing's general essence',[16] of being as the truth of beings – and it thereby opens us up as much to that which works in the shoes, to the equipmental of the equipment, the thingliness of the thing, as to the work as opening. Essence is pregiven, *vorgegeben*, to the artist, and regiven in the artwork – and therefore the relation between work and thing is not simple mimesis, *Abbildverhältnis*; rather, if the work is a copy or representation of the truth of things, of the being of beings, it is because it regives the truth of the original presence of beings. The work of art is not original giving, but an original regiving of a gift that has already been given, a second-hand gift as good as the first, an eternally fresh giving, as pure and perfect today as it ever was. In this way, truth happens in the artwork each time anew, just as 'the sun is new every day',[17] just as the Pythagorean theorem is no more or less true each time we think it, as the experience of pleasure and pain cannot be a representation, but always a presentation, another absolutely singular event.

But how is original presentation possible? Could we ever be certain of differentiating a regiving of truth from its representation? Or the uniqueness of experience, insofar as it is unique for everyone, every time? And can the purity of presentation be maintained once it has been represented in the work of art? Like the lecture itself, does not the work of art show the impossibility of pure presentation? Demonstrate how truth cannot happen in the painting? How representation threatens even the being of beings, the singularity of experience, the Pythagorean theorem and the rotation of the planets, presentations that are always also representations – not only because the work could be a forgery, but because at its limit, that which Heidegger takes to be the most difficult of thoughts, that which is simple and pure and original and absolute, cannot be thought *qua* thought, or happen *qua* happening, and thus cannot happen in the work of art, at least without compromising its simplicity, purity, originality?

Regardless, 'The Origin of the Work of Art' insists upon the event of truth in the painting: the shoes open up or deconceal the truth of beings – for 'art is the setting-itself-in-the-work of truth', the '*Sich-ins-Werk-Setzen der Wahrheit*'.[18] Or is it? For as the lecture asks, albeit with reference to connoisseurs and critics, art dealers and art historians (and here the charge against the art market can also be the most effective form of advertising), a question precisely designed to distance the work of philosophy from that of everyone else: 'in all this busy activity do we encounter the work itself?'[19] And if we do not, is it because we cannot? If the text reacts upon itself, is it not more or less 'busy activity' in which the truth of the painting is not yet encountered, or never encountered, either because it has not yet been properly encountered, or because it could never be encountered? Then can the difference between the work of philosophy and the busy activity of art history be maintained? Or does the text stand before us like the shoes, a test that we perhaps cannot pass?

In fact, Meyer Schapiro, the art historian, thinks the philosopher fails the test because he gets the painting wrong: the one to which Heidegger refers is 'clearly de la Faille's no. 255',[20] not peasant's shoes, but 'the shoes of the artist, by that time a man of the town and city'.[21] For the art historian therefore, the philosopher has 'retained from his encounter with van Gogh's canvas a moving set of associations with peasants and the soil, which are not sustained by the picture itself. They are grounded rather in his own social outlook with its heavy pathos of the primordial and earthy.'[22] Heidegger does not realized that the painting is a 'piece from a self-portrait' – for he has misses 'the artist's presence in the work'.[23] The subject of painting is always the painter, and the philosopher overlooks that which is 'personal and physiognomic in the shoes'.[24] The subject of the painting is the painter – or a part of the painter, a 'sacred relic'[25] – and this desire for expression, successful or not, is a desire for appropriation: the artist always says that the work, or shoes, are due to him or her.[26] If the shoes then are worn by someone, they are thereby marked by their connection to the feet – they bear the trace of the person who wore them, so that the subject of the painting is not only the artist, but also the owner, possessor, thief, or inventor of the shoes. Schapiro therefore insists that the shoes are 'more likely pictures of the artist's own shoes, not the shoes of a peasant'.[27]

Yet here, there is neither argument nor evidence, both of which would be essential in order to fulfil art history's own criterion of truth; rather, there is second-hand testimony, hearsay from Gauguin, who – the art historian informs us – shared van Gogh's quarters in Arles in 1888 and remarked that 'in the studio was a pair of big hob-nailed shoes, all worn and spotted with mud; he made of it a remarkable still life painting' – for these were, reportedly, the shoes the artist wore on his missionary voyage.[28] Yet as

Schapiro admits: 'it is not certain which of the paintings with a single pair of shoes Gauguin had seen at Arles',[29] and the credibility of the witness begins to unravel. Even further, there is no assurance that Gauguin's assertion is not itself an interpretation of the painting at best, or an imaginary projection at worst – and even if the artist had given the painting a title like 'My Shoes!', 'that would change nothing in the effect produced, whether or not it is sought after consciously'.[30] For what could convince us that the image of shoes corresponds to the things themselves, any more than to an image of shoes? Are the shoes in the studio those that the art historian sees in the painting? Is the painting not rather a translation or transformation? But if so, then of what? And could we ever know that the artist painted the shoes which stood before him and not those of his imagination? Or confirm that the painting can be attributed to the artist, not to another, or to nobody at all, even after we have gathered and corroborated all the testimony of all the witnesses? Or that the image of shoes – if that is actually that which is to be seen in the paint – is itself not a projection or interpretation? And could we ever be sure that nothing that did not belong to the shoes in the studio, not even the paint itself, crept into the painting of the shoes – with or without intent? In other words, can we be sure that the art historian's assumed correspondence between presentation and representation is possible? Or is there far more always something that remains unrepresented and unrepresentable?

Even further: the art historian insists that the subject of the painting must be confined to that which he, Schapiro, sees, namely, a portion of the artist himself, a sacred relic. But here the art historian fails to see that which can be seen in the painting – for seeing is not simply a matter of necessity – and is it not possible to see the equipmentality of equipment in the shoes? The earth and world of the work of art? The happening or non-happening of truth and untruth? Or the very failure of thought – both the philosopher's and the art historian's – to think the work of art? Indeed, in attempting to limit his sight, the art historian cannot see the impossibility of his own limitations – for he cannot stop the painting from going beyond the artist, the art historian, the philosopher, even beyond art itself. The subject of the painting runs away from us, and runs away with itself, escapes and escapes our notice (even when noticed), remains at large, multiplies implications, transgresses the frame. And even if he attempts to correct his short-sightedness, by some prosthetic, glasses or eyes, his own or someone else's, or through surgery, the art historian would only see through the medium of his instrument – for he cannot see that he cannot see. Then if Heidegger knows that the shoes are not of peasant origin, that his attribution is incorrect, or inconfirmable, or inconsequential; it may be in order to show not only that the arguments of art history concerning attribution cannot be solved, neither by the most minute empirical investigation nor by further advances in research technologies, but just as much that they do not address the work of artworks – so if Schapiro is right, he is wrong. And the art historical critique directed against 'The Origin of the

Work of Art' demonstrates not that the painting is a function of philosophical phantasy, imagination or projection, but that art historians will be art historians, framed by their own frame – for Schapiro doesn't prove but presupposes that truth is correspondence, not *alētheia*, and that the shoes in truth belong to the artist.

Yet what about the painting? Have we yet seen what is there to be seen? Certainly the artist seems to have painted a pair of shoes, although the philosopher – coming face to face with a van Gogh, or that which he takes to be a van Gogh, encountering or thinking that he is encountering a 'great work of art' – assumes that the two shoes must be thought as together, gathered and held in a conceptual framework or *Gestell*, in one whole, unified product. But there is no conclusive evidence, no certainty that the thing in the work is a pair of shoes, no less peasant's shoes.[31] Once untied, removed from the feet, they no longer make a pair, or at least, they are always threatened with a mix-up – and perhaps the subject of the painting is far more the absent feet, or some other more or less suitable appendage. Nevertheless, insofar as the philosopher couples the shoes and ascribes them to a peasant woman, and insofar as the art historian attributes the pair to the artist, both fail to recognize the threat of singularities, mismatched shoes, as well as the threat of simulation, pure repetition, mechanical reproduction, the continual flow of identical products off an assembly line; and both miss that which is there to be seen, the many, *viel* – for if they both seek restitution, to return the shoes to their owner, peasant or a painter, they actually attempt to appropriate the shoes for themselves. Giving implies taking; giving the shoes to you, I take up the role of giver for myself – for it is due to me or through me that you have received the gift, the gift of shoes, meaning, truth, identity, difference: I am the cause and ground of your reception. So the subject of the painting becomes far more the viewer: not the shoes, but the one who looks – the artist has painted us. And the shoes look at us, look at us looking at them, looking at us. Similarly the philosopher and art historian are not simply the makers of meaning or interpretation, not merely the appropriators or collectors of paintings – for the gift must be received by someone, anyone, the artist or the audience. Even further, if the painter paints, subjects the shoes to paint, makes art come to be, presents a painting, and painting itself, to us; then the shoes are a self-portrait of the painter as the maker, the giver of the gift, or the painter as paint, or as shoes. And the painting therefore, is a painting of shoes, us and the painter; or of the strife of earth and world, art, the happening of truth, an essential ambiguity, the being of beings, things, thingliness, serviceability, equipment; or of representation, presentation, interpretation; or of the riddle of the painting that cannot be answered, but only seen, or the secret that only becomes secret when it is told; or of the gift, taking and being given. Indeed, not only do we not know what is inside or behind the shoes, but we do not even know what is there to be seen, what shoes are in truth, or if the painting is a painting of shoes at all, that is, if the shoes are not simply equipment – and perhaps shoes do not serve us in walking, do not connect but far more disconnect our feet from the earth, attempt to translate the touch of our toes, while demonstrating their untranslatability, revealing the locus of a loss or lack, an infinite difference and unbridgeable gap between us and the earth, spectator and work of art, a failure of participation or translation, *metalēpsis*, between idea and thing (Plato) – but pure ornaments, frames around feet, as useless as a work of art, or a frame of a painting; or removed from the feet, lost objects, abandoned forms, or perhaps a fetish, foot-trap or strap-on, or the shape (or lack) of the foot's convex (penis), and the concave form sometimes enveloping the foot (vagina, mouth, anus, nasal cavity, belly-button, ear, circumcised or not).[32] Indeed, the subject of the painting has become even more indeterminate, even more ambiguous, and we don't even know if the painting is therefore a portrait of shoes (or what appear to be shoes), or is not a portrait at all, but a landscape, the ground on which the shoes rest, that which the shoes hide, or the shoes as landscape, or a painting of a particular place and time, or of the particularity of this particular, or of nothing at all, not of shoes (a pair or non-pair, of a peasant woman or city-dweller) or any other subject, or a painting of a painting – a forgery of an original, or of a forgery, or an original – or a copy of a painting, representation of a representation, or a painting simply of paint, of colour, brushstroke, shape, line, plane, perspective or light, and of the act of painting, a painting of the remains of movement, the artwork as the detritus of work, of the work that art does, or the residue of thought, instinct, indeed, of life itself; or not of the painting at all, but of the frame, the painting as frame of that which is in the painting or of the frame around the painting, framing the frame, or seeing as framing – so then the origin of the work of art would be framing, self-framing, just as art itself, as *poiēsis*, comes out of improvisation, *ex tōn autoschediasmatōn*.[33] And even if the painting paints shoes, it paints all these other things as well. Thus it may prove quite impossible to confirm not only *that*, but *what* the artist painted, if he painted at all, whether he painted peasant's shoes, shoes of the artist, one shoe twice, the shoe and its double, the same shoe with a difference, the shoes in his mind, or in ours; or to find the limit of painting, of art in general – if this is the work of art, namely, to inject what 'The Origin of the Work of Art' calls an essential ambiguity into the artwork, where the threat of forgery becomes as palpable to aesthetics as that of sophistry to philosophy, where the riddle of art is as essential as that of thought – for perhaps the painting of shoes is not a painting of shoes at all; perhaps the painting is a painting of everything but shoes.

    And is this not precisely the point? Namely, that the *work* of art as the work of *art*, or *Art*, is the work of attempting to demonstrate the essential ambiguity at and of the origin, of the task of posing the riddle of art, just as thought's work is to see the riddle? Is this not the happening of truth – the posing of an unanswered and unanswerable riddle? Not only the riddle of the origin of art, but just as much of the origin of work (of art and thought alike)? And therefore a reposing of the riddle as riddle? Or would the riddle then too be just another answer? An answer posing as a riddle, or an apparent or fake riddle, a *Scheinrätzel*, an even more under-handed way to reappropriate and repossess the origin of the work of art? Merely the latest avatar in the long line of strategies deployed to stop the riddle from riddling? The newest form of philosophical self-deception? Would the philosopher then be anything more than just another riddler? And 'The Origin of the Work of Art', the most truthful or lying riddle?

3.4

Regardless, the lecture insists that the truth that comes to light in the artwork, does so clandestinely, in an under-handed way, *unter der Hand*. But if something can here surreptitiously slide into the shoes, work in the work, the equipmentality of equipment or the being of beings, then perhaps it can do so elsewhere as well. Indeed truth is at stake, the truth of the work of art, the truth of great art, *großen Kunst* – for 'only such art is under consideration here'[34] – although the extent to which the lecture could differentiate great art from the less great or non-great remains uncertain, not to mention the great business of great art forgery. And in this great kind of art, the artist is supposed to be inconsequential in order to let the work stand and reveal its truth, just as we are supposed to encounter the work in its own world, not torn out of its own sphere, and placed in some kind of collection or subject to market forces.[35]

So what is great art? After van Gogh, Heidegger gives the example of the temple at Paestum. Here great art is at work in its world, or at least in a world that is no more, that the work used to inhabit, perhaps once upon a time, although that too has yet to be confirmed, if could be. And here art is no longer representational. Non-representation then, is supposed to characterize the temple and allow us to encounter the work and working of art, earth and world at work in the artwork – but if this criterion fails to be fulfilled, the lecture's reflection on work and truth may fail as well. It is therefore essential to find a way to access the work of art – for nothing about the work can be discovered as long as it does not stand alone, in itself, as long as the pure self-subsistence of the work, *das reine Insichstehen des Werkes*, has not shown itself. But as 'The Origin of the Work of Art' itself asks: 'Is the work ever in itself accessible?'[36] And if the answer is negative, if access to the work itself is denied or delayed, refused 'for the time being' or promised as a possible future, or uncertain, if the door to the temple does not open up on to the work itself, then the entire project may be threatened. The lecture therefore suggests: in order to gain access to the work, 'it would be necessary to remove it from all relations to something other than itself'.[37] And if this is impossible, then either the project is sunk – or this is not the project. Then although the artist's task may be to produce an independent work, the goal may be unreachable – but worth reaching, and therefore worth striving for, an idea or ideal with regulative use-value; or the impossibility of the task may be the goal, or may be designed to point us elsewhere, away from the task of discovering the self-subsistence of the artwork, towards another, one perhaps less lofty, and towards artwork that is perhaps less great. As the text insists: no work stands outside of all relations, and the key is to determine in which relations it stands and belongs – for only then can we approach the happening of truth in the work of art. Indeed, the self-subsistence of the work has fled, if it was ever present, because the world of the work has perished, if it ever existed – for 'world-withdrawal and world-decay can never be undone',[38] if they ever were done in the first place.

Still the question of truth persists; and the lecture therefore deliberately selects a building, a Greek temple that portrays nothing, that *bildet nichts ab*, and 'cannot be ranked as representational art'[39] – for even if the temple bars our passage to its original world, even if the work fails to maintain its self-subsistence, it should nevertheless open up the question of the relation between work and truth. But does the temple really portray nothing? Absolutely nothing? Or does it always also portray something? And can 'The Origin of the Work of Art' maintain the difference between representative and non-representative art, *bildende und nicht bildende Kunst*? Or is their difference perhaps designed to breakdown? And what then happens to the truth that art is supposed to let happen in the temple? Have we here encountered the essence of art, the nature of art's work or its origin?

On the one hand, the claim that unlike painting, architecture portrays nothing seems quite superficial, if not downright wrong. Buildings can and often do represent something: a sculpture of the divine, votive offerings, as well as tragedy; or allegorically, *allo-agoreuei*, as in the case of the Sydney opera house, sailing ships; or as each of New York's World Trade Centers before September 11 represented the other. So architecture is never purely non-representational – and it always represents at least one thing, namely, itself. So too the temple at Paestum is only that which it is *qua* self-representational or reflexive, as the being that represents its being, and not nothing, or both that which it is and that which it is not, as well as that which is and is not. And architecture is always also a portrayal of its matter and form, stone or wood; or of the worker, of the carpenter's hands, the labourer's back, of the body that constructed it; or of the architect who designed it, or the architect's idea, the building in the mind; or as equipment, a tool or mechanism for calling and permitting the arrival of the gods, the temple represents the people who live and work in it, their earth and world; or a portrait of the forces and institutions that are concretized in its foundations; or of space, of that which it includes and excludes, of the spaces that traverse its spaces, of the spaces of space, and of space itself, of that box that serves as a threshold between that which is and is not the temple. And architecture always also represents the unrepresentable – not merely of the god that religion invites into its space, but of the order, 'right orders', the physical and mathematical laws of architecture, the laws of harmony that serve the Greeks in architecture as well as music and poetry, in building and making – for the temple represents frozen music (Schlegel). Indeed, the musical proportions of the lyre are just as valid as the formal relations of Paestum (Goethe): 'The column's shaft, and triglyph rings / I almost think, the whole temple sings.'[40] And just as the Renaissance laws of perspective worked out by Albertini and da Vinci can work to produce the feeling of pleasure and pain, the experience of beauty, so too with the temple's Pythagorean form – for the right ordering of columns are the universal laws of life itself (Hölderlin): 'As if rest' on thin columns / on right orders, new life.'[41] So the temple is a representation of life's newness as well, and a portrayal of history, its own history as well as that of a world, and of time itself. Indeed, even according to 'The Origin of the Work of Art', if the temple brings to light the essential worlding of the world, the happening of being of beings, the art at work in the work of art, the temple's light and shadow, and not only of the light of a clearing that lightens and darkens the truth, but just as much of the light that lets truth happen, both the *light* of truth and the *truth* of the light, then the temple can always also portray light and truth. If the temple encloses and protects mortals and immortals, gathers the four-fold, serves as a kind of cave for representation: the temple is a representation of that which does not cave in, but rather gathers – and the representations are not only on the wall; they are the walls themselves. So if the lecture deliberately selects a building, a Greek temple that portrays nothing, it is because it is always also a portrait of that which does not portray. Portraying nothing then, the temple portrays quite a lot.

On the other hand, Heidegger's formulation says just the opposite – or more precisely, it is ambiguous to the point that it may be impossible to be certain of its meaning: 'a building, a Greek temple, portrays nothing'. In other words, the temple portrays nothing that cannot be represented. And if Paestum allows us to step inside it, to enter into the clearing that it has lighted; it is not only to allow the four-fold to reveal its presence, but just as much to conceal that which can never present itself. Architecture lets us step into nothingness, lets us encounter the nothing. The temple's representation of nothing, however, is precisely non-representational – for nothing cannot be portrayed, just as Parmenides knows that 'nothing is not';[42] and as Heidegger, after *Being and Time*, explicitly thinks the 'not' and nothing in 'What is Metaphysics?' Indeed, this is the way in which architecture comes into being – for every artwork takes up a relation to the things themselves, to beings in the world, and thus to the being of beings, in order to articulate what they are, their *Wasgehalt*, their particular content, and how they are, their mode of being, their *Seinsart*, just as the construction of the temple is an interruption or break-in, *Einbruch*, into the totality of beings, into the earth and world of the Greeks. In this sense of 'breaking and entering', *poiēsis* is a criminal attitude, a violent transgression of the law of beings in the world; it is the way in which artistic production works: breaking into the temple at Paestum, we find that it contains nothing – not merely that it is now empty of beings, but that nothing itself is in some way there, present as that which the presence of beings works to conceal, as that which allows the work to come to presence, permits the temple to first come into being, conceals itself so that the being of the four-fold can be that which it is. Indeed, that which is or is not portrayed in the temple stands in an essential relation with that which is not, this nothing that is or is not portrayed, because it can never be portrayed. And the *technē* of the *archē-techton* consists not only in exploiting nothing in order to let the being of the temple come to be, but just as much in representing the unrepresentable, constructing a site for that which cannot be. Building thereby, gathering the four-fold, and nothing else, *sonst nichts*, presupposes the being of beings, and nothing further, *weiter nichts*, while working to clear and illuminate a site for the four-fold, that which allows entrance into beings themselves, and nothing more, *darüber hinaus nichts*. So like thought, architecture *is* only in relation to being, and therefore always also in relation to that which being is not, nothing. When the temple then seeks to be something, itself, it only shows itself over and against something else, some other, an *Andere*, namely nothing, *Nichts* – and it finds that it is that which it is, representational or not, only by virtue of that which it is not, nothing. In this moment, architecture works in reverse, shows itself as the opposite of that which it is supposed to be: it should not represent anything, no beings, but serve to open up a place for them to gather, a *syn-agogue* for the four-fold – but it ends up serving nothing. Thus the temple at Paestum, like all art, works for nothing, the other of being, of the being of beings; and simultaneously, it works for that which is essential to beings, the being of their being, the being of beings that allows them to work. So nothing is essentially that about which architecture knows nothing, but when building begins, it calls for nothing – as the lecture insists: if architecture portrays nothing, it is because 'it has recourse to what it rejects'.[43]

But taking up nothing, the temple takes it as something that it is not – for an absolute difference is supposed to lie between being and nothing; and nothing is not a thing or a being, but nothing. That which the temple portrays should be nothing, but in the moment that it is, it is not, and is not what it should be – for nothing must both be and not be. And the work of architecture cannot, therefore, be nothing – for nothing is supposed to be absolute non-being (although the nothing is prior to the 'not' and negation alike; they are only possible on the basis of a more originary nothing that is 'formally impossible', but metaphysically essential).[44] And if the temple's nothing is not to be thought or comprehended, *erfassen*, but encountered, *begegnen*, and announced, *bekunden*, as already given; we must not imagine, but experience nothing, not merely its concept, like that of infinity or zero, but the nothing itself, *das Nichts selbst*, authentic nothingness, *eigentlichen Nichts* (although an inauthentic or 'sham' nothing may threaten here as well).[45] Between the portrait or form of nothing and nothing itself then, an essential difference – but the nothing should not even have difference; it should be without distinction, pure non-difference. Thus the portrayal of nothing is a sign or indication that the encounter with the temple's truth happens neither in the production of some kind of empty or non-place, nor in some idea of negative space, but in relation to the nothing that is. And architecture's nothing, like a building's self-representation, is an opportunity to encounter nothing insofar as art works to let us step out into nothing, open up the temple, or clear an opening for nothing.

Stepping into the temple at Paestum then, we are supposed to encounter nothing, not as an everyday thing in the world, not as a being, nor as the being of beings, insofar as this would conceal the nothing (although we have not yet shown *that* or *how* we could do so, nor *that* or *how* nothing could be encountered), but as the nothing that encircles all beings. In stepping into the temple then, we encounter the nothing, but we are not afraid – for our relation to that which we fear is a being, fear *of* something determinate – rather we are filled with the angst that reveals the nothing.[46] Indeed, for Heidegger, angst has a fundamental relation to nothing insofar as it is always 'angst for', not this or that being, but precisely for nothing. No other encounter affects us like angst – for in no other experience are we supposed to relate to nothing. And the encounter with nothing is angst ridden for us because the totality of beings slips away. We hover or float, *schweben,* and our proper place among beings, the place in which we feel *at home*, is no more: we are confronted with the uncanny, *Unheimlichkeit* – for we are no longer at home. In fact, experiencing angst for nothing, we are no longer who and what we are; we simply are there, *Dasein.* And with angst, we can no longer even speak, no longer even say that we are or are not – for language always implies being.[47] The fundamental affect of angst opens up the nothing: 'in angst, the nothing is encountered at one with beings as a whole'.[48] The nothing therefore, is not the negation, annihilation or extermination of beings; it is their slipping-away. In this sense, nothing is not simply a passive no-thing that we experience, but that which impresses itself upon us by repelling us, the cause of our anxiety, the ground of our encounter with groundlessness, *Ungrund.* In this way, 'nothing itself nihilizes'.[49] Standing over and against the totality of beings as their absolute other, the nothing reveals beings as a whole; and beings in relation to their being, as not nothing. Even further: the nothing makes the revelation of beings first possible – for nothing brings us before beings, and allows beings to open themselves up to us. Nothing is the opening that permits the relationship to beings – for if we are there, in the temple at Paestum, it is because our essence means: 'holding-out-into the nothing'.[50] We are always already out of ourselves, more than ourselves, beyond ourselves, transcending ourselves; we can therefore relate to others, to beings, to that which is not us. Thus nothing belongs to the essence of what it means for us to be there in the temple, as beings – for nothing too belongs to being. As Heidegger insists (continuing Hegel's thought that nothing is not simply over and against beings, but in relation to being itself – for *'pure being and pure nothing is therefore the same'*):[51] 'the nihilizing of nothing happens in the being of beings'.[52] Then nothing nihilizes even if we remain unaware of its action, and whether we deny and negate it or not. So nothing shows itself as that which lets our day-to-day negations be, makes possible our privations and refusals, no-sayings, our representations and non-representations – for we are the place-holders of the nothing, and our finitude the mark of its presence. The questions of logical negation therefore, questions asked and answered by the ancient thought of non-being, *mē on*, or the medieval thought of that from which created beings come, *ex nihilo*, the opposite of beings and of God, can only be answered, for Heidegger, on the basis of a more original investigation into the essence of nothing (although that too may demand a yet more original investigation, investigation of the investigation for the origin of the origin, or an infinite investigation that leaves everyone investigating everything and everyone else) – for as 'The Origin of the Work of Art' insists (and it is perhaps here that the lecture gives the clearest indication of how we should take the claim that the building portrays nothing): 'This open center is therefore not surrounded by what is; rather, the lighting center itself encircles all that is, like the nothing which we scarcely know.'[53]

So the temple at Paestum portrays nothing – either nothing at all, or the nothing, or the four-fold, or something else; but only if we have found something that, Heidegger insists, hits the mark, something *Triftiges*, an account that is valid for the phenomena, that encounters the encounter, to the extent this is possible. And if not, then not – then at least we could say that we can rule the account of architecture out. Indeed hitting the mark, the task of articulating the nature and essence of the work of art, seems to be the goal of the lecture.

Two threats however, now show themselves. First, what if the difference between representative and non-representative art, between painting and building, cannot be maintained? For if the examples seem to lie safely within their respective genera, they cannot then serve to determine their limits. When painting becomes architecture, building with colour and shadow or painting with space and stone, constructing a house that looks like a shoe or painting to the point of abstraction – and we couldn't even be sure that architecture and painting had not already become something like sculpture – when any or all of this happens, then even the examples the lecture provides become questionable. And either 'The Origin of the Work of Art' takes this process of selection seriously, *Ernst*, or as a joke, *Scherz* – but if the former, is it because only 'great art' respects the law of genre? And if the latter, is it because it means to point us elsewhere in the search for the essence of the work of art? Or is generic self-implosion not the work of art? The demonstration of the failure of all attempts to fix the artwork within boundaries and to maintain an essential difference between representative and non-representative art, a distinction perhaps far more motivated by art historians and art markets, than works of art themselves, at least to the extent these can be distinguished?

Yet second, not only is the lecture threatened by the examples it introduces in order to hit the mark – the structure of the account itself is threatened by the mark it is supposed to try to hit, by the inability to account for its account. The temple is supposed to open up the nothing and let the four-fold and its being arrive – but 'it shows itself only when it remains undisclosed and unexplained'.[54] No explanation or disclosure is possible (not even that one); and this holds not only for the temple's earth, but for its world and truth as well – for that would immediately betray it as that which it is not: explaining the unexplainable, disclosing the undisclosable, cannot hit the mark; rather the lecture demonstrates the inexplicability and undisclosability of the work of art (as well as the lecture's), the impossibility of a non-explanation of the non-explainable, or a non-disclosure of the non-disclosable. In other words, the structural impossibility of knowing, thinking or encountering nothing reappears when we confront the work of art – and we come no closer to hitting the mark by not hitting it, or knowing that we cannot hit it, or hitting upon its unhitability, which once again means that we fail to hit it. But is that not precisely the point of the lecture? The attempt is all we have, the eternal recurrence of the infinite presence of the task, perpetual failure of the account to take account of the work of art and of itself, even to take account of failure.

Regardless, like the shoes,[55] the temple does not just portray nothing; it is also a thing and equipment, and the art of the architectural work of art lies not in its utility, its sheltering function, nor in its ability to invoke the gods – although the equipmentality of equipment, like the purposiveness of form, can neither account for the art of the temple nor think the way in which the artwork works, nor the work of art itself, if anything could; rather for Heidegger, the temple brings the withdrawal of the Greek world into unconcealedness, allows mortals and immortals to come into presence, to gather there on the earth that supports them and to which they (and we humans as historical-decisive beings) belong. Heidegger calls this character of the temple, the four-fold, *das Geviert*: here earth and world, mortals and immortals are allowed to be that which they are, to show that they are originally united, not merely collected or enframed, how they are in truth. And the temple is the opening up of this truth – for insofar as art works to set up a world, to disclose its earth, reveal the essential differences of earth and world, the unifying tension of their struggle, the *agon* of mortals and immortals, *ens creatum* and *ens increatum*; it must allow the thingly character of the building, along with its equipmentality, to withdraw, and conceal its work, if it is to work. The temple works to open up a clearing in which the four-fold can come to light – and as the light or lighting itself, the work of art conceals itself in order to function. In fact, like light, the temple is that clearing, that something that is nothing, that is necessary, but can never be seen; and although we can never look into the lighted clearing without being blinded, we need it to happen in order for beings to reveal themselves, in order for the unity of the four-fold to be and be that one which it truly is. So just as being lets beings be that which they are by withdrawing, the temple works by concealing its work in providing the place, *Ort*, for the gathering of the four-fold – although concealing may be just another kind of revealing, the undisclosed and essentially undisclosable, *die wesenhaft Unerschließbare*, as a disclosure, the unexplained or unexplainable as an explanation – and this is its beauty, *Schönheit*, the way, *Weise*, in which the temple's lighting throws open the truth.

Yet what about this truth? For in truth, truth – not simply as *adaequatio* or correspondence, but as unconcealment, *alētheia* – is supposed to be the essence of the true, *das Wesen des Wahren*. So what is the truth of truth? And the lecture itself brings us here a warning – for it insists that in posing this question we find ourselves already entangled in a curious tangle, a *merkwürdige Verstrickung*, in that which we should be disentangling. We must be able to stand outside of truth in order to determine its essence, in order to say what it is in truth, but then we can say nothing about it; and if we enter into the truth, we can no longer determine its essence – for we have tainted the evidence, corrupted the essence of that which we were supposed to determine. Thus 'inside' or 'outside' – although these obviously cannot be considered simply spatial determinations, such as being in or out of the temple – we find ourselves unable to even seek the truth.

Indeed, as the lecture asks with respect to the question the essence of truth: 'Is it only a curiosity or even merely the empty hairsplitting of a conceptual-game, or is it – an abyss?'[56] Yet this question, this threat not only to the essential question of the essence of truth, but just as much to 'The Origin of the Work of Art', is never answered, although truth means essence of the true, *Wahrheit meint Wesen des Wahren*.[57] Then if truth is neither a curiosity nor hairsplitting, neither a *Merkwürdigkeit* nor a *Spitzfindigkeit*, how is it an abyss, *Abgrund*, *abussos*? In fact, it is the abyss' infinity, its constant openness and essential ambiguity, that also characterizes truth, or truth as abyssal – for in truth, we are always in the truth and the untruth. Here *alētheia* means concealing unconcealment, the unconcealment of beings prior to agreement or conformity of thought and thing; it is the presentation or self-showing or opening – if this is indeed possible – prior to representation, the coming to presence in the clearing or lighting or nothing, the original unconcealing that is concealing, as well as deceit, falsity, copying, forgery, lying, refusal, dissembling and revealing. In this way, truth is never simply unconcealment, never pure and unalloyed; it is always also riddled with concealment – *alētheia* is a concealment. Then if every revealing is a concealing, and vice versa, so too with unconcealment itself: original unconcealment is a concealment, just as presentation is a representation (although Heidegger's introduction of dissembling, *Verstellen*, and refusal or failure, *Versagen*, may come back to plague the lecture, as well as its understanding of truth, to make us wonder about that which *alētheia* itself conceals, or what it serves to mask, how it puts itself forward as another, as that which it is not and could never be, how it must be taken and mistaken for another, and how it must fail in any attempt to show itself, or even wonder about the extent to which this semblance is itself a dissemblance, how this failure fails). Thus truth is concealing unconcealment and unconcealing concealment; or as the lecture puts it: truth is, in its essence, un-truth, *die Wahrheit ist in ihrem Wesen Un-Wahrheit*.[58]

As abyssal however, *alētheia*, truth and untruth, is not merely a contradiction, some kind of logical paradox to be resolved or refused, nor can their relation be just determined and set-up as an essential presupposition, nor is it a conceptual movement designed to supersede their relation in some sort of original unity or synthesis, to fold the four-fold up into a collection, like some perpetual motion machine that could serve to re-establish the ground as shifting – yet even less can it be ignored, forgotten or overlooked – for the truth of truth is not simply the unconcealment of the idea, the coming into the light of beings, not merely the light or lighting, nor the demonstration of correspondence, *homoiōsis*, *veritas* as *rectitudo*, nor the *certitudo* of assertion understood as *symplokē*, *connexio*, nor validity, objectivity, or legitimacy. Rather by posing the question of truth as the question of the essence of truth understood in terms of the truth of truth, we propose an empty advance into the emptiness of the abyss. With *alētheia*, we never touch down on the secure firmament of truth, nor have we determined the certainty of untruth; we fall into an abyss. And even the discourse of clearing and light and being cannot save us – for these too are essentially darkness and obfuscation and the nothing, although the abyss is not simply nothing; it is that which opens itself as the essence of truth and lets it be. And this is why Heidegger names truth the 'abyssal middle'.[59]

Yet once the essence of truth is marked out, once the abyss shows itself, once it opens up, it closes down – for in asserting its abyssal-character, in taking up the yoke or frame of abyssness, *Abgründigkeit*, it becomes that which it should not be, namely, non-abyssal; just as in determining the chaotic nature of nature, we attempt and fail to master it. As 'The Origin of the Work of Art' warns: 'There is much in being that man cannot master. There is but little that comes to be known. What is known remains inexact, what is mastered insecure.'[60] In other words, if truth is an abyss, then the (perhaps fatal) step is taken, away from lack, negation, nihilization, and towards a 'positive' or 'affirmative' truth – then truth is not an abyss, but *un*-ground is un-*ground*, *Ab*-Grund is Ab-*Grund*.[61] Or again: 'The open of the ab-ground is not groundless. Ab-ground is not – like a groundlessness – the no to every ground but rather the yes to the ground in its hidden expanse and remoteness.'[62] And if truth is not a *Grund*, but an *Abgrund*, it is still, or once again, a *Grund*, and the ground is the essence of truth, *der Grund ist das Wesen der*

Wahrheit.[63] We cannot mean what we say and say what we mean – nor even know, think or experience it, and the thought of *alētheia*'s abyss in 'The Origin of the Work of Art' doesn't answer the question of the essence of truth – on the contrary, it gives the question in order to show that no answer is possible; even the abyss fails to encounter its own abyss. And thought should determine what is ownmost to emptiness itself, the essence of the empty, *das Wesen der Leere*, to the abyss, and hence to the essence of truth, of the truth of truth – but if it can't, it won't, and thought's goal may not lie in its inability, but elsewhere. The abyss therefore, is that which can never be true or untrue, the truth or the untruth, nor the relation of both – for it is the original non-relation, divorce before marriage, or more precisely the failure of truth to even get to the copulation or privation of *a-lētheia*; and it may therefore never show itself, never not escape notice, not even as that which conceals or doubly-conceals itself, concealing its concealment, not even as that which opens up and closes down – for it is the trap into which truth falls, even before it covers up its fall, even before it conceals the evidence, and conceals its concealment, buries the body and buries the burial, even before it unconceals the trap it conceals, the trap of its own trap.

If truth however is an abyss, and if the work of art is the happening of the abyss, then art is an abyss as well. And here perhaps we raise more questions than we can answer – which may just be the abyssal work that art and thought share – for how does the abyss of truth lie at the core of art? How must the essence of the abyss set itself to work in the work? Can it then be or not be, present or absent, in the work? And how must the abyss be so it can happen as, or even must happen as, art? Or can it not? And if the truth of art is abyssal, how is it that art *is* at all?

3.5

Still, after the painting comes the temple, and after the temple the poem; or after the Dutch, the Greeks, and now the Germans. But are we any closer to the origin of the work of art? To the nature or essence of art? Certainly the lecture moves from 'Thing and Work' to 'Work and Truth' to 'Truth and Art' – but then are we not to expect 'Art and. . .'? And would 'Art and. . .' lead us to the origin of the artwork? Or back to 'Art and Thing'? Or is the investigation not far more endless, coming to no end, from no beginning, so that the search for the origin of the work of art, like the truth of the artwork, opens up onto an infinite abyss? But would this then bring us any closer to art? Or if the question of art remains unanswered, even unanswerable, and perhaps unquestioned, would this perhaps be the unquestioned – or unquestionable – question of 'The Origin of the Work of Art'? Or evidence that the origin was not even sought? A feigned or faked quest for the origin that could never be found?

Regardless, the lecture repeats that art is the origin of the artwork and the artist, that origin means source of essence; and Heidegger repeats the question that has perhaps driven the lecture from the start: 'What is art?' And answers: Art is the happening of truth. But then, he proceeds to explain the explanation: the happening of truth is the conflictual unity of earth and world, not merely the workly character of the work, nor simply that it was brought forth out of unconcealedness by the artist's activity, the artifice of the artificer; but rather the emergence of truth as un-truth, opening up a place for the arrival of truth and being, that sets up the frame, the gathered-placement or em-placement, *Ge-stell*, in order to let a unique being, a pure singularity, come to presence. In this way, truth establishes itself in the artwork (thereby demonstrating its uselessness – for strictly speaking, insofar as art begins where equipmentality and utility end, it is useless, although as the happening of truth, it is perhaps more desirable than utility itself, if we could in fact differentiate the two, disentangle the useful from the useless, to the extent this would be useful or useless, and this too may be far from certain), and createdness is expressly created in the created being. So art has a particular way of letting truth happen by which the being of a being presents itself to us as unusual, *ungewöhnlich*, presents the fact that it is something, and something unique, or clears and conceals that it is not simply nothing, a way that is not merely the subjective activity of an artistic creator, but that which lets the work stand on its own as independent, and therefore just as much the work of preservers, of those who resolutely transcend themselves, not in order to parry the extraordinary or *Un-geheure* in the work with the ordinary thereby submitting it to the economy of the art market, but to open themselves up to the work of opening up that the work accomplishes, and that means to encounter not only the happening, but just as much the becoming of truth.[64] Indeed, art is the advent or arrival, the *Ankunft*, of the truth of what is, and as such all art is essentially poetry – although the lecture admits that the essence of poetry remains questionable, a not yet thought through question, if it could ever be thought through – but poetry is not merely a linguistic form, like communication or expression; it is language understood as letting 'that which is' come into the open for the first time as something that is, like the naming that first makes a being into what it is, that nominates it to a place where it is no longer nothing; and thus language is a privileged mode of creation insofar as it marks the general poetizing, as opposed to *physis*, of which painting and architecture are special cases, a poetizing whereby truth comes into being and is preserved, that is, historically founded as bestowing, grounding and beginning. Thus in its essence, art is an origin, a primal leap, *Ur-sprung*, a particular way of letting the truth of what is originate in the work.

Yet has 'The Origin of the Work of Art' then answered the question of the origin of the work of art? The lecture insists: 'the answer to the question, like every genuine answer, is only the final result of the last step in a long series of questioning-steps'.[65] Indeed, the answer remains in question, infinitely open

– for if art is an origin, and an origin is a particular way, an *ausgezeichnete Weise*, in which truth happens and becomes, well then: What is so particular about the way? What is so special or extraordinary about art? Or is it really not extraordinary at all, but rather the most ordinary of ways? And can we maintain the difference between the ordinary and the extraordinary, familiar and unfamiliar, or the usual and the unusual? And what happens when everything ordinary becomes extraordinary? When the unusual becomes usual, like some kind of inverted world, where wrong is right, evil good, unjust just? Or where truth happens everywhere all the time? Or in a state where art is regulated neither by the market nor by individual preservers, but by the state itself – and such that some such art is degenerate, relegated to the realm of non-art, *ent-artet*? When the self-determination and self-sufficiency of the work of art is decapitated? Or where it shows itself as a feign in the first place? In other words, when the creators and preservers of the happening and becoming of truth themselves become subject to the creation and preservation of a somehow motivated creation and preservation? Or does this not demonstrate that creation and preservation, those of 'The Origin of the Work of Art' included, is always motivated? And could we ever be certain that truth had, is, or will happen in the work of art? Is this not a feign as well – for who would believe us, if we insisted that here, with this work of art, truth is happening? Could it be verified with some kind of objectively valid or universal criterion? Or if not, then could you be sure that I was not lying if I told the truth? And could you not be faking if you swore it happened, the experience of the happening of truth – and then swore that you were not faking? Or is it rather that art reveals that truth is always happening, in every work of art and non-work of art, in every being whatsoever, to the point where both everything and nothing is art, and where truth happens everywhere and nowhere? And have we then here, in the work of art, not also come upon the double-concealment of truth, the concealment of the concealment? And hence of that which cannot even be revealed as concealed – but which remains as the interminable riddle of art, the riddle that cannot even be seen?

In fact, all of our questions here – this answer that is not an answer, or question that is no longer a question – both prove and disprove the insistence that 'each answer remains in force as an answer only as long as it is rooted in questioning'.[66] Each answer leads both back to the question it answers and forward to the question of its answer. The question of the origin of the work of art always also begs the question of the question, of questioning, of the origin of the question, of the answer that is a question and the question that is already an answer. So the question of the origin of the work of art is an answer to a question; although not the question of art and its origin, but the question with which the lecture begins and ends, namely, the question of the origin of questioning.

The 'The Origin of the Work of Art' therefore poses, or reposes, the questioning of origin at the end: 'Do we know, which means do we give heed to, the nature of the origin?'[67] And this is the questioning of the lecture's first line: 'Origin here means that from and by which something is what it is and as it is.'[68] Art is an origin, but what is an origin rooted in questioning? What is that questioning from and by which the origin is what it is? Certainly, an origin is an origin, an original leap – but what kind of questioning is that?

But the lecture does not end with Heidegger-the-philosopher's questioning; it continues with a quote from Hölderlin-the-poet: 'With difficulty leaves / What dwells near the origin, the place.'[69] And here the philosopher is both showing that the (finite) answer is rooted in questioning – for the poet gives an infallible sign (for what?) for the either-or decision of historical experience, at least for the Germans, whoever they may be, and whatever the sign might mean, insofar as it too stands not as an answer, but a questioning, yet another sign in need of a reading, more marks demanding interpretation, and interpretations of interpretations – and that (infinite) questioning is essentially uprooted and uprooting, that roots presuppose roots *ad infinitum*, so that answering the question of the origin shows that it cannot be answered. Every answer a question, every question an answer – so that at the moment that 'The Origin of the Work of Art' gives heed to the nature or origin, it can't find the origin because it can't seek it. Thus 'what art may be is one of the questions to which no answers are given in the essay. What gives the impression of such an answer are directions for questions.'[70] And if we take the lecture seriously here – although it introduces the possibility of a false impression, a mere *Anschein*, and if we could have the wrong impression here, we may in fact have it everywhere – then the riddle of art remains, the riddle of the origin, of the question and answer, of the work, and the riddle of the riddle. The riddle is not solved, solved as insolvable, as the riddle of the riddle, just as the questioning remains questionable.

3.6

The riddle of art then, of the origin of the work of art, remains. But the lecture gives a hint as to where we may begin again to look for a start, if looking is at all the way to solve it, or demonstrate its insolvability, and see that it cannot be seen, or question its questionability. The Reclam edition of 'The Origin of the Work of Art' reads: 'the Introduction composed by H.-G. Gadamer contains a decisive hint for the reader',[71] although whether the lecture, originally given in 1935/36 actually belongs to the later writings (the post-*Kehre* thought or not, if there really was a *Kehre*, a turn in Heidegger's thought), remains to be seen. Regardless, Gadamer writes – and this may or may not be the hint to which Heidegger hints: 'An overcoming of the concept of aesthetics itself is necessary.'[72] Indeed Hegel tried to accomplish this by insisting that art no longer represents the highest instantiation of truth; rather insofar as it is superseded by religion and philosophy, the system of science wherein the concept of the concept, like the truth of truth, becomes not merely potential, but actual in the speculative logic of Absolute Spirit's self-externalization, aesthetics shows its limits – and art falls short precisely because its truth relies on another to provide its concept. But Gadamer claims that Heidegger and Hegel are not that far from one another: they both seek to overcome aesthetics, the opposition of subject and object, thought and thing, so that the work of art is neither the product of genius nor a function of nature; but while for the latter, the truth of art is superseded and completed, *aufgehoben und vollendet*, in the truth of the philosophical concept, so that it only *really* happens in the totalization of Spirit; for the former, truth happens already in the artwork.[73] Thus supersession is unnecessary – for if the work works, it is self-sufficient, a complete unity, in itself, not for another. Unlike Gadamer however, Heidegger does not insist upon an essential difference between his own thought and that of Hegel's; rather he suspends such judgements: 'the truth of Hegel's judgment has not yet been decided'.[74] And Heidegger may be much closer to Hegel than Gadamer thinks, particularly if Hegel too thinks not only the non-totality or incompleteness of the artwork, the infinite open always waiting for the finishing touches of Spirit, but just as much its totality and completeness, the finitude of the work. The overcoming of aesthetics is at issue, and if Hegel doesn't do it, then according to Heidegger, it is because he remains dependent upon metaphysics, the history of the philosophy of art that stretches back through Kant and Baumgarten's subjectification of art to the Greeks (although the riddle of art can only be seen by thinking that which lies prior to objectification as well). The question becomes not only how to overcome the subject/object and form/matter economies that, along with its oppositional philosophemes, governs the discourse known as aesthetics, if such an overcoming would indeed ever be possible, nor simply how to retrieve a one-sided subjective or objective theory of the work of art, if such a retrieval could ever be accomplished, but rather: How can we approach the riddle of the origin of aesthetics itself? How can we remain rooted in questioning?

And here 'The Origin of the Work of Art' hints once again: aesthetics presupposes that art is the object of sensuous apprehension in the widest sense, *aisthesis*.[75] The overcoming of aesthetics would be an overcoming of *aisthesis*, and the origin of the work of art can no longer be thought in terms of sensation. So another hint: '*all art*, as the letting-happen of the advent of the truth of beings as such, is *essentially poetry*'.[76] The question of the origin of the work of art therefore becomes: What is the origin of poetry? But this is a question that 'The Origin of the Work of Art' doesn't question.

3.7

So the question 'What is the origin of the work of art?' becomes 'What is the origin of poetry'? Nietzsche asks this question:

> We must now avail ourselves of all the principles of art considered so far, in order to find our way in the labyrinth of *the origin of Greek tragedy*, as we must call it. I do not think I am unreasonable in saying that the problem of this origin has as yet not even been seriously posed, to say nothing of solved, however often the ragged tatters of ancient tradition have been sewn together in various combinations and torn apart again.[77]

But perhaps Aristotle asks the question more essentially:

> Once tragedy and comedy came to light side by side, each initiating a turn toward each sort of *poiēsis* in conformity with their own nature, some became makers of comedy instead of iambs, and others became producers of tragedy instead of epics, because the latter forms were greater and more estimable than the former. Now, to go further in examining whether tragedy is or is not by now sufficient in respect to its kinds, in order to judge it both by itself in relation to itself and in relation to the spectators, is another account. But regardless of that issue, it came to be from an improvisatory beginning.[78]

Or again: 'Since to imitate is natural for us, as well as harmony and rhythm (for it is manifest that meters are proper parts of rhythms), from the beginning those most naturally inclined toward them, advancing little by little, generated *poiēsis* out of improvisations.'[79] Indeed, *poiēsis* is *ex tōn autoschedias-matōn*; art is *ap' archēs autoschediastikēs*. The origin of the work of art is improvisation.

But (continuing the questioning, and answering) what does it mean to think improvisation as the *archē* of *poiēsis*? Does it mean that the beginning is improvised? That beginning is improvising? Then the *archē* would be improvisational because it improvises as an improvisation, originates as improvising, as original improvisation: the *archē autoschediastikē* is *ex tōn autoschediasmatōn*.[80] And if art is originally improvisational because improvisation is the origin of art, what is the meaning of improvisation? What does it mean to improvise? To improvise the beginning? Originally improvise? Or if improvising is the meaning of beginning itself, what does it mean to begin?

In fact, the Greeks thought improvisation as *autoschediazō*, doing something off-hand, impromptu, *ad hoc*, *ex tempore*. The root of *schediazein* is *schein*:[81] having, holding, keeping, standing and bearing, preserving or maintaining, guarding and protecting, as well as being able to, having the power or force to; but also being engaged with or used for, or simply being (*kalōs echei*, *thaumasas echō*; in English: 'we *have* our health' means 'we *are* healthy'), as well as orienting and steering a course, or doing something with continuous aspect in time. But improvisation is not only *schediazein*; it is *autoschediazein*, that which one does to and for oneself insofar as one does it to and for another, auto-improvisation. If we improvise on something, it improvises on us: action upon the other is action of the other; action reaction. Holding onto something is holding onto ourselves holding, just as it holds itself in being held, gives itself to be held – having is self-having, holding self-holding. Protecting another, we protect ourselves as protecting and protected, just as they protect themselves: protection *qua* auto-protection. So the state of wonder at another, is also wonder at oneself, self-wondering, and the wonder of wonderment.

But improvising is not just 'improvising on'; it is self-improvisation, improvisation of the self, or self as improvisational; hence as self-having, auto-affective and auto-affecting – for improvisation is the origin of self (*autos, ipse*), self-originating, that out of which the self comes to be and is. So if we improvise in art and science, it is because we are self-improvisational. We improvise not only our improvisations, but also ourselves, *autoschediazein*.

Improvisation then, is the origin of improvisors and improvisations. But what is improvisation? What does it mean to improvise, the self or an improvisation? To originate in improvisation?

Zeus declares to his son: 'You are our messenger, Hermes, sent on all our missions. Announce to the nymph with lovely braids our fixed decree: Odysseus journeys home – the exile must return. But not in the convoy of the gods or mortal men. No, on a lashed, makeshift raft [*schedia*] and rung with pains.'[82] Indeed, Odysseus' raft is an improvisation – not because it is improvised, nor because it floats, carries and supports, has and holds, nor simply because it has been framed out in such a way as to form a structure that saves or permits crossing, and keeps Odysseus from drowning. On the contrary, the raft is an improvisation because improvisation is a raft, because the raft is the origin of improvisation.

What then is a raft? The Greeks call it *schedia*, frame.[83] Before it is a world constituting *Gestell*, the raft is Odysseus' universe; it keeps the oceans out, the man in, protects and supports, grasps and holds. The raft improvises the god-forsaken exile's return. So if the raft is an improvisation, it is not because it floats or frames; if it floats or frames, it is because it is an improvisation. The raft is neither simply holding in standing-reserve nor gathered-emplacement; it is making and doing, the origin of art and the arts, the sciences, poetry and music, tragedy and comedy; it is that original improvisation out of which improvisation and self-improvisation come.

The question then, perhaps questioning once again: If improvisation is the origin of art, and if the raft is the origin of improvisation as the frame, what does it mean for the raft to be our universe?

Notes

1   See *PLT*, 17/56, 69/57, 75/63; and Heidegger's 'Addendum', 85/71.

2   *PLT*, 18/2, translation modified.

3   *PLT*, 18/2, translation modified; A. Danto, 'The Artworld', *Journal of Philosophy*, 61/19, 1964.

4   In fact, the text ends with Hölderlin, or more precisely, with an indication of a confrontation with the origin and 'The Origin of the Work of Art', a sign that, Heidegger insists, stands before the Germans. Indeed, riddles upon riddles – and if we stand before these riddles, then why should the Germans be singled out to withstand the test? Why should the Germans be faced with Hölderlin's work, and not the French or Turks or Jews or Asians? Or does the lecture introduce the Germans at the very end not to answer the riddle of the origin of the work of art, nor to pose the riddle of the riddle or question of the question, but to raise the Germans themselves to the level of a question, 'the German question'? Is this simple, old-fashioned racism – albeit one that perhaps stretches throughout Heidegger's writings in such a way that each of his texts could be renamed: not 'The Origin of the Work of Art', but 'The German Origin of the Work of Art'; not 'Letter on "Humanism"', but 'Letter on "the Germans"'; not merely the 'Self-Determination of the German University', but the 'Self-Determination of the Germans'; not simply 'Only a God can save Us', but 'Only a God can save us Germans'; not just *Being and Time*, but *Being and Time and the Germans*? And does the introduction of the Germans not force us to reread the entire *lecture* in the light of the question of Germans? For the text then shows itself as concerned not with art, but with Germans, with the question: What is German? And who are Germans? And if these questions cannot be answered? They don't seem to be here, if they are anywhere, ever, perhaps because Heidegger assumes the questions to be non-questions, or because he takes them to be easily answered, positively or negatively, with those who have lived in Germany for over a hundred years, through the Nazi years, or by those whose mother-tongue is German, although that might not be sufficient for excluding Turks born in Germany, or those whose character, if not physical features, correspond to that which the Germans normally call German, although this too may prove impossible to verify, especially if Germany is full of all sorts of characters, those like Kant and Heidegger who want to stay put in the *Heimat*, and those like Nietzsche who can't wait to get out. Indeed, these are the kind of questions put in the *Spiegel* interview (Nr. 23/1976) such that when asked, 'You assign in particular a special task to the Germans?', Heidegger answers: 'Yes, in the sense of a dialogue with Hölderlin.' And when pushed to clarify why the Germans are specially qualified, he responds: 'I have in mind especially the inner relationship of the German

language with the language of the Greeks and with their thought. This
has been confirmed for me today again by the French. When they begin
to think, they speak German, being sure that they could not make it with
their own language.' On what Heidegger calls the Asiatic threat to
European philosophy, see my translation of 'Europe and German
Philosophy', *New Yearbook for Phenomenology and Phenomenological Philosophy*,
Noesis, 2007.

5   *PLT*, 77/65.
6   *PLT*, 23/7.
7   *PLT*, 26–8/11–13.
8   *PLT*, 24/8.
9   *PLT*, 28/13.
10   A. Danto, 'The Artworld', *After the End of Art*, Princeton, 1997.
11   *PLT*, 31/16.
12   *PLT*, 33/17.
13   *PLT*, 35/20.
14   *PLT*, 35/20.
15   *PLT*, 37/22.
16   *PLT*, 36/22.
17   Heraclitus, Fr. 6, Aristotle, *Meteor.* B2, 355a13; *PP*, 201.
18   *PLT*, 38/24; translation modified.
19   *PLT*, 39/25.
20   *NHG*,136.
21   *NHG*, 138.
22   *NHG*, 138.
23   *NHG*, 139–40.
24   *NHG*, 138.
25   *NHG*, 141.
26   See *TP*, 261ff.
27   *NHG*, 136.
28   *NHG*, 140–1.
29   *NHG*, 141.
30   *TP*, 278/317.
31   As Derrida insists: 'nothing proves it' (*TP*, 264/301).
32   *TP*, 267/305.
33   Aristotle, *Poetics*, 1448b19-24; see below sec. 3.7.
34   *PLT*, 39/25.
35   *PLT*, 39/26.
36   *PLT*, 39/25.
37   *PLT*, 39/25.
38   *PLT*, 40/26.
39   *PLT*, 40/27.
40   'Der Säulenschaft, auch die Triglyhe klingt | Ich glaube gar, der ganze Tempel
      singt' (Goethe, *Faust II*; my translation).

41   '*Wie auf schlanken Säulen ruh'* | *Auf richtigen Ordnungen das neue Leben*'
      (Hölderlin, 'Paestum', my translation).

42   6, Simplicius *in Phys.* 86, 27–8; 117, 4–13; *PP*, 247.

43   *BW*, 98/4.

44   *BW*, 100/6.

45   *BT*, 178.

46   *BW*, 103/9.

47   *BW*, 103/9.

48   *BW*, 104/10.

49   *BW*, 105/11.

50   *BW*, 105/12.

51   Hegel, *Science of Logic*, 82; *Gesammelte Werke*, Bd. XXI, 70.

52   *BW*, 106/12.

53   *PLT*, 51/39.

54   *PLT*, 45/32.

55   And the shoes? Is there something in the shoes, or rather far more
      nothing, or the nothing? Then the encounter with non-representative art,
      if it indeed exists, would have no priority over representative art, if it
      exists, in opening itself up for the arrival of the four-fold or letting the
      nothing happen so that being can come to presence. Indeed everything
      that the lecture argues with respect to the temple could have been
      accomplished with the shoes, and will be possible with the poem to come
      – thus either the selection is arbitrary or merely pedagogical, designed to
      make the work more accessible, although it may have just the opposite
      effect, and that may be the point, namely, to demonstrate the
      inaccessibility of that which we take for accessible, the closure of that
      which opens itself to all comers. In fact, if the series of examples moves
      from the apparently more concrete to the apparently more abstract, it is
      to show that any work of art – no matter which kind, especially if the
      difference of kinds cannot be maintained, as long as it is 'great art', and
      nothing has yet determined how we might make this kind of selection – is
      a happening of truth.

56   *PLT*, 49/36; translation modified.

57   *PLT*, 49/36.

58   *PLT*, 53/40; cf., *GA65*, 356. Of course, *alētheia* means not only
      unconcealment – for the alpha is not just privativum, but also
      copulativum, alpha-unity, alpha-collective, alpha-congress or alpha-
      intimate; hence co-concealment, synlanthanic, the togetherness of that
      which escapes notice. As Plato reminds us: in the naming of Apollo,
      where the alpha is substituted for *homo*, the *Apollōna* means the same as
      homopolōn, and the only difference is that the second *lambda* is added to
      avoid the ominous sound of *apolōn*, destruction (*Craty.*, 405d). His
      attributes are four-fold: music, prophecy, medicine and archery. And
      Apollo's alpha harmonizes them all; he is the purifier and the washer and

absolver from impurities: 'or again, the name may refer to his musical attributes, and then, as in *akolouthos* [follower, attendant] and *akoitis* [bedfellow, spouse], and in many other words, the *a* is supposed to mean 'together'; so the meaning of the name Apollo will be 'moving together', whether in the poles of heaven as they are called, or in the harmony of song, which is termed concord, because he moves all together by a harmonious power, as astronomers and musicians ingeniously declare' (*Craty.*, 405c6-d3). Thus every privation of truth is itself a copulation, every separation occupies a communication, every dissolution of disharmony closes with harmony, every negation slips into an affirmation. Then if we follow Shakespeare and 'let copulation thrive' (*King Lear*, IV, vi, 116), perhaps we should not wonder that it does so as privation – for *alētheia* signifies that which conceals unconcealment together. J. Sallis also cites P. Friedländer's 1928 comments in this regard: not only is Heidegger's historical reconstruction untenable, but for example, Hesiod's use of *alētheia* means not the hiddenness and unhiddenness of being, but those who do not forget; and in Homer, it usually occurs with verbs of assertion, thereby referring to the genuine, coherent or correct (*Delimitations*, Indiana University Press, 1996, 176ff; cf., *Platon*, de Gruyter, 1954). Heidegger responds in 'Hegel and the Greeks' (1958): 'It is not that unconcealment is "dependent" upon assertion; rather every assertion already needs the realm of unconcealment' (*PM*, 335/443; translation modified). Nevertheless, the question of the truth of truth, of the uncertainty of *alētheia* as revealing and concealing, or the effect of uncertainty on *alētheia*, has not yet become questionable.

59 *GA65*, 331.
60 *PLT*, 51/38.
61 *GA65*, 379. Indeed, this also seems to be the structural problem of all negative theologies. See J. Derrida, 'How to Avoid Speaking', *Languages of the Unsayable*, Columbia University Press, 1989.
62 *GA65*, 387.
63 *GA65*, 379.
64 *PLT*, 60–2/48–51.
65 *PLT*, 68/57; translation modified.
66 *PLT*, 68/57.
67 *PLT*, 75/64.
68 *PLT*, 17/1.
69 '*Schwer verläßt | Was nahe dem Ursprung wohnet, den Ort*' (*PLT*, 76/64; 'Die Wanderung', Bd. IV, Hellingrath, 167; 'The Journey', verses 18–19; my translation).
70 *PLT*, 85/71.
71 *PLT*, xxiv; *UKR*, 5.
72 *UKR*, 100.
73 *UKR*, 107; *PLT*, 78/65; Hegel's *Lectures on Aesthetics*, Vol. 12, Stuttgart,

1953, X, 1, 134; 135; 16. Similarly, J. Taminiaux argues that just as for Aristotle's *Nicomachean Ethics*, *poiēsis* is the origin of the work of art, the *ergon* of *technē*, it is a deficient activity because its end or *telos* lies outside of itself, in another, namely, in the work ('The Origin of "The Origin of the Work of Art"', *Reading Heidegger*, Indiana University, 1993, 393).

74 *PLT*, 78/66.

75 *PLT*, 77/65.

76 *OWA*, 70/58, translation modified.

77 *BOT*, §7, translation modified. Nietzsche continues: 'This tradition tells us quite unequivocally *that tragedy arose out of the tragic chorus, and was originally only chorus and nothing but chorus*' (*BOT*, §7; translation modified). And the origin of the chorus? Nietzsche responds: 'Let us recall our surprise at the *chorus* and the *tragic hero* of that tragedy, neither of which we could reconcile with our own customs any more than with the tradition   until we rediscovered this duality itself as the origin and essence of Greek tragedy, as the expression of two interwoven artistic impulses, *the Apollinian and the Dionysian*' (*BOT*, §12; translation modified). But music is that which has the capacity to give birth to myth, particularly tragic myth – for myth is merely the objectified image or symbolization, the translation or reification, the imaginary representation of music (*BOT*, §16). Nietzsche concludes: 'With this conception we believe we have done justice for the first time to the original and so astonishing significance of the chorus' (*BOT*, §17; translation modified). But the origin of music? Although I cannot demonstrate this here, I might venture to suggest that, for Nietzsche, it lies in (the dual concept of Dionysian-Apollinian) freedom: 'Myth protects us from music, while on the other hand it first gives music the highest *freedom*' (*BOT*, §21; translation modified; my italics).

78 1449a2-10.

79 1448b19-24, translation modified.

80 In this way, Aristotle responds to the question: Why is there something rather than nothing? Improvisation. What is change, *metabolē*, from something into something, or nothing into something, *genēsis*? What is the being of becoming in general? Improvisation. And if the *archē* of *poiēin*, making and doing (in art and politics, ethics and *epistemē*, in the human soul and life itself), is improvisational, then it may be necessary to reread Aristotle's entire corpus, both insofar as it thinks *archē* as improvisational, and insofar as it is an improvisation itself. The multiplicity at the origin is a multiplicity of the origin. Aristotle is quite precise: art comes out of improvisations (plural). If these improvisations are to be improvisational however, it is because they all have an improvisational origin. Improvisation is always improvisations, just as improvisations are improvisational because of improvisation.

81 *Schein* however, is also the origin of *schesis*, the way in which something is,

its state or condition; and of *schēma*, its form, shape or appearance, the way it shows itself; but also of *schetērion*, a check or remedy, like a *pharmakon*. See Plato, *Phaed.*, 229c-d, 274e; and J. Derrida, 'La pharmacie de Platon', *La dissémination*, Seuil, 1972; 'Plato's Pharmacy', *Dissemination*, University of Chicago Press, 1981. For Derrida's discussion of invention, albeit without reference to *autoschediazō* or improvisation, see *Psyché*, Galilée, 1987–1998.

82   *Odyssey*, 5.33, Penguin, 1996, 153. See also Plato, *Phaed.*: 'But, my dear good Phaedrus, it will be courting ridicule for an amateur like me to improvise on the same theme as an accomplished writer' (236d; translation modified). See also the 'Interpretive Essay' in S. Scully's *Plato's Phaedrus*, Focus Publishing, 2003, 91, 108, 132–3. And in *Menex.*, for example, Menexenus says: 'You are always making fun of the rhetoricians, Socrates. This time, however, I am inclined to think that the speaker who is chosen will not have much to say, for he has been called upon to speak at a moment's notice, and he will be compelled almost to improvise' (235c). Socrates responds: 'But why, my friend, should he not have plenty to say? Every rhetorician has speeches ready-made, nor is there any difficulty in improvising that sort of stuff' (235d; see also, *Menex.* 236b; *Euthy.* 278d). In Plato's dialogues, a philosophical *poiēsis* that is always simultaneously a dialogue on dialogue, it could be argued that improvisation is the character of a character. Sometimes in Plato, *autoschediazō* seems to have a pejorative sense of a lie or fabrication; hence, to act unadvisedly. For example, 'Here perhaps one of you might interrupt me and say, But what is it that you do, Socrates? How is it that you have been misrepresented like this? Surely all this talk and gossip about you would never have arisen if you had confined yourself to ordinary activities, but only if your behavior was abnormal. Tell us the explanation, if you do not want us to improvise it for ourselves' (*Apol.* 20c-d, translation altered). See also, *Euthy.* 5a, 16a; *Craty.* 413d, in *Collected Dialogues of Plato*, Princeton University, 1985. Aristotle seems to use it in this derogatory way in the *Politics* to refer to a random decision (1326b19).

83   *Ath. Mech.*, 10.1.

4

Still far from pondering the essence of action

4.1

So sophist, fascist, philosopher. Maybe. Who can be certain? But some kind of man. And if human, not a humanist – or so it seems from the 'Letter on "Humanism"'[1] – but what is that? In fact, this is a question for a letter, a piece of correspondence, presumably – composed in 1947, which appears as an essay, no longer a letter, under the revised title, 'Letter on "Humanism"', with 'Humanism' in quotation marks, or simply 'On Humanism', without the quotes – and here an *avertisment*, a clear warning to the reader is attached:

> First edition, 1949: That which is said here was not first thought out at the time it was written down, rather it follows the course of a way that was started in 1936, in the '*Augenblick*' of an attempt, to simply speak the truth of being. – The letter still continues to speak in the language of metaphysics, and knowingly so. The other language remains in the background.[2]

Indeed, in the blink of an eye? So on the one hand, a flash of insight that attempts to grasp the things themselves, with the mind alone, their *eidos*, essence, in the moment, as they present themselves, their presence and being, and the being of their being, in order to express its truth. On the other hand – as the quotation marks indicate – an '*Augenblick*' that is not an *Augenblick*, and the mask is dropped, the glance reveals the possibility of a secret, feign, a wink pointing to that which it is not, or that which was not thought out at the time, the unthought. And an attempt, a *Versuch*, may be a failure or a success, successful or not – just as the *Augenblick* reveals both the attempt and itself. If we see this blick however, catch sight of this eye-sight, moment of the moment, instant's instant, is it because the attempt, started in 1936,[3] to simply speak the truth of being, has not been accomplished, not yet, or because it cannot be accomplished, an impossible task, one that we know to be so, and yet one in which we persist? Or one that is only accomplished in remaining unaccomplished? Or in order to demonstrate the structure of truth? The truth of truth? Or that even this truth may not be true? Or to show the limits of speaking, of language? Or in order to convince ourselves of our own power of persistence? The will to truth, rather than no will at all? To comfort ourselves in our failure? Or is it rather to keep us on track, honest and loyal to the original task of 1936 to speak the truth of being? There is nothing that can assure us this is true – but also nothing that assures us it is not. Then the *Augenblick* perhaps stands as an indication that the attempt resists a certain interpretation, as much as the *Augenblick* itself, as much as its interpretation.

But Heidegger's warning doesn't stop there: the 'Letter on Humanism' speaks the language of metaphysics, and it knows it. There is no pretence here – or is there? – to have transcended metaphysics, no claim to have gone beyond good and evil, to think that which metaphysics cannot, or even to speak a non-, anti-, un-, pre-, post- or a-metaphysical language; on the contrary, the letter remains within the language of metaphysics (perhaps because the attempt to speak the truth of being remains metaphysical, at least as metaphysical as the attempt at self-knowledge). If the pretence to metaphysics however, or the thinking of an even more profound essence of metaphysics, the movement towards an even nearer nearness of the receding metaphysical horizon – if all this is itself a pretence, if the letter makes a pretence to know itself, it is perhaps because it knows that it cannot know itself. If the letter is a pretence of non-pretence, the knowledge of ignorance (and none of this seems certain), it is not only because we cannot get out of metaphysics, but because there is no outside. Knowing that it speaks the language of metaphysics then, like *Being and Time's* destruction or destructuring of metaphysics, may not be enough to overcome it, although it might call it into question or doubt, just as it might serve to perfect metaphysics, conceal it by revealing it, leaving us more metaphysical than metaphysics. Then knowing that it speaks metaphysically, the letter may attempt to be honest and without pretence, and to speak the truth of being as metaphysical, to speak philosophically – although like the '*Augenblick*', this honesty could always be 'honesty', honestly lying, pretence to non-pretence, attempting to successfully fail in speaking the truth and untruth of being – or not.

Regardless, knowing that it speaks the language of metaphysics, the letter not only shows how metaphysics works, its pretences and non-pretences, lies and truths, but also how does not work. Heidegger's warning however, does not stop there – for the other language, *die andere Sprache*, remains in the background? Which other language? The other of metaphysics. Is there a language that succeeds in speaking the truth of being, and in getting out of metaphysics? Is this a poetic language, like that of Schiller or Hölderlin? Or would *poiēsis* too remain true to metaphysics? Is this the language of the other beginning, *der andere Anfang*?[4] And once there is one language in the background could there be others, background of the background, not only other languages, but other backgrounds – for the introduction of the background into the letter calls the foreground into question, and not just the attempt to speak the truth of being, but the foreground as foreground? So if the other language remains in the background, it may be because it must, because it can or cannot speak the truth of being, or seek to, or because it cannot speak to metaphysics, because translation or communication (that which Plato thought as *metalepsis*, participation, sharing or having a share in something through getting and having given)[5] is impossible.

But if the other language remains in the background, then the foreground is suspect: humanism, the matter of the letter, and the letter itself, leave their backgrounds unspoken – and knowingly so. Metaphysics may speak in the foreground in order to keep the background a secret, conceal it, to preserve itself – and perhaps its other as well; but not only that which is foregrounded – for the foregrounding itself always leaves something in the background. And if the letter conceals another language by revealing the language of metaphysics with its attempt to speak the truth of being, then the letter leaves something in the background as well. Once the background is introduced into the letter, language, metaphysics, the language of metaphysics, the other language, the attempt to speak, the truth – once a background is even possible, it is actual, and the letter cannot be, nor could it ever have been, trusted. Metaphysics in the foreground is threatened by that which lies in the background. And the 'Letter on Humanism' is no exception to the rule, some kind of honesty in the name of trust, some will to truth condemning dissimulation and ruse, some attempt to speak in clear or straightforward language, as opposed to the *technē* of deceit, without ambiguity or artifice or cunning, without secrets and lies; on the contrary, it embodies the rule itself. The truth of the letter, the double-*logos* of *alētheia*, the law of the law – all this seems suspect.

And Heidegger knows it when he addresses the letter 'On Humanism' to Paris in the Fall of 1946, to Jean Beaufret – the war is over, let the war begin – a letter that is already a response to a letter that remains in the background, as much as the unmentioned and unmentionable war, nationalism and the German contempt for the French, their apparent superficiality of thought in the name of a *joie de vivre*, as if that were indeed superficial. Then if Beaufret's letter is an attack or defence of France, no wonder that Heidegger responds with counter-attack and counter-defence – action and reaction, thought and counter-thought, movement and counter-movement, thrust, parry and repost. But maybe this is only foreground.

4.2

Regardless, Heidegger's 'Letter on Humanism' is written to answer a question – or rather, three questions, at least to grapple with one in order to shed light on two others: 'How can we restore meaning to the word "humanism"?'[6] Repeated twenty-eight pages later: 'How can we restore meaning to the word "humanism"?'[7] Second question: 'But if *humanitas* must be viewed as so essential to the thinking of being, must not "ontology" therefore be supplemented by "ethics"? Is that effort not entirely essential which you express in the sentence "What I have been trying to do for a long time now is to determine precisely the relation of ontology to a possible ethics?"'[8] Although this question has already been asked: 'Soon after *Being and Time* appeared a young friend asked me, "When are you going to write an ethics?"'[9] Third question: 'How can we preserve the element of adventure that all research contains without simply turning philosophy into an adventuress?'[10] Three questions of the letter then, in order to raise the question of humanism, three questions asked, although perhaps not answered. And what if the questions remain unanswered? What if they cannot be answered? Why raise these questions, if they are not or cannot be answered? In order to direct the quest for an answer, or non-answer? To approach an answer? Or in order to demonstrate that no answer is possible? And no response adequate? Or to maintain the questionability of the question? So perhaps we cannot restore meaning to the word 'humanism'; the relation between ontology and a possible ethics cannot be determined, or not determined; we cannot preserve the element of adventure without turning philosophy into an 'adventure' – would this then make the questions questionable? Or the answers answerable – or unanswerable?

Yet even before the questions are posed, the first line of the 'Letter on "Humanism"' insists: 'We are still far from pondering the essence of action decisively enough.'[11] Heidegger's text then apparently goes on to do just that, namely, to reflect upon the essence of action – not as utilitarian cause of an effect, but as *Vollbringen*, fulfilment, accomplishment, (aspectual) completion. And the essence of accomplishment is unfolding, *producere*, that which is, namely, being. Thinking then, pondering, is neither a *technē* in the service of *praxis* or *poiēsis*, nor some kind of intellectual theory reactively constructed in order to save a space for thought within the hegemony of science and logic and grammar; it is the action that is complete insofar as it unfolds or manifests being by bringing it into a relationship with us through language. In this way, according to Heidegger, we dwell in the house of being and guard it (although unlike the dogs of Plato's *Republic* – Or is it so unlike? And what happens when the wolf plays guardian of the sheep shed? Or when, feigning care for being, under the sign of circumspective concern, the thinker takes up residence in the house of being, claiming language to be its home, insisting that 'those who think and create with words are the guardians of this home'[12] and those who don't are not? Or when thinking, under the pretence of letting itself 'be claimed by being in order to speak the truth of being',[13] actually claims being and language and the house for itself? In other words, when the engagement of being by and for being is a con game, a legitimation of will or power, a justification for desire? And could we ever be certain that it is not? – we not only recognize and differentiate friend from foe, to the extent this is possible even for the city in speech, but let thinking be claimed by being so that it can say the truth of being).

If we however, think the essence of action as the thinking and speaking that accomplish being by letting themselves be claimed by and for being, have we then pondered enough? What is enough? When is enough enough? And how would we know that we have been claimed? How could we ever be certain that we have accomplished that which is? Or unfolded something fully, into its fullness, *in die Fülle*? That our action was complete and not continuing? And can we maintain the difference between letting and let, an action that is being done and one that is done? Can we be certain about the difference between complete and incomplete aspect? How could we decide that we have thought the essence of action decisively enough? If the essence of action lies in a thinking that accomplishes through letting – then what is the essence of letting? How can we accomplish the thought of the action of letting? Or can it far more never be accomplished? Can we never accomplish the thinking of the essence of action, or bring the thinking of being to completion, accomplishment, for that matter? Or is thought accomplished in thinking, just as acting we have acted, are seeing and have seen, are thinking and have thought? In the fullness that, lacking fullness, is being full in lack and has been fulfilled? The decisiveness that, as never decisive enough, is a *telos*?[14]

Indeed, if pondering the essence of action is complete *qua* incomplete, it is because incompleteness belongs to the essence of action's completion, or to action's essence itself. Then we both have and have not pondered the essence of action long enough, decisively enough – for its essence is only to be thought as unthought and unthinkable. The will to essence shows itself as not only incomplete, but incompleteable, completely complete as incomplete. And when incompleteness is raised to the level of action's essence, wherein both action and its essence remain essentially incomplete, completely incomplete, the essence of action and inaction shows itself to lie in the inability to act: we cannot complete anything; we couldn't even start. The essence of action then would be a spectacular failure, complete incompleteness. And the thought of the essence of action as incompleteness would remain incomplete – for if the action of thinking is itself an action, it is an action that can never be completed.

We cannot then think the essence of action decisively enough. Thus we cannot complete the action of thought, the thought of action, cannot let being live in its house, nor hope to serve as the guardian of its interests, nor thereby reveal it to language or maintain it in speech, nor can the letter on 'Humanism' complete the thinking of 'Humanism' – or it can only do so if it leaves it incomplete. And if we presume that thinking is complete insofar as it thinks, if we presumably presume, only *vermutlich*, that such action is the simplest or highest because it concerns the relation of being to humans, then our presumption will be our undoing[15] – then we cannot think the essence of action, the human as actor or indweller, thinker, speaker or writer; then we will never be able to respond to Beaufret's question, or questions, not only because they can never be put, nor simply because the letter's thinking is unable to actualize its own actions, but just as much because being too, insofar as it manifests or reveals itself, shelters, houses, relates, claims, opens, comes, lights, is, gives – whatever – in all of this, being's actions remain incomplete and incompleteable.

As incomplete then, the 'Letter on "Humanism"' continues to ponder the essence of action – for if incompleteness is complete, it is no incompleteness at all, but far more its other, complete. The successful failure denies the possibility of failure by reinterpreting, reappropriating, revaluing. But thinking the unthought *qua* unthought is a continuation of thought. The letter thereby demonstrates our inability to completely ponder the essence of action, to finish with it even as imponderable – it shows not only that thought cannot complete what it starts or even start what it successfully fails to complete, but just as much that the action of the letter, presumably at a distance, cannot be completed. And if the letter on humanism is to remain incomplete, unfinished and unfinishable, then like Beaufret, we will probably never be finished reading it.

Heidegger however, writes the letter – incompletely complete, so incomplete (like *Being and Time*, or any text that is presumably complete) – only to, along with the history of philosophy as metaphysics, condemn writing in writing: thinking becomes inflexible in writing, seems to be completed, and it is difficult to maintain the multidimensionality of language. Like Plato's attack on *poiēsis* however, at the end of a poietic work, the *Republic*, if it is taken to the letter, *à la lettre*, cannot be what it seems. As the 'Letter on "Humanism"' insists: on the one hand, speech remains in being and lets being rule; on the other hand, 'writing offers the healing pressure of deliberate linguistic composition'.[16] In fact, both speech and writing are subject to grammar, and the metaphysical forms of subject and object. And although there is no hierarchy of speech over writing, or phonocentrism – for in writing there is a sort of necessary constraint or wholesome limitation, the essential law to which thought submits – if we find that our formulations lose flexibility, we thereby gain the pressure to write precisely, to practise the rare 'handicraft of writing'.[17] Beaufret's questions then, do not call for a visit to Paris – for the letter demonstrates that the presumed clarity of the immediate discussion, the apparent clarity of the question, and its answer, the seemingly open window to the soul that the voice provides, that the hearer hears what the speaker speaks, or what the writer writes, that we could read the letters before us, gain clarity rather than confusion – all this is itself suspect. Indeed, if Heidegger writes the 'Letter on "Humanism"' rather than taking off for France, it is precisely to put the healing pressure of the medium on both correspondents, and on us. The difficulty of maintaining multiplicity in writing seems to call for a particular kind of action with respect to metaphysics, for an attack on logic and grammar, the destructuring of its truth and hegemony, not merely for the reactive rescue of thought as *theoria* over and against doing or acting, nor simply the justification of philosophy as applied – it calls for a spectacular failure in the attempt to ponder the essence of action decisively enough, to maintain the difference between aspectually complete and incomplete thought. So if 'thinking has been stranded on dry land',[18] it may have to enter another element, becoming wet – but then, well we too, may have to get wet, not in order to go back or retrieve some lost philogenetic home, some return to nature, origin before the origin, but becoming fish, learn to swim in a foreign element, cut new gills in our throats, breathe water, if we can, as if we haven't been doing so all along.

4.3

Regardless, the letter remains the 'Letter on "*Humanism*"'. But what is that? Heidegger gives a clue in another text: 'The beginning of metaphysics in the thought of Plato is at the same time the beginning of "humanism."'[19] And warns: 'So that we could experience and know for the future what a thinker left unsaid, whatever that might be, we have to consider what he said. To properly satisfy this demand would entail examining all of Plato's "dialogues" in their interrelationship. Since this is impossible, we must let a different path guide us to the unsaid in Plato's thinking.'[20] Impossible indeed, and perhaps nothing we could do would allow us to authentically experience and know the unsaid. The text however, does not begin with humanism, but with a translation of the allegory of the cave – for Heidegger insists that herein lies the doctrine of the ideas, and the idea of ideas, the idea of the Good, that is, Plato's doctrine of truth – and the beginning of 'humanism'.[21]

So into the cave, Plato's or Socrates'. Here everyone is tied up in the dark watching images of humans and animals, like in a dream. Or not everyone: some face forward and watch the shadows of the figures wrought in stone and wood projected on the wall, others produce and direct the show behind them. The prisoners however, know only the world of the cave – not themselves, nor one another, nor the source of the shadows, but only the shadow-play. Sight is available, but since the prisoners talk and name the things they see, they also hear each others' voices and echoes, as well as the sounds of some puppeteers and of silence. As human, the prisoners have the other bodily senses as well, in addition to language – for these prisoners are like us, and must be so in order for the allegory to work (Although as Glaucon insists: insofar as they are not like us, this is a strange image with strange prisoners. And what if this is Plato's point? If the allegory of the cave is designed to cave-in? If it is internally inconsistent, and knowingly so? If Plato both produces and destroys the image? An image or shadow-play of us, for us, as well as an image of truth, our truth and the truth? What if the allegory is another example of Socratic irony?)

Socrates continues: in naming the images of things, the prisoners assume they are naming the things themselves, *ta onta*, beings, *die Seiende*, and the echoes of voices they ascribe to the shadows. The prisoners think the shadows of the artifacts are real, true, *alēthes*, reality, the revelation of things themselves (although why they would take them to be more true than their own bodies, or the evidence of the senses, or language, remains unclear). But the shadows are not the prisoner's only reality – for sight is only one way in which we access the real, whether our bodies are tied up or not; and the prisoners could use other means to determine the true. (Or would the prisoners not even know that the images are not them, that their thoughts and senses belong to themselves? Would the prisoners know that some things move while they cannot and that they were strangely fettered while others – for they are said to take the images to be humans and animals themselves, namely, others – are not? And would they not know up from down, left from right, orienting themselves and their world with respect to the body? So if Socrates limits his description of the prisoners' powers to sight, is it in order to show the limits of the allegory, and of sight, especially if it is taken for the pathway to the true and the truth?).

But Socrates continues: a prisoner is released and compelled to stand up, turn his head and walk – the body kicks in – he is forced to look at the theatrical apparatus that others used to produce images for him. And looking towards the light, *pros to phōs*, the fire above, source of his error, origin of the mistake of taking the image for the real, copy for the original – or at least one source, for the puppeteers must surely be blamed as well, as much as the prisoner himself, if he failed to use his other senses or reason to discern that something was amiss – seeing all this he feels pain (as if he didn't feel it all along, as if his bonds no longer hurt, and his atrophied body no longer functioned, not to speak of the problems of nourishment and evacuation – but this is only an allegory, in which memory, imagination and thought are not yet permitted). It is the sensation of pleasure and pain, however, that would have already clued him into the fact that vision is not enough, nor that it ever functions alone, but with other senses and faculties.

Regardless Socrates insists: the light from the fire would make the former prisoner at first unable to recognize the original objects used to produce the shadow-play; and if he was shown how the trick was done, if he was told that objects were nearer to reality than images, if he was turned towards more real things and saw more truly, he might nevertheless claim that the things he formally saw were more real than the things he sees now. If the eyes deceived, there is no reason to believe them now. (And is the prisoner really closer to reality? Or has he merely replaced one copy with another? Whose reality is more real – the spectators' or the producers' – for both see images: the former take them for real; the latter use them to produce images on the wall? Then would the prisoner be so wrong to deny that the things he was now forced to look at were any more real than the things he saw before, if the truth has degrees? Would the prisoner be any nearer to beings, to the truth of beings? Or would he merely be nearer to the truth of the objects through which images are made? And was he not perhaps nearer to images before, when he was in chains – for then the images were more real, now they are less so; then they spoke, now they are just a trick; then he could indulge the pleasure of the eye, now the magic is gone; then the image was an original, now it is only a copy; then an experience, now an 'experience'?) The chained prisoner is nearer to the being and truth of images, the image as image, the true image; unchained he is nearer to the being and truth of objects, the object as object or more true object, and to the knowledge that he did not know – both are more, and less. Unchained, the prisoner confronts the objects, source of his illusion, only to find that they appear as well; images are yet another prison – for corrected vision here grants only a more perfect illusion. Sight is augmented by the other senses (and now memory and reason), to produce an experience of reality, but neither the experience nor the reality of beings – insofar as they appear, are phenomena – can be trusted. (Is release then too not just another deception?). And not only the objects, the figures of humans and animals in stone and wood – for these too prove to be only representations (not things themselves, if such things exist), fakes, doubles, forms. (Who can tell if the puppeteers themselves are not puppets, props proper to another shadow play, always another, yet to be revealed, one to which we will, one fateful day, be released?) Then if the prisoner wants to go back to the world of shadows, it is because it was one where representation could not threaten presentation: things showed themselves as they were, a (shadow of a) dog was a (shadow of a) dog. And the pain is less – for the light from the fire burning in his former prison, the source of the sound and light show in the cave, a little sun or little light, is itself a smaller copy, an allegory or reduced double of the big sun above. (But then the big sun too is a double of the little sun, or allegory of an allegory.)

And Socrates continues: the problems of the cave prisoner are not overcome, merely displaced – for the prisoner is dragged up out of the cave, away from the light of the fire and into the light of the sun, *eis to tou hēliou phōs*, in order to repeat the pain of looking towards the light itself, *pros auto to phōs*, now looking at shadows, likenesses and reflections in water, appearances in the heavens, the heavens themselves until presumably he looks at the sun itself, in and of itself, *auton kath' hauton*, in its own place, *en tē hautou chōra* (if he can, and like Socrates, we may only suppose or believe or hope or fear, *oimai*, as opposed to know, that it would perhaps be possible, presumably maybe, if not immediately and completely, although perhaps mediately or incompletely, that we would not ruin our eyes, be blinded looking at the light itself, if we could ever do so), and concludes or recognizes, correctly or perhaps not, that it is the cause of everything both in and out of the cave. (But does the exit out of the cave only open up another cave, an infinity of caves? Has Socrates not set the prisoner an impossible task as possible, thereby demonstrating its impossibility, an incomplete and incompleteable task, showing that con-templating the sun itself would always remain unaccomplished and incomplete, a would-be or should-be look – for the only truth is that we cannot look at the truth of the sun: the light of the light is not the light, is not visible in the light? Or has Socrates not given the prisoner an uncertain task, perhaps presented as certain, to see the sun not by reflection or images or mediation, but in and by itself, immediately and completely in its true nature? Is it not clear that not only could he never accomplish such a task, but that he could never be sure that he had in fact seen the sun, and precisely not an image of the sun, a reflection or representation of the sun? Doesn't the sun itself always have the look of the sun, even if its true nature is a representation of it in its true nature? Does Socrates then set up an infinite task as finite in order to show its infinity? And would the teaching of the cave not be that there is no outside the cave; that insofar as ideas appear at all, present themselves, are present, they are subject to the law of representations; everything is an allegory for everything else – and allegory collapses, implodes, leaves no escape, *alēthes*, from the prison-house of shadows and light? So if Plato has what Heidegger calls a doctrine of truth, *Lehre von der Wahrheit*, a teaching written on the walls of the cave, is it that the truth lies not in that which escapes notice, but in that non-noticing from which there is no escape, *alētheia*, the unnoticed or unnoticeable unforgetting of the lie, the remembering of forgetting as incomplete and incompleteable? Then is the truth of the allegory that the allegory is not true?).

Regardless, Socrates shifts directions (from metaphysics, ontology, epistemology to ethics and politics – at least to the extent their difference, like that between completeness and incompleteness, can be maintained) and asks: Would the freed prisoner now be happier? Indeed, one who knows he is in prison is perhaps happier than one who does not; the life of the seeker of wisdom is preferable to that of the bondsman, not just 729 times, but essentially better than that of the honoured prize-winners who count success in dollars and cents – for according to Socrates, the second habitation (from which there too is perhaps no escape) is preferable to the first even though it does not pay, and the (impossible, infinite, incomplete, perhaps uncertain) task of getting an education or seeking wisdom will grant us a happier life than one spent competing for the rewards of cave dwellers, even if it continues to escape us. But if there is no argument for life outside the cave, it is perhaps because none is necessary – the entire *Republic* is argument enough for Glaucon to choose the company of those like Homer, landless serfs and other such assorted riff-raff, of which we might count Socrates and Plato. Like the allegory of the cave, the dialogue is a demonstration of philosophy as the good-life, and an embodiment of justice as well – for here no argument would convince, no rational or logical defence is possible; we must see for ourselves if we prefer a different kind of not seeing, or trying to see, but not seeing, that which can never be seen. And even under the threat of death, one to which Socrates eventually succumbs – which is not to say that we would escape it (for it too is inescapable, *alētheia*), but simply that it might not yet be the right time, the right way – it's worth the risk to try to live out of the cave, in another cave, or maybe even between caves.

And here, with the threat of death, Heidegger's translation of the allegory of the cave comes to an end. But Plato continues: 'This image then, dear Glaucon, we must apply as a whole to all that has been said, likening the region revealed through sight to the habitation of the prison, and the light of the fire in it to the power of the sun. And if you assume that the ascent and the contemplation of the things above is the soul's ascension to the intelligible region, you will not miss my surmise, since that is what you desire to hear. *But God knows whether it is true.*'[22] Indeed, it is only a god who could know if the allegory of the cave is true – we however, are no gods; and we might therefore rightly ask whether it is perhaps quite false, even intentionally so, a trap for Glaucon and would-be-Glaucons, irresistible if not inevitable, or if not exactly false, then perhaps neither false nor true, a judgement that only a god could make, if there is one, or many, if the God is not dead, although nothing proves that even the gods could decide with certainty. And although it is a true account or *logos* that Glaucon longs to hear – namely that we can get out of the cave and see things themselves and the source of sight – desire, *thoumos*, can never be trusted. Then if Socrates knows what Glaucon wants, and if we too perhaps share his desire (for a *logos* in which all things are one, *hen panta*, or a thought of being, of that which is, that never was nor will be, since it is now, perfect, all together, one, continuous), the allegory may be far more a tool of (inescapable?) seduction than an image of truth.

And in fact, everything here remains on the level of images, seeming: the phenomena or appearances must appear, show themselves – as must the idea of the Good as the cause and master of appearances in the visible and intelligible world, and the necessary condition for intelligent *praxis*. But the (intelligible) phenomena of (visible) phenomena only show us phenomena – which may be Plato's doctrine of truth – and in this way we could be better off than those who believe they are dealing in the real. In other words, the truth of the allegory of the cave, of the theatre played out here and above, the truth to which we must refer in order to act with wisdom in public and private, is that which appears to be the truth. Then knowing that we do not know (the truth of appearance – for it too is an appearance) because we cannot know, in or out of the cave, with or without the idea of the Good in sight – this may be acting wisely, wisdom, justice itself. And the allegory of the cave consists neither in getting out of the cave, nor in the contemplation of forms, looking at the sun itself; rather it is the story or *logos* of our education and uneducation, *paideia* and *apaideia*, with respect to images, phenomena – so not merely a history of intellectual development, but phenomenology, and we don't simply come to know the being of beings, the idea of ideas or the sun in and of itself, but how they show themselves. Thereby, we come to know the nature of ourselves, and our education, by turning the entirety of our souls towards the truth, towards that which we fail to notice because it cannot be noticed, that is, towards the appearance of failing itself, a failure from which there is no escape, as well as that which never appears.

Heidegger however argues: the allegory of the cave contains 'Plato's Doctrine of Truth' insofar as it concerns not merely the self-representation or self-showing of beings, but the actual being of beings, the *idea* as that which shows itself, the *Sichzeigende* in the self-showing of beings through which they present themselves. The fire in the cave, an artificial light constructed by humans in order to represent things as real, is not the truth; but rather the sun outside (an image of the idea of ideas, an allegory of the form of forms, the Good, that is really and truly not an image) that grants the natural light in which *physis*, being as a whole, is in relation to the ideas, the forms. The vision however, of the difference between the look of what beings are and the look of what they look like (if we can maintain their difference), always only provides another look: in the cave, the identity of identities; out of the cave, taken for truer, *alēthestera*, more inescapable, the difference of identities – and just as we saw the light of the fire along with the shadows in the cave, so too out of the cave we see the light of the sun along with the things themselves. the ideas. Outside the cave however, we reach the stage not merely of the more true, but of the most true, *ta alēthestata* – although as Heidegger recalls: 'in fact. Plato does not use this designation at this point'.[23] And in order to make the allegory of the cave work, Heidegger must refer to a different section of the *Republic* (Book VI, where the discussion is of philosophers, not prisoners, the proposed leaders of the state, although this too must be seen within the context of the entire dialogue, a perhaps incompleteable task, or at least one that is not here completed). If Plato refuses the most true however, it may be because the truth of the teaching, of the allegory of the cave, of allegories themselves, always only offers the truer. That which we see outside the cave would be nothing like the most revealed or most unhidden. nor the inescapable whatness of a being, the *Was-sein*, and the ideas would not be the most self-showing of beings; but we would only arrive at that which is perhaps more true, not the truth – and not by getting out of the cave, but by realizing that we never get out.

Heidegger however insists that the prisoners are freed from their bonds at the moment they look at the ideas of things and see that which is to be seen in the appearance of an appearance, the presence of the idea in the look: the truth. Education (always in relation to uneducation, as escape is to the inescapable), the movement away-from, the formation of the unformed, is taken to be grounded in the truest truth. After returning to the cave therefore, the former or free-prisoner, upon seeing that which is taken for truth among the imprisoned-prisoners (Once a prisoner, always a prisoner? Could we count ourselves among the producers of shadows, rather than consumers? And would we find another life perhaps better? One spent in contemplation of all things under the sun? Or in the cave struggling to liberate others, while trying to save our necks?), after seeing once again that which they take for true, learn that concealing lies in the nature of unconcealment, and *Verborgenheit* in *Sichverbergen*: appearance belongs to truth itself. As Heidegger writes: 'hiddenness as self-hiding permeates [and therefore, governs] the essence of being and thus also determines beings in their presentness and accessibility ("truth")'.[24] But this is not even the most true, although it may perhaps be more true than the truth of the most true. For at the moment that truth falls from its claim to be the one and only truth, the truth that Glaucon might well desire, at this moment it in fact becomes more true, and this may not only be all we can hope for, but precisely what Plato means (and Heidegger as well?).

With respect to truth however, or the truer, the truths of the cave – although this may have less to do with Plato or his teaching, than with Glaucon and his learning – everything revolves around light. Indeed for Heidegger, the allegorical power of the cave – if the allegory is to be allegorical – lies in the metonymic chain: shadows, firelight, fire, day, daylight, sunlight, sun, the shining of the light, the shining forth of that which appears, *das Scheinen des Erscheinenden*, the appearance of that which appears, look of the idea, *eidos* of the *idea*. And light (as that which allows that which appears to appear, allows sight to first happen), comes from the sun. The *idea* for instance, is that which presents itself in the form of the look of a being: it is the pure appearing, the possibility of the look. A being can present and represent itself as something, in the form of itself or another, look like itself or another, because that which it is, its being understood here as 'whatness', shines forth or appears – *idea* is the original that *eidos* copies. And 'the essence of the idea lies in its ability to shine and be seen'[25] – for it is through shining that beings come to be, come to presence, present themselves; and here presence is the meaning of being. Thus everything relies on seeing: truth is the unconcealment of that which appears, the seeing of that which is to be seen in the look, apprehending the idea – for 'access is necessarily achieved through a "seeing."'[26] Indeed, whether with the eyes or the mind, sight (and all its problems) remains the dominant metaphor of Western metaphysics and phenomenology alike. And the sun, the idea of the Good, *hē tou agathou idea*, is the possibility of seeing with the eye; as well as the origin of the appearance of beings, their appearances and that which appears, of light (and shadow) of itself, and of our power to grasp the truer with the mind.[27]

According to Heidegger then – although the allegory of the cave does not, *doch nicht*, certainly not, *gewiß nicht*, deal with *alētheia*[28] – 'Plato's Doctrine of Truth' lies in the proper interpretation of the allegory of the cave. And from this moment in the history of Western metaphysics, truth will no longer be thought as unconcealment (nor as that from which there is no escape) – for its meaning will be found in the essence of the idea of the Good; and its method will be a kind of corrective looking, *ortheteron*, thought or *nous* through *eidos* to *idea*, to that which is more real than shadows on the wall, to that which is present prior to representation, the ontological originals. Then truth no longer means *alētheia*, but *homoiōsis, adaequatio*, correspondence of thought and thing, ideal and real; or the correct seeing and right method through which knowledge articulates beings themselves. And the lovers of wisdom understood as friends of the forms will identify the highest idea with the truth, the idea of the Good with the highest and first cause, namely God. The locus of truth shifts from things in the world (*alētheia* of beings) to us, the correctness of our look, the right reason of a subject's method, its true or false relation to objects. So the interpretation of the allegory of the cave is the beginning of the end: that which begins with the unconcealment of beings and their being, is translated through the onto-theological constitution of metaphysics and its thought of God as the beingest of beings, to culminate in Nietzsche's interpretation of truth as value and the death of God.

Originally however, as Heidegger insists: 'there is a necessary ambiguity in Plato's doctrine'.[29] Truth is a *notwendige Zweideutigkeit*, both *alētheia* and *orthos*, unconcealment and correctness. The double-meaning of truth however, that drives the development of Western metaphysics, points not only to an ambiguity in Plato's dialogue – it reacts upon Heidegger's text as well. The ambiguity that Heidegger finds and names Plato's 'Doctrine of Truth', threatens the truth that the text 'Plato's Doctrine of Truth' claims to lay bare. As Heidegger argues: any attempt to ground the essence of truth as unhiddenness in metaphysics does not adequately question, but only clarifies, *erklärt*. We come to know more clearly that we do not know because we cannot know, that we cannot even know that we do not know, but only more or less know that we do not know. The allegory of the cave then, offers the theory of the ideas as a conception of truth in order to point to our inescapable predicament: if we think truth in terms of sight and light, empirical or transcendental, with the eyes or the mind, then we never 'see' the truth – for we never get out of the cave, or the cave of the cave; on the contrary, our horizon is the phenomena of phenomena, the show of shows, the point of pointing out, look of looks or things or ideas. Then neither the theory of the ideas and ultimately the idea of the Good (a conception of truth that is perhaps far more a critique of those like Glaucon, those who might hope for a simple dogmatic truth, a teaching or doctrine of truth to be learnt and repeated) nor the truth that Heidegger gleans from them and assigns to Plato, the ambiguity of truth as unconcealment and correctness, can be the truth (or at least only a god could know); rather the truth is that the truth cannot be 'seen', revealed or correct, for the truth of truth lies not in the noticing of that which escapes notice, but in that from which there can be no escape, that which can never be noticed.

If the theory of the ideas however, is not Plato's doctrine of truth, then too perhaps Heidegger's explanation is not Heidegger's. For if Plato designed the allegory of the cave to implode, and if Heidegger knew it, we might not be surprised to find that Heidegger thinks the next cave, perhaps more true, but not the truth, or merely the truth that beings cannot be known in truth, and maybe Heidegger knew that as well – for the title of Heidegger's essay, '*Platons*

Lehre von der Wahrheit', means not only 'Plato's Teaching of Truth', but just as much 'Plato's Teaching from the Truth', both about the truth and on the ground of the truth. Here Heidegger indicates both that Plato's word is not the word of truth, the truth and not the truth and that Plato does not even lead towards the truth – perhaps because such an approach is impossible, an infinite task – but away from it.

Still Heidegger maintains that Plato's concept of truth as eidetic unconcealment remains true to metaphysics insofar as it grasps through looking, apprehending, thinking and speaking in relation to that which can be seen with the mind's eye. The entire metaphorics of representation however, means that the question of the essence of unconcealment is 'not even yet adequately asked'[30] – for the positive of the negative conception of truth, the affirmative of the (alpha) privative that lies in the essence of *a-lētheia*, has not yet been experienced, which is not yet to say that it could be, and perhaps an adequate questioning of truth as unconcealment would be impossible as well, just as the claim to have experienced the positive essence of truth might very well be the denial of the truth of truth. Indeed, neither an adequate conception of truth nor an adequate experience of questioning, nor of the experience of the fundamental character of being (none of this would be adequate, reach far enough) – not because it had not yet extended itself, hard and long enough; but because the question of the essence of truth as (completely) incomplete can never be adequately asked. As Heraclitus reminds us with respect to the soul: 'You would not find out the boundaries of the soul, even by traveling along every path; so deep a measure does it have.'[31]

And it is precisely this question of the soul, the boundlessness of the soul, or of our inability to find its measure, the truth of the human soul, that confronts the doctrine of the ideas as a problem – for what would be the idea of the soul, or how could we assign an essence to that which is essentially boundless? But it is this task that metaphysics – from Plato to Nietzsche, according to Heidegger – assumes in order to accomplish its role in education, the turning of the soul towards the truth, that is, the *paideia* of the cave. Here education is only possible on the basis of a conception of the soul of the human being – and that is why 'the beginning of metaphysics [a beginning to which there is essentially no end?] in the thought of Plato is at the same time the beginning of "humanism"'. The human being, standing in the centre of beings, never as the highest being, but nevertheless as a being, becomes the focus of metaphysics: Platonism is a humanism, anthropology – and thereby determinate for our essence, as rational animal or moral actor, as immortal in soul or substance, as person or personality, individual, cause or effect, function or creator of common sense or society, as subject, body, differentiated, or as the bearer of rights and responsibilities.

Plato therefore is the bridge between metaphysics and humanism, as well as between Heidegger's 'Plato's Doctrine of Truth' and the 'Letter on "Humanism"'. Sartre and Beaufret merely mark the latest translation and continuation of Platonic humanism. If Plato however, does not succeed in formulating a conception of humanity as thinking through the looks of ideas to reality, to immortal truth, or because he cannot articulate a practice of judging reality rightly and in accordance with its value in relation to human values, or because he fails even to assure that we could, as with Protagoras, serve as the measure of all beings and being itself – and perhaps this is precisely Plato's point – then is it because he is a humanist (a word and thought that remains alien to Plato – a Heideggerian projection or mistranslation), or not? And if not, where does that leave Heidegger's destruction of metaphysics?

4.4

But back to the letter – for Heidegger does seem to take the question of humanism seriously in the 'Letter on "Humanism"'. Or does he? For as soon as he poses the question, 'How can we restore meaning to the word "Humanism"'? he ridicules it: 'I ask myself if that is necessary.'[32] And the refusal of the question means that the intention to retain the word humanism is not only unnecessary, but damaging and suspect: bad question, wrong question, wrong assumption, bad Beaufret, bad formulation, bad language, metaphysical. The 'Letter on "Humanism"' then appears to defend thinking against humanism (and against the dictatorship of the public realm and the They, the insistence on the subjectivity of subjects, selfhood or persons). Humanism as metaphysics amounts to the denial of the thinking of being. Putting thought into its non- or pre-metaphysical element thus seems to be the goal, the other beginning – for only here can we perhaps confront the mystery or secret, the *Geheimnis* of being, if it's a secret at all, if we could keep the secret, or if its secrecy would thereby be destroyed, if the mystery would not be diffused, like so much smoke and mirrors, light and shadow, at the very moment of confrontation, if this confrontation would not even be confronting, or if the secret would only be a secret if it were told.

   And for Heidegger, neither the business-like calculations of science and business however, nor the formal emptiness of logic, could approach the essence of language as the house of the truth of being, could comprehend the incomprehensibility of being, the mysteriousness of the mystery, the secrecy of secrets – for the metaphysical explication that something is inexplicable, is merely a more effective way of denying inexplicability.[33] Rather, the letter claims that we must learn to exist in the nameless – for the promise of a nearness to the mystery of being, a nearness to come, maybe, is supposed to lie with the renunciation of names, resistance to the familiar, openness to being claimed by being. But clearly, naming the nameless, like becoming familiar with the resistance to the familiar, leaves thought open to the charge of metaphysics. Like the trick or *technē* that Odysseus ('Nobody') uses against the

Cyclops – if the mystery were opened, it would not be mysterious. And the 'nameless' name demonstrates that the refusal of the name brings us only closer to the mystery, if there is one, if the lack of a name doesn't simply camouflage a lack, or the return to metaphysics, perhaps the most metaphysical of all metaphysics, under the sign of the secret. Behind the mask of the mystery then, another mask, just another mask, infinite masks – otherwise it wouldn't be mysterious. If the secret could be told, it wouldn't be a secret. Thus perhaps the letter is supposed to point us in another direction?

Regardless, the letter suggests that we must let being claim us, thereby think not only of being, but of ourselves. In this way, Heidegger runs up against the question (that he presumably raised in *Being and Time* with Dasein) that Kant placed at the foundation of critical philosophy – What can I know? What should I do? And what may I hope? – each question corresponding to a field of inquiry (cosmology, psychology, theology; or science, ethics, religion), but unified in the question. What is the human being? As Kant insists in the Introduction to his *Logic* (1800): 'We can basically count all of these as anthropology because the first three questions themselves refer to the last.'[34] And this is the question asked and answered, perhaps in being asked, in one way or another, the question of the determination of our essence, the *humanitas* of *homo humanus*, the freedom and nature of human beings, by metaphysics from Platonism through Christian thought to Marxism. This is the question answered in relation to the ground of our humanity, the history of our history, nature of our nature, human beings in relation to the world in its entirety, the unity or totality of beings. Thus the answer to the question of the meaning of human being depends upon the answer to the question of the meaning of being; and if we can't answer this question, then the project of 'humanism', perhaps like every project of metaphysics, is sunk.

The letter therefore begins with the first determinate characterization of human being in Western philosophy: *zōon logon echon* translated (metaphysically) as *animal rationale*. Here for Heidegger, because metaphysics does not think and experience, but only 'represents' beings in their being, or equates thinking with representation, because metaphysics does not think the ontological difference between beings and being, and thereby does not ask the truth of being – because of all this, metaphysics cannot ask the question of the essence of human being, and cannot think the truth of being. The *failure* of metaphysics however, is not merely the failure of *metaphysics* – for the question remains inaccessible to all representational thinking. As Heidegger insists: 'being is still waiting for it itself to become thought-provoking to humans'.[35] But if being is still waiting, it may be doing so for a long time, maybe forever. And does being not wait because it is most worthy of thought while it waits? *Qua* waiting? Because being means that which can never become thought-provoking? Or that which becomes thought-provoking in waiting? Not just a representation of the unrepresentable, the name of the nameless, but rather that thinking which cannot think itself? The impossibility, and thus infinite deferral, of thought's attempt to think thought? And if 'we cannot see around our own corner',[36] just as being cannot think the thought of itself, then can non-metaphysical or non-representational thinking open up the mystery of being, learn the secret? Or is this designed to turn our souls away from metaphysical humanism? Towards that being that lies in wait?

In any case, the letter presses on to characterize the metaphysical characterization of the human being: we are animals, but not essentially. Here, the traditional philosopheme of identity and difference functions under the sign of species and genus. The 'Letter on "Humanism"' is quite precise, or at least as precise as the *Rektoratsrede* – for Heidegger uses the exact same words he used in 1933, secretly or unconsciously quoting himself without quote marks, and without emphasis: 'One can proceed in this manner.'[37] In other words, we can situate human beings as beings among beings, outline our specific difference, more or less precisely, and thereby pave the way for natural science, biology, medicine, and the metaphysical representations of our essence as subject, person, spirit. All this is correct, but not true; one can proceed in this manner, but this is the manner of metaphysics, a way of closing us off to the question of our essence as claimed by being – for in truth, we stand outside of ourselves, temporalized in the light of being; and not a species mark (featherless biped or rational), but a way-of-being that differentiates us from other beings. As the letter insists: 'This way of being is proper only to humans.'[38] Or so it seems – for Heidegger immediately qualifies: our way of being is our own, but only 'as far as our experience shows'.[39] It is therefore quite possible that our experience of human existence (ex-istence, or ek-sistence, Dasein as ecstatic inhering in the truth of being) has been limited, or that the interpretation of our experience has been faulty, or that our experience of thought has shown us what we wanted to see, what we put into it, or what we are capable of experiencing. Our way of being characterizes our essence – but only insofar as our experience of our way of being shows. And we must keep open the possibility that our experience does not show our essence to us, at least not yet, as far as our experience goes, or perhaps because it cannot show it, because essence or being is not a function of experience, or of an experience of thinking, or because the showing of experience itself is a show, a representation of essence or way of being, a showing that simultaneously does not show, revealing as concealing, just as the show of showing, as oneself or as another, can be the most effective way of showing nothing, and therefore – the show goes on – of showing that which cannot be shown. Can we then demonstrate that the difference between the metaphysical representation of species difference is so different from the experience of the thought of our way of being? Or does Heidegger here not remain loyal to a certain somehow motivated metaphysics that stretches from *Being and Time* to the 'Letter on "Humanism"', 1927 to 1949, perhaps more metaphysical than metaphysics, insofar as it merely works out its next logical step? Has the letter not replaced one species difference with another, and knowingly so? Or is ex-istence too designed to fail as a means of fixing the smallest qualitative difference between us and other beings? And does the letter therefore not show the impossibility of differentiating us from them? Is it not a refutation of any humanism or anti-humanism that attempts to provide a test, mark or sign of human difference – be it a way of thinking, reason, or a way of being, existence? That claims to possess a shibboleth, and is ready to apply Ocham's razor? And knowingly so?

The letter therefore, takes pains not to speak of the experience of other beings (How could it?), not to claim knowledge of the life of stones, or plants and animals or gods; it concentrates on the way in which our essence lies in ex-istence – not a universal, but a way of being, 'which is different from the metaphysically conceived *existentia*'.[40] And even *existentia*, insofar as it remains loyal to metaphysics, cannot be used to think us, rocks, plants and animals, adequately. Heidegger insists: 'Here it remains an open question whether through *existentia* – in these explanations of it as actuality, which at first seems quite different – the being of a stone or even life as the being of plants and animals is adequately thought.'[41] Indeed, *bleibe hier als Frage offen* – it remains an open question we know that rocks and plants are beings, but of their *actualitas* we can say nothing. Nevertheless the 'Letter' must attempt to differentiate humans from animals, plants and rocks – not on the basis of essentialism or subjectivism, but through 'this other thinking that abandons subjectivity'.[42] And Heidegger acknowledges that this cannot be the fundamental ontology or existential analytic of *Being and Time* – for if the third division of the first part, 'Time and Being' was held back, it was because thinking failed, *versagte*, to adequately articulate the reversal or turning away from the subject.[43] In other words, Dasein's difference from other beings is a difference that doesn't make a difference, a difference that cannot be maintained, but a demonstration of the kind of thinking that fails. From 1927 to 1962, thirty-five years, from *Being and Time* to 'Time and Being', thinking fails to adequately speak the essence of human being – for it continues to turn out just one more metaphysical avatar of the subject. This failure however, is not just a failure; on the contrary, insofar as it seeks a more fundamental difference between us and other beings, attempts to articulate a more original relation to them, it shows how metaphysics works. Everything in the 'Letter' turns on remaining loyal to metaphysics, to the logic and discourse that allows science to function, permits us to realize the dream of becoming the masters and possessors of nature.

When it comes time for Heidegger to articulate the essence of metaphysical thinking, the kind of thinking that appears to abandon subjectivity in order to ground it in fundamental ontology, he does so in the *Introduction to Metaphysics*. Here Heidegger attempts to delimit human being over and against other beings: 'World is always spiritual world. The animal has no world, nor any environment.'[44] And as worldly, we are in language: 'For to be human means to be a sayer. Human beings are yes- and no-sayers only because they are, in the ground of their essence, sayers, the sayers. That is their distinction and also their predicament. It distinguishes them from stone, plant, and animal, but also from the gods.'[45] Here the attempt is to think the *logos* of the human – not a zoological, biological, historical, psychological, physiological or anthropological definition, but a metaphysical determination; and to clarify the extent to which it can or cannot maintain its difference from the others. The essential elucidation of the human is not finished with the existential analytic of Dasein (on the ground of the attempt at fundamental ontology) in *Being and Time*. The question remains: Are we human beings? Or is the human a determination that begins and ends with metaphysics, a determination imposed upon us, perhaps *a posteriori*, perhaps by and for us, either to legitimate natural science, the powerful discourse of rights and responsibilities, the art industry's belief in genius – or to be overcome (with Nietzsche), thereby reversing Platonism? Thus another circle: if metaphysics functions via essentialism, the determination of the *humanitas* of the human, it must first show that we are humans, so that it can then give us our meaning. But are we human?

For Nietzsche, according to Heidegger, we are human insofar as we are a transition, a bridge, 'a rope strung between animal and overman'[46] – but to the extent that Nietzsche remains loyal to metaphysics, he articulates the essence of the human over and against the animal and super-human. For Heidegger however, the human and its overcoming are both metaphysical: we are not humans or *homo sapiens*; we are not men, or Man, or animals, and therefore we are not not-animals, but nor are we just rational animals. Still metaphysics would have us be animals, beasts endowed with reason, in order to differentiate us from other animals, like dogs, so that we can kick them around, or eat them. Thus speaking in the name of metaphysics, Heidegger insists: 'a mere animal, e.g., a dog, never represents anything, it can never represent anything *to itself*; to do so, it would have to, the animal, perceive *itself*. It cannot say "I," it cannot speak at all. By contrast man, *according to metaphysical doctrine*, is the representing animal, the one that has the property that it can speak.'[47] Indeed, the *homo faber* of representation, according to the teaching of metaphysics, by means of metaphysics, in collusion with metaphysics – although at some point, we must certainly ask whether this metaphysics is not itself a construct, an *a posteriori* projection, a whipping-boy or strawman – all of this metaphysics in the name of Man, the *humanitas* of the human, in our name, although perhaps we haven't even thought of it, because the most thought-provoking thought '*in our thought-provoking time is that we are still not thinking*', *daß wir noch nicht denken*.[48] But will we stand for it? Will we have it? Will we will it?

And in the 'Letter', where essentialism is the essence of metaphysics, the essence of human being lies in language:

Because plants and animals are lodged in their respective environments but are never placed freely in the lighting of being which alone is 'world,' they lack language. But in being denied language they are not thereby suspended worldlessly in their environment. Still, in this word 'environment' converges all that is puzzling about living creatures. In its essence language is not the utterance of an organism; nor is it the expression of a living thing. Nor can it ever be thought in an essentially correct way in terms of its symbolic character, perhaps not even in terms of the character of signification. Language is the lighting-concealing advent of being itself.[49]

So according to the teaching of metaphysics, we are essentially different from plants and animals: we have what they lack, not only hands with opposing thumbs, but language understood as the lighting-concealing advent of being itself. An abyssal difference opens up between us and other living beings. But how can we be certain that we have leaped over this abyss and arrived at an adequate thought of their being – or can we not? How can we be sure that plants and animals lack language, or can we not? How could we certify that being itself does not arrive with the dog? That being's lighting and concealing are not present with the plant? Indeed how could we be sure of the advent of being in others, any other, if we can't even be sure it's happened to us? Or is Heidegger perhaps demonstrating that every thought of essence no matter how abstract or concrete, every attempt at empirical or transcendental diaeresis no matter how metaphysical, every desire to provide the adequate thought of *existentia*, every formulation of our essence no matter how Heideggerian, is destined to end in failure? That the line metaphysics constructs between kinds, the borders between stones and plants and animals and us and gods, like those between countries or species, are themselves metaphysical constructs? Or that every achievement of determination, every definition and *logos* – even that we are a transition – provided to answer the question of essence is itself not only an answer, but always also a question? The answer to the riddle is a riddle? Then just as Oedipus, in riddling the Sphinx's riddle with Man, leaves the essential riddle of Man intact – perhaps tragically, and this may very well be the tragedy of tragedy – so too by insisting upon language as the advent of being, metaphysics leaves the mystery of being mysterious (a mystification?). Metaphysics teaches the doctrine of essence – and if Hegel places this at the centre of his *Logic*, then it is perhaps with reason – but the metaphysical determination of essence, of the essence that precedes existence, may just be an unsolved and unsolvable riddle, even for Heidegger, or especially for Heidegger, and knowingly so, or at least the letter may show that an adequate execution and completion of this other thinking, this other beginning, one that abandons metaphysics, would always be inadequate and incomplete.

4.5

The reversal of metaphysics too however, inadequately abandons metaphysics; inversion is reversion. As Heidegger insists: 'Time and Being', as a mere reversal of *Being and Time*, is a failure of thinking – remaining loyal to the language of metaphysics, it cannot think the truth of being, and failing to notice its own loyalty, its own failure, it cannot notice the unnoticed, nor escape that from which there is no escape. Although here it seems like everything is reversed – not only in 'Time and Being' and *Being and Time* – a reversal so obvious that it becomes suspect, that we perhaps begin to question whether in the attempted reversal something necessary remains irreversible, just as the wounds of spirit do not heal without scars, the spoken word cannot be unspoken, just as translation cannot escape the untranslatable: no apology, not now – but just as much there in the 'Letter on "Humanism"'. For in the letter, the metaphysical doctrine "essence precedes existence" is not simply inverted, as in the Sartrean 'existence precedes essence',[50] which remains loyal to metaphysics and its experience of the oblivion of being, while continuing to maintain 'the human as end and as superior value'[51] in order to claim that 'human being is free, human being is freedom'.[52] Rather as Heidegger insists in *Being and Time*: 'a statement about the relation of *essentia* and *existentia* cannot yet even be expressed',[53] *noch gar nicht ausgesprochen* – the question of the relation is in the preparatory phase, whether it ever gets out of it or not, whether it could or not, or whether the preparatory is not its opposite, final; and whether being in Heidegger's letter as the ground or origin of the differentiation of existence and essence constitutes a reversal or not, remains open (closed as open?), a question that can only be answered on the basis of thinking being, and thinking, if and how being claims us.

   Regardless, one thing is clear: Heidegger's thinking of ek-sistence cannot mean metaphysical substance – the destruction of which took place in *Being and Time*, although the success of this destruction may be a failure insofar as it deploys the usual metaphysical reversal, however knowingly, a turning no longer of the soul, but of thought – for it is upon this ground that humanism interprets us as rational animals, persons, subjects, spirits or souls or minds in bodies. Indeed, the letter insists that we do not rule over being, as subjects over objects; rather – and this may be a kind of metaphysical reversal – we are thrown from being into the world, and into the truth of being. 'Whether and how [*ob es und wie es*] beings appear, whether and how God and the gods, history and nature, come forward into the lighting of being, come to presence and depart, is not decided by humans';[54] *nicht der Mensch*, but just the reverse: the decision lies with being. But everything here is not supposed to be reversed. Yet if the shift of responsibility, ground, origin, cause, from us to being is not the other or flip-side of metaphysics, Heidegger must show why not – or if the non-reversal, in spite of all attempts to the contrary, is in fact a reversal, is it perhaps in order to demonstrate that every thinking of being is metaphysical? Is the letter's failure its success? And if the reversal of metaphysics is metaphysical ('whether and how' being is effect or cause, thrown or thrower, decided or decider, appearance or origin, lighted or lighting), then does the letter not point us elsewhere?

Still following *Being and Time* and 'Time and Being' – in spite of its necessary failure in thinking, in apparent disregard for the incomplete saying of the turning or reversal – the letter insists upon the experience of thinking, of ecstatic existence, care, speaking, homelessness and dwelling, the experience of being, or of its oblivion.[55] If representational thought is metaphysical, then experience is our only hope, *ein erfahrendes Fragen*, the 'step-back through which thinking enters into an *experience* of questioning'.[56] And dwelling in the truth of being is supposed to be that which first yields 'the experience of something we can hold onto'.[57] But what if we cannot hold onto being? Or experience? What if experience yields that which we cannot hold because it cannot be held, or held onto   but that which withdraws? Then what if we can only hold onto that which escapes our grip? Holding something that we cannot hold? And what if the step-back that is supposed to enter the experience of questioning itself demands yet another step-back, the step-back from the step-back? Would the letter not announce or report, give a *logos* or bear witness to the failure of experience? The impossibility of experiencing questioning? The inadequacy not only of expression to experience, but of experience to truth? But what is the meaning of experience? And what would it mean to fail in the thinking of experience? To step-back into the failure of experience? To experience the failure of experience?

Certainly experience here cannot be Hegelian – for as Heidegger insists in his reading of the *Phenomenology*,[58] that is, the 'Science of the *Experience* of Consciousness': the metaphysical conception of experience is subjective, always in relation to consciousness, or Absolute Spirit – we are the ones who experience being, who move from natural consciousness to the point of Absolute Knowing, who follow the dialectical moments of the *Science of Logic* from being through essence to the concept. Indeed for Heidegger, if Spirit externalizes itself in us as our experience of history, it is not because our experience belongs to Spirit, but so that it can be near us, *bei uns* – and if we find not only that we cohabit with Spirit, but that we in fact are Spirit, it is only because Spirit is taken to be Absolute Subject. So for Heidegger, Hegel is a one-sided metaphysical thinker. The *genitivus subiectivus* lies between experience and consciousness: consciousness is subject, the subject that is and is experiencing science. Hegel's truth is the subjective concept, 'the subject-object-relation of the Absolute Subject in its subjectivity'.[59] But if Heidegger gives priority to the subject for metaphysical experience – against Hegel's explicit insistence on two-sided thought, the unity of subject and object, the total multiplicity of consciousness and nature, and the experience of consciousness in the *Phenomenology* as a moment, a precursor to the *Science of Logic*, the science that Heidegger admits is the actual science,[60] the warm-up for the complete System of Science, wherein neither subject nor object, neither consciousness nor Spirit have priority, but rather the relation of both – then is it in order to take Hegel's concept of experience for himself, the original-relational unity on the ground of which experience is first possible as impossible?

Regardless, for Heidegger the truth of experience is prior to subject and object; it is a way of being and how we are in the world. Experience is the pure presentation of questioning-thinking, prior to representation and expression, prior to any transcendental ground or condition of possibility, preontological and pretheoretical – not only the pure phenomenological seeing of beings showing themselves as themselves, not simply the pure look of being, but our pure relation to beings, to ourselves, and being's relation to us. And questioning-thinking is an experience insofar as it lets being and beings come to presence, just as questioning-thinking must learn, according to Heidegger, to experience being itself.

What then would it mean to experience being? To experience the thought of being not as a being, but as the It itself, being as such – for being is, in the letter, Its self, *Es selbst*?[61] How would we be certain that the experience is authentic? Especially if it is an impossible one, a thought that cannot be accomplished or completed, that remains outstanding or elusive – especially if being is constantly in withdrawal? Would it then be the experience of the lack of experience, failure to accomplish or inability to complete? Or is Heidegger perhaps pointing out how experience itself is metaphysical? And can experience, whether that of the subject, of our lives or deaths, or of being, successful or not, complete or incomplete, not be faked, if it isn't always a fake, an original experience of a copy? In other words, experience is supposed to be that which individuates, always only belongs to me, like my death, *solus ipse*: my experience of the question of being is mine – but if it is only mine, how could I confirm that I had it, that is, without referring to the experience of another, a reference which would precisely disconfirm that it was mine and only mine?

And experience can be used, a mark of distinction, sign of the elite, should or would be sovereign, status symbol of those who know, the one who is supposed to know the one who is able to experience questioning. Heidegger himself marks this possibility in his reading of Aristotle's Heraclitus story: 'The visitors [who go to see the thinker thinking] want this "experience" not in order to be overwhelmed by thinking but simply so they can say they saw and heard someone everybody says is a thinker.'[62] But how can we tell the difference between those who have been overwhelmed by the experience or event, and those who only say they have been? Will we see some kind of tell-tale sign at the heart of their stories, an aura around their heads, mark on their hands or chain around their necks? Or will we merely see them project an *a posteriori* explanation onto the inexplicable? Or is the experience of being overwhelmed by thinking an experience they could never have seen or heard, perhaps never could have had?

Indeed, if they were overwhelmed by thinking, then they weren't overwhelmed – and didn't think. And if we were overwhelmed by the experience of thinking, nor could we confirm it (either way). Like the miracle, *l'avenant*, of the messiah that changes both the being of those who experience it and their concept of experience itself, thinking would become an object of faith – we think that we've thought, but are not in a position to think that, and if we did, we wouldn't be able to speak about it. This experience of thinking then, like all such claims, would be an absolutely singular event, violation of the laws of nature, discontinuity in the uniformity of experience, transgression of the law of cause and effect (in the service of another law); which is why Heidegger insists that thinking attempts, although it may not be able to succeed, at least not in succeeding, attain for the first time, *zum erstenmal*, which would perhaps be the only time, something simple; which is why being remains mysterious, secret, *geheimnisvoll*, untold and untellable, unconfirmed and inconfirmable.[63] All singularities however, *qua* singular, unheard of, never before seen, must be witnessed – for it is the testimony of the thinker that first gives an event its singular status. Yet if someone must always bear witness to the experience of thought (at least the experiencer), it is impossible to derive *a priori* any connection between testimony and reality, between the thinker and their thinking. In fact, no testimony is sufficient to establish that the event of the experience of thought has happened   there is always a counter-argument; forged thoughts, faked miracles, bribed witnesses; thinking appears no longer to happen; and the testimony of the thinker is always opposed by an infinite number of witnesses. As Hume insists – having found an essential uncertainty that threatens all philosophies of experience: not only 'the miracle destroys the credit of testimony, but the testimony destroys itself'.[64] In other words, if the non-metaphysical experience of thinking happened (successfully or not), the norms of metaphysical experience and empirical observation (to which we bear witness everyday) would be destroyed – we could not trust the custom of our own mundane experience, if this kind of thinking abounded. And uncorroborated testimony is no testimony at all, merely a private or personal claim – for singularity without repetition could not even be said to be singular. In this sense, like all purely private experiences, like all singular events, the experience of thinking is beyond all testimony – for testimony means: repeating the unrepeatable – otherwise it would not be singular – but in this very repetition, the miracle is no longer miraculous, the singular no longer singular, the experience no longer mine. As Celan would have it: *Niemand zeugt für den Zeugen*, no one bears witness for the witness, no one fathers for the Father, thus no one experiences for the experiencer – for the experience of thinking cannot be repeated. The experience of questioning is an article of faith.

The singularity of the experience of thought however, is also not singular at all – it is constant: every experience, of every moment of every day, not just that of thought or death, would be singular, unrepeatable, whether the experience of a subject, or the event of the arrival or withdrawal of being, adequately or not, completely or not. At this moment however, not only the credit of testimony, but the credit of experience itself is threatened – we can no longer believe anything that is said because we cannot even bear witness to our own experience. And just as the singularity of every event, every experience, every question, everything new – or every trace of newness in an event, every partially new experience, like the impossible possibility of my death – destroys the credit of testimony, it simultaneously destroys itself.

In this sense, there is no reason to trust that the letter speaks of an experience of thinking, that it has ever happened, and it could just as well be that Heraclitus is just warming his hands by the stove. The 'Letter' testifies to an experience of thought to which there can be no testimony (and if it could be lying here, or at least could not establish that it is not, how can we trust it anywhere?). Then the text reacts upon itself: the expression of the experience of thinking destroys thinking as much as it destroys itself. And nor does it matter if the letter is only supposed to point the way, refer to or formally indicate, prepare a path towards the experience of thinking, a path that we are to walk alone – for not only is the preparation an experience, the sign a sign, not only is walking of the path to the experience itself an experience, and subject to all the problems of the experience of thinking, but we could never be sure that the path led anywhere, even if we got to the end of it, even to the path itself; and this may be why Heidegger calls the collection of texts in which he publishes 'Hegel's Concept of Experience', *Holzwege*, paths in the woods leading nowhere, that is, leading to the wood.

The problems of experience however, do not end there – for experience (as much as ex-perience, xed-out-experience, ~~experience~~, *erfahren* or *erleben*, even if it does not return to a subjective empiricism) seems essentially metaphysical: and the experience of thinking is itself an experience, the experience of an experience: an infinite regress of experiences opens up, and the experience of each experience would itself require an experience in order to be experienced, which is obviously impossible. But is that not Heidegger's point? The experience of reading the letter, of thinking that is brought on by the letter, not merely seeing the phenomena of the words, nor understanding the concepts, but rather being claimed by thinking, by questioning being, the experience of being claimed by being – all this is supposed to be a 'step-back through which thinking enters into an experience of questioning'. The step-back however, is a step-forward, on the way to that which lies prior to the instantiation of subjects and objects, whether it presupposes the event of original experience, the pure presentation of being there, the arrival of thought and questioning and being to which it strives, or not. Repetition does nothing to alter the metaphysics of experience, and the step-back implies an infinity of steps – but experience remains metaphysical, although it no longer belongs to a subject.

The experience of experience then (if we have it, or if we think we have or had it, we can't say what it was, or be sure that we had it, so perhaps we didn't have it, but we assume we had it, arguing from effects to causes, or taking a step-back that it had us, which perhaps amounts to the same thing, or simply makes matters worse), means that we can't trust that what we experience is what we experience, nor that the experience could ever happen. And if we find ourselves changed by what we call the experience, we can never confirm our experience, or the experience of change. So experience seeks to tell us about experience, but it can only speak about itself. And if it splits itself into experience and experience of experience; it comes no further, but merely repeats the economy of experience on another level. Then if Heidegger says what he means, he doesn't, which means that he may never have said what he meant, or could say what he meant, but that means that he might in fact say what he means all along, and maybe not. And once introduced, the experience of experience cannot be excluded, bracketed out, eliminated; it is not some kind of instrument or medium that could be applied and then removed, nor something we could doubt or confirm (for not only would we never be sure we got rid of it, but we could never be sure it never came back). Then the only thing we can trust is that we cannot trust. And experience may be what it seems, but maybe not.

If thinking or questioning then, or the question or the arrival of being, is supposed to be an experience, not only is every saying of it sure to be inadequate, but the 'Letter' perpetuates and refines this inadequacy, enacts a displacement, inaugurates a stepping-back that continues, albeit differently or more radically, the logic and language of metaphysics. Experience is no longer a purely subjective representation, but the pure presentation of the event (perhaps, but perhaps not, who could be sure?). And this may be the point: a demonstration of the limits of experience, not simply human experience, but any experience whatsoever. By identifying the experience of questioning thinking then, as the of the subjective experience of thinking, Heidegger articulates the latest avatar of metaphysics. Hence the letter continues to speak in the language of metaphysics, and knowingly so, continues to offer the experience of metaphysics and the metaphysics of experience. But as Heidegger insists elsewhere: 'Experience is the source that is standard not only for art appreciation and enjoyment, but also for artistic creation. Everything is an experience. Yet perhaps experience is the element in which art dies. The dying occurs so slowly that it takes a few centuries.'[65] Is the experience of questioning then, not the element in which the question dies?

4.6

Regardless, the 'Letter on "Humanism"' continues to respond to the question of the *humanitas* of the human being with reference to being. The question of

the meaning of being (asked and answered provisionally in *Being and Time*
with '*the transcendens pure and simple*')[66] is raised again by Beaufret's use of the
French *il y a*, which Heidegger insists translates the German *es gibt* imprecisely
(although the German is no less an imprecise translation of the French, or the
English – for what translation is not imprecise?): it gives being, *es gibt das Sein*,
il y a l'Être.[67] Being is not a being; it gives being, in German; it has there being,
in French. In this way Heidegger attempts to secure for the Germans
something German, something given to them, not so they can lord over
beings, but so they can belong to the world along with other peoples, become
the shepherds of being in their own way[68] – and whether he can do so or not
remains to be seen, or not, that is, whether he could ever get the gift of being,
German or not, receive anything originally given, without giving something
back, a counter-gift or exchange, whether the unidirectional and self-giving
gift remains loyal to metaphysics too; or whether the gift of being *qua* given is
given prior to the gift, just as the question of the meaning of being is
questionable insofar as it is raised; or even whether the gift is ever a gift, not
far more a burden, a moment of shame, or attack, poison, *Gift*, so that It
wouldn't give being, but rather burden being, embarrass it, so that being
would embarrass itself, attack itself, poison itself.

   The German impersonal however, 'It gives being', signifies, or formally
indicates, that which gives being, the It, being itself – for being is the It, or the
It, the *Es*, is being, *das Sein*. And if being gives itself, it is because the essence of
being is self-giving. To be means to be given, to give itself: being means giving.

   What then is the meaning of giving? Clearly giving cannot mean simply
handing over a possession, a present to be opened up, used and discarded;
rather giving is opening – to give means to open. And if being opens up the
region or there, the *Da* in which giving gives, and gives itself in the opening, it
is because giving and opening both are as well. In this way, being gives being
by letting beings come to be, open themselves up and come to light. In the
'Letter' therefore, the question of the meaning of being becomes the question
of the lighting itself, *die Lichtung selbst*.[69] And beings come forward into the
clearing that the lighting provides, come to presence and go out of presence –
for the truth of being is that which gives beings, human beings understood as
Dasein included, by giving itself as the lighting.

   So being means lighting? And lighting? Lighting is that which being gives,
and in the light of being, beings show themselves. But lighting is not simply a
thing, being or empirical light, nor a universal concept or form, the light of
lights; lighting is that which first lets these lights come to light. And here
Heidegger must be careful to differentiate his phosophorics from those of
metaphysics: being is the giver of light, the *phōstáros*, that which gives Dasein a
place to be. Metaphysics however, and the entire scopophilic economy of
showing and seeing, only recognizes the appearance, the *idea*, only
categorically represents the look or *eidos*; only allows the certainty of that
which is perceived with the mind alone, only accepts the sightless vision of

concepts or the intellectual intuition of an essence grasped – it therefore conceals the truth of being as lighting. So as the lighting itself, being is the truth that lets beings be, be seen and known. But does this here not return being to the (Platonic) logic of light? Does the thinking of lighting (rather than the seeing of being) fail even more spectacularly than in *Being and Time* – and that may be precisely the point – to speak any language other than that of metaphysics, albeit knowingly so? And if this is the case, is there any break with the metaphysics of light, or reversal of the economy of seeing, or rather its continuation, perpetuation, perfection? For as the letter insists: the lighting is that which gives light the region in which it can light, just as it gives being the clearing in which it can come to presence.

But not simply lighting – for the 'Letter' insists that it *gibt sich und versagt sich zumal*, 'gives itself and refuses itself simultaneously'.[70] Being gives and fails to give, speaks and is silent, is and is not. The lighting lights itself and cannot set itself alight. The lighting is supposed to open itself up for that which it lights and for itself, just as being is supposed to let beings be and be itself. The 'Letter' articulates this simple truth with 'It gives being', or 'there is being', or 'being is the lighting itself'. But if thinking fails to speak the simplicity of being, or if every thinking speaks the simplicity of being, it is perhaps not just the fault of being, but of thought, of the thought of simplicity, thinking the simple truth – and for at least two reasons.

On the one hand, the metaphysical will to simplicity could be an unfulfillable desire. We cannot achieve the thought of being or essence; only approach it, getting nearer and nearer, but that is, as in Zeno's paradox, always doomed to remain infinitely far. Still the dream of the simple essence, *das einfache Wesen*, always remains to be dreamt, a possible dream, possible *qua* impossible, infinitely possible/impossible, always outstanding, on the way to being thought, like an idea regulating the practice of thinking, an inexhaustible source, question that can always be asked and asked again – for as Heidegger insists: 'this and this alone is the primary question for a thinking that attempts to think the truth of being'.[71] And in this sense, the attempt at simplicity succeeds in only approaching its goal, successful failure, climbing to the nearness of the nearest, *die Nähe des Nächsten*.

On the other hand however, in this attempt, thinking could also fail to think the simple essence of being – and it is for this reason that we never get any nearer to being than we've ever been. Then the attempt to think the truth of being, to raise the question of the meaning of being, is a kind of feign – it brings us no nearer to the source. In other words, the attempt to think the unthinkable can be taken seriously, *kein Scherz, nur Ernst* (and here we may fall into the kind of nihilism against which Nietzsche warns, the kind of *resentiment* that forms the height of pessimism), or it can be taken as the most joyful of jokes. Then the progress of science is erected upon the ground of an unfulfilable wish; and the metaphysical dream of simple essence is not only unachievable, but undreamable, failing even at failure. Is this not the (noble) lie that thought is getting closer to the truth? And if it is a lie that works, a dream that functions to this day, that which we desire to hear, then the primary question for thought maybe far more: Who asks for the pure and simple, the absolute, *schlechthin*? And to what end? Why do we want it? Is this not the question of the question and the meaning of meaning?

Still, if the question of the simple essence and truth of being cannot be answered from the start, if we fall infinitely short, no matter how hard we try; then it is perhaps there that the truth is to be found, in the unanswerability of the question of the meaning of being, the refusal of the lighting to show itself as itself, especially if we look at it, not only our failure to think the truth, but far more truth's failure to allow itself to be thought. The attempt to think the simple essence of being then, would point to both the sham of simplicity, the deception of continuing to perpetuate it as *telos*, as well as the lie that lies at the core of questioning, of that which belongs not to the question, but to the desire for the question or answer, questionability or answerability – and thus it would point to the structurally necessary failure of thought in the face of thinking. The difference then between metaphysics and thought would lie in their ability to acknowledge and bear the truth that they cannot think, that the approach to being is impossible, that the search for the source is in vain. As Kant notes: in mathematics, where Lambert proves that π is incommensurable since no adequate solution in terms of rational or irrational numbers is possible, 'at least the impossibility of a solution can be known with certainty'.[72] Or as Gödel proves: in every consistent axiomatic system, there exists at least one proposition that is undecidable. Or as Heidegger insists when turning to the other of being, to the question of the nothing, *das Nichts*, immediately after *Being and Time*: 'The elaboration of the question of the nothing must bring us to the point where an answer becomes possible or the impossibility of any answer becomes clear.'[73] So if the question of the meaning of being is always already an answer, and if the answer is essentially impossible, *die Unmöglichkeit der Antwort*, then the task is to think the essential impossibility of the question.[74] As Heidegger writes: 'the indeterminateness of that in the face of which and for which we become anxious is no mere lack of determination but rather the essential impossibility of determining it'.[75] But while metaphysics creates and preserves the desire for nearness to being, the desire to think being, the will to essential simplicity, thought thinks that it cannot think (although nothing yet assures us that we would be able to differentiate the two, that we could once and for all determine with certainty whether the 'Letter on "Humanism"' belonged to metaphysics – for the way up and down, as Heraclitus reminds us, like the way in and out, are the same – or whether it went over and beyond humanism, *Über den Humanismus*, to something else).

4.7

Three questions however remain (to be answered, left unanswered, perhaps *qua* unanswerable). And Heidegger appears to respond to the first question about restoring a sense to the word 'humanism' by attempting to think the essence of humans more primordially (an attempt also attempted in *Being and Time* to overcome the subjectivism of *animal rationale* through the thought of our existence as throwness, as essentially being-in-the-world, the ek-sistence whereby we become not lords of beings, but shepherds of being, *Hirt des Seins*). Of course, as Heidegger himself notes (a note on which he here refuses to comment, a refusal that is itself a refusal, or non-commenting comment – because it is not untrue?): 'it is everywhere supposed that the attempt in *Being and Time* ended in a blind ally', that the *Versuch* finished in a *Sackgasse*.[76] Is this because shepherding being is merely another way of lording over beings or being, just as the *throw* of being is the throw of *being*? Heidegger's answer: from *Being and Time* to the 'Letter on "Humanism"', 'whether the realm of the truth of being is a blind alley or a free space',[77] a *Sackgasse* or *das Freie*, is a conflict that cannot be settled, *kann nicht geschlichtet werden*. So no answer, at least not yet, and then perhaps never – rather, unending conflict.

Then having raised and re-raised the first question of the sense of the word 'humanism', and having responded with reference to the destruction of metaphysics and the fundamental ontology of *Being and Time*, the letter continues to the second question, the question of 'ethics', not rules for living or some kind of criterion for judging right and wrong and good and evil, rather the question. What is ethics? But any application of ontology and ethics, any question of their relationship, presupposes that we know what we mean by ontology and ethics. Heidegger insists: 'we must ask what "ontology" and "ethics" themselves are'.[78] The questioning of ethics here however, is simultaneously its refusal – and what better way to not answer a question, than by seeming to ask or answer it, perhaps even more fundamentally than it has ever been asked or answered before? What better way to refuse the question of ethics than by reposing it as ontology? And if we ask what ontology and ethics are, do we do so ontologically or ethically? Then in order to ask what they are, do we not already have to presuppose that we should do so (ethics), or want to (psychology) or that we are able to (logic) or that we can (ontology)? Thus, does the question of ontology and ethics not presuppose that the question has been asked and answered? Or that the asking is an answering?

Regardless, the argument for the question of the being of ontology and ethics is bracketed out so that the letter can unfold or reveal the being and essence of ethics, the *ethos* of *anthropos* that (through translation) the *humanitas* of *homo humanus* forgets. Here Heidegger recalls Heraclitus' fragment: *ēthos anthrōpō daimōn*, 'Man's character is his daimon'.[79] Indeed, this translation is almost literal: our character is identified with the divine. Heidegger however,

translates in his own way: 'the (familiar) abode is for man the open region for
the presencing of god (the unfamiliar one)'.[80] This translation wants to allow
the truth of Heraclitus' thought to appear, to speak to us, say to us that which
can be said – for *ēthos* also means living-place, the space in which animals and
human beings dwell, that which is ownmost to us, our accustomed haunt or
joint, and thereby the source of our customs, norms, rules, laws, morals.
Insofar as this place opens up a space for us to live, it allows us to be that
which we essentially are (finite, mortals); and not that which we are not
(infinite, divine). Yet the opening of the place of our *ēthos* also makes it
possible for that which belongs to us as our other (the infinite, the divine) to
approach us; and if we are not separate from the divine, the infinite, it could
not come hither. In this way, our *ēthos* reserves a place for the other – and our
role in its arrival is not simply a passive waiting, nor a merely active seeking; it
is an active passivity, a passive activity, that opens and preserves a space for
the arrival of a stranger god or daimonic guest. Our *ēthos* therefore, being
ours, must be such that it can open up to the other; the character of our
existence must be such that we can be there for the *daimon*.

   And here, Heidegger is trying to question and think prior to the
metaphysical conception of human being as *zōon logon echon*, before Aristotle's
insistences that 'nature, as we often say, makes nothing in vain, and man is the
only animal whom she has endowed with the gift of speech',[81] before Kant's
characterization of us an 'animal capable of reason (*animal rationabile*)',[82] and
even before *Being and Time*'s own thought of us as that being which in its being
'is concerned *about* its very being'.[83] Indeed, Heidegger is attempting to
question and think before Sartrean existentialism and Marx's insistence that
our humanity is to be found in society, that we are social-historical beings,
products of the mode of production and that the nature of human beings is a
cultural artifact, an effect of material conditions; to question and think before
the theological claim that the humanity of *ens finitum* is to be found in *ens
infinitum*, in our relation to the Absolute, or the Other, before we are 'children
of God', and life is merely a momentary resting place on our way to heaven;
and before the medieval contention that humanity is not that which we are,
but what we learn, *paideia*, whereby we differentiate the educated *homo
humanus* from the *homo barbarus*, the one who is not Greek, speaks no Greek, but
only BaBaBa.

   Indeed, all these translations of Heraclitus are certainly correct; they may
not however, be quite true, or just – for they think the being of human being
in a way that is no longer pre-metaphysical. But Heraclitus warns: 'Not
knowing how to listen, neither can they speak.'[84] And for this reason, 'the
Lord at Delphi neither speaks nor conceals, but signs'.[85]

   So if the word 'is' is not in the Greek (*ēthos anthrōpō daimōn*), it is not, as
philology insists, because the linking-verb 'to be' must be supplemented in the
text, nor because it is somehow always already given, nor because it is simply
a fragment, but because the connection or relation between our character or

dwelling-place and the daimonic or presencing-of-god is not that of being –
but more intimate – because a *logos* that claims our character 'to be' the divine
would have to abstract from our divinity in order to arrive at being, because
our infinity and otherness is not a question of being. But if Heraclitus'
leipontological *logos* takes account of us, it is because it is not (and would not)
think with being, but far more constitutes a *thinking without being*. And the
question here would be not only how to think without being, but just as much
how to write and speak without being, and to live without it – not simply its
lack, but the *technē*, the knowing skill embodied in a long tradition that
extends from Sophocles' 'many wonders, none more wonderful than
anthropos',[86] to Keats' 'Ode to a Grecian Urn': 'Beauty is truth, truth beauty,
– that is all / Ye know on earth, and all ye need to know.' Thinking without
being, Heraclitus' thought may now be translated: 'human's character
divine', or 'dwelling of humans – divine'.

Heraclitus then thinks the divine as intimate to us, to *anthropos*. But what is
that? The essential unity of *anthropos* lies in the face: we are the man-faced
being, *anēr-ōps*, the one whose aspect is neither that of animal nor god – not
the mere *face à face*, but 'the other [who] *continues* to face me, to reveal
themselves in their visage';[87] not one of our perspectives, this countenance as
opposed to another, but our aspect itself, that which continues to efface itself
in the facing, whether it multiplies its faces, its masks or masquerades, or not –
there dwells the divine. Thus in thinking with or without being, facing is the
aspect that characterizes our divinity – for aspect is the *ōps* of *anēr-ōps*. With
the thought of human aspect, however, Heraclitus has not only revealed our
daimon, but shown how we dwell with the divine or provide an open space for
its arrival. But here, have we yet taken up the task of thinking the truth of
human being, that from which there is no escape?

In fact, before Heraclitus' philosophical anthropology, Homer reminds us:
the godlike human, *isotheos*, is not *anēr*, but *phōs*, light.[88] So not anthropology,
but 'phosology' is the science of the essential truth of human beings. If Homer
however, is able to speak our essence in poetry, it is neither because he is a
poet, nor because phos is poetic; but rather if we can be poetic, it is because we
are phos. Then insofar as we come to light as light, *phainesthai* as *phōs*,
phosology is phenomenology, the science of the being and unity, time and
aspect of *phos*.

It is no wonder then, when Heidegger comes to the third question of the
letter, he turns to poetry, *das Dichten* – for 'poetics is truer than the exploration
of beings',[89] But here Heidegger insists: in the thinking that brings being to
language, ambiguity threatens, *die Zweideutigkeit droht*; and not just here – for
as the *Introduction to Metaphysics* warns: 'every essential form of spirit stands in
ambiguity',[90] remains a *double-entendre*, that is, charged, sexually or otherwise,
laden with another meaning, ready to discharge. And it is precisely this kind
of *double-entendre* that marks the letter from the start – for when Heidegger
seeks not to deny, but affirm thought's poetic essence in bringing the advent of

being to language, he cannot avoid the multiplicity of meanings, cannot stop the multiplication of significations generated when language speaks, not us, and knowingly or not.

Indeed, ambiguity is the danger, *die Gefahr*, and discord, *die Zwietracht*, the threat – but if this is to remain part of the adventure of philosophy, as Beaufret asks, the danger must be accepted, even affirmed. It is therefore as essential to differentiate the dangerous from the innocuous – to the extent this is possible – as to separate the adventure from the adventuress, or adventurer (as it will be to delineate technology's saving power over and against the threat of enframing).[91] So the letter claims that bringing the advent of being to language is supposed to be the matter of thinking, the work of essential thinkers insofar as they think the same not just the identical, *das Selbe* not *das Gleiche*.[92] The difference however, or the difference of differences, lies with thought's will to risk: 'To flee into the identical is not dangerous. To risk discord in order to say the same is the danger.'[93] The letter however, does not exhort us to risk ourselves, bet our lives rather than our money, in order to speak the same differently; it merely speaks the danger, gives a warning sign. How then are we to know that we have said the same and not the identical? Or the identical in the guise of the same? If ambiguity threatens, if the same is itself ambiguous, and if it always also contains elements of the identical? Or is it the opposite, namely, that we could never say the identical, never think the identical identically – for identity is just as much an abstract identification as the thought of identity? Or is it not possible that the identical and the same could be identical and not the same? And if they were the same, could we mark the moment that their difference becomes unambiguous? Or would this betray the very ambiguity that threatens, would this disambiguate the very danger that the same is supposed to maintain, make the ambiguous unambiguous?

Indeed, ambiguity threatens – throughout the entire 'Letter'. The double, the *double-entendre*, that which could be heard in what is said or unsaid, meant or not; and the *Zweideutigkeit* of language as it speaks, the threat of the threat, reacts upon Heidegger as well. Thus at the very end of the letter, when insisting that 'it is time to break the habit of overestimating philosophy',[94] can we be sure that this estimation is itself not an underestimation, or just another overestimation? In asking less of philosophy are we asking more – or in fact less? And is the thinking to come announced in the letter, the thinking that is supposed to think more originally than metaphysics – will this thinking ever come? Or has it come? Or does it come in not coming, like the advent of the arrival of being? Or all of these? For thought is supposed to descend to the poverty of its provisional essence, no longer claim to become absolute knowledge or wisdom itself, but rather realize itself as the 'love of wisdom', the loving directed towards wisdom, *Liebe zur Weisheit* – but if being underway to wisdom is itself wisdom, a higher wisdom *qua* lower, more true because less so, then can it still claim to be underway? Or is this just sham? Or is it spoken in the other language, the language that remains in the background, in which the letter does not speak?

Notes

1   *BW; GA9.*
2   '1. *Auflage 1949: Das hier Gesagte ist nicht erst zur Zeit der Niederschrift ausgedacht, sondern beruht auf dem Gang eines Weges, der 1936 begonnen wurde, im "Augenblick" eines Versuches, die Wahrheit des Seins einfach zu sagen. – Der Brief spricht immer noch in der Sprache der Metaphysik, und zwar wissentlich. Die andere Sprache bleibt im Hintergrund'* (*GA9*, 313n; my translation).
3   Exactly what Heidegger means with this date remains unclear, for although in the 1946 note he refers to, 'Hölderlin and the Essence of Poetry', *BW*, 236/49 ['Hölderlin und das Wesen der Dichtung', *Hölderlin und das Wesen der Dichtung*, Langen, 1937; 'Hölderlin and the Essence of Poetry' *Existence and Being*, Regnery, 1949], he could also be thinking of the Nietzsche or Schelling lectures, those on the 'Fundamental Problems of Metaphysics', or the Leibniz/German Idealism or Schiller or Hegel seminars, or the colloquium on 'Overcoming Aesthetics', or of (as the editors insist) the *Contributions to Philosophy*, all in 1936 (or maybe even some private matter?).
4   Plato, *Parm.*, 131a. The Platonic theory of participation as the relation of things and the ideas can now – perhaps finally – be thought as translation.
5   *BW*, 195/7.
6   *BW*, 224/35.
7   *BW*, 231/43; translation modified.
8   *BW*, 231/43.
9   *BW*, 240/53. Turning philosophy into an adventuress? So philosophy is (once again) a woman? Or is Heidegger referring to another one of his adventures? The metaphor's sexism, like that of the Thracian maid, remains in the background.
10   *BW*, 193/5.
11   *BW*, 193/5.
12   *BW*, 194/5.
13   Aristotle, *Meta.*, 1048b17-35. Here Aristotle thinks aspectually: actions are one not merely in terms of time, but with respect to the way something is done, accomplished or not, complete or incomplete, *energia* or *kinēseis*, an end in itself or in another – at one and the same time or not. The science of teleology is dependent upon phenomenology *qua* science of aspect.
14   *BW*, 193/5.
15   *BW*, 195/7; translation modified.

16   *BW*, 223/34.

17   *BW*, 195/7.

18   'Plato's Doctrine of Truth', *PM*, 181/142.

19   *PM*, 155/203.

20   Plato, *Rep.*, VII, 514a2–517a7. Here the allegory is plucked out of context, out of the middle of the *Republic*, the reflection on the essence of the *polis* that perhaps first makes it possible, and set up as the means by which to determine not merely Plato's pedagogical teaching or our nature with respect to its education and lack thereof, but his 'doctrine of truth', assuming that he has one, a perhaps necessary injustice, wilful abbreviation, an expedient short-cut designed to cover over the insufficiency by acknowledging it, or conceal the impossibility by labelling it impossible.

21   Plato, *Rep.*, 517a8ff; my emphasis.

22   *PM*, 170/221; translation modified. For Heidegger, the history of Western metaphysics has allowed the fundamentally Greek conception of truth as unconcealment, *alētheia*, to remain hidden, preferring to think it as a kind of representative thinking that culminates in truth as correspondence of thought and thing, *adaequatio intellectus et rei*; but before they can correspond, beings must present themselves as unconcealed, open themselves to our view, and the ground of our representations: in the cave they show themselves as shadows, in black and white, and the prisoners take the appearance of things as identical to things themselves; outside in colour, and in relation to their appearance, we see the difference between the appearance and that which appears – or at least we think we see, or perhaps we simply want to see, like Glaucon, desire to hear that we can and do see.

23   *PM*, 171/223; translation modified. Here education means *Bildung*, branding our souls through an image, *durch ein Bild*, formation through the forms, or more precisely, through truth as image, through the truth of the forms, to the truth of the Good itself.

24   *PM*, 173/225; translation modified.

25   *PM*, 173/226.

26   The idea of the Good however, as Heidegger insists, cannot be taken morally or amorally; although 'whoever wants to act and has to act in a world determined by "the ideas" needs, before all else, a view of the ideas' – rather, the good is the highest because it is the best, because it is that which makes everything possible, the source of all lights, the origin of all beings or goods. If the ideas then are the being of every being, then the idea of the ideas, that which allows them to be ideas, give beings their look, is the last and first of ideas, beginning and end, *idea teleutaia*, the idea of all ideas and the shiniest of all shines, the shiniest shiny – and that named the idea of the Good. And the sun is like the Good insofar as it gives the light whereby everything can possibly be seen (*PM*, 176/229).

27 And therefore we must ask to what extent the interpretation has nothing to do with Plato but, and this is a familiar complaint, only with Heidegger? To what extent it forces Platonism upon Plato, the doctrinaire upon that which refuses doctrine, a teaching upon the philosopher who could not teach, or accept money for teaching, unlike the sophists, because he did not know? As B. Magnus notes with respect to *KPM*: 'Many decades after its publication, after all of its deficiencies had been discussed to death, Heidegger told a friend of mine: "It may not be good Kant, but it is awfully good Heidegger." I feel the same thing can be said of Heidegger's Nietzsche studies: They may not be good Nietzsche, but they are first-rate Heidegger' (*Nietzsche's Philosophy of the Eternal Recurrence of the Same*, K. Löwith, University of California, 1977, xvii). Maybe the same thing can be said of Heidegger's reading of Plato.

28 *PM*, 177/231.

29 *PM*, 182/238.

30 Diogenes Laertius, IX, 7; *PP*, 203.

31 *BW*, 195/7.

32 *BW*, 199/10.

33 *Kants gesammelte Schriften*, dc Gruyter, VIII, 343; cf., also, *Werke* VI, Suhrkamp, 1958, 448, A26; translation modified; Heidegger, *KPM*, 206–7.

34 *BW*, 203/14; translation modified.

35 *GS*, 374.

36 *BW*, 203/14; translation modified; *RR*, 490/30.

37 *BW*, 204/15.

38 *BW*, 204/15.

39 *BW*, 205/17.

40 *BW*, 206/17.

41 *BW*, 207/19.

42 *BW*, 208/19.

43 *IM*, 47/34; cf., Derrida, *De l'esprit* and *Geschlecht I-IV*.

44 *IM*, 86/62.

45 *WCT*, 60/27; translation modified.

46 *WCT*, 61/27–8; translation modified, my emphasis.

47 *WCT*, 6/3.

48 *BW*, 206/17–18. Heidegger's formulation in 'The Origin of the Work of Art' is somewhat different: 'A stone is worldless. Plant and animal likewise have no world; but they belong to the covert throng of a surrounding into which they are linked. The peasant woman, on the other hand, has a world because she dwells in the overtness of beings, of the things that are' (*PLT*, 43/30).

49 *EH*, 26.

50 *EH*, 74.

51 *EH*, 39.

52   *BW*, 209/20; translation modified.

53   *BW*, 210/22; translation modified.

54   *BW*, 210/22, 217/28.

55   *BW*, 222/33; translation modified; my emphasis.

56   *BW*, 239/51.

57   'Hegels Begriff der Erfahrung', *HW*, 111–204; all translations are my own.

58   *HW*, 193.

59   *HW*, 192. See my *Hegel and the Problem of Multiplicity*, Northwestern University, 2000.

60   *BW*, 210/22.

61   *BW*, 233–4/46; Heidegger's quotation marks.

62   *BW*, 212/24.

63   D. Hume, *An Enquiry Concerning Human Understanding*, 110.

64   *PLT*, 77/65.

65   *BT*, 38; *BW*, 216/27, here not in italics. This is just one indication that Beaufret doesn't seem to understand that the meaning of being is less at issue than the question of the meaning of being and its questionability.

66   *BW*, 214/25.

67   *BW*, 218/29.

68   *BW*, 211/23; 216/27.

69   *BW*, 215/26.

70   *BW*, 216/28.

71   *CPR*, A480/B508.

72   *BW*, 98/106.

73   As Heidegger insists: 'the question of being as such is the encompassing question of metaphysics, then the question of the nothing proves to be such that it embraces the whole of metaphysics' (*BW*, 110/120).

74   *BW*, 103/111.

75   *BW*, 222/33.

76   *BW*, 223/34.

77   *BW*, 232/44.

78   *PP*, 247, 211. R. McKirahan translates: 'a person's character is his divinity' (*A Presocratics Reader*, Hackett, 1996, 40). C. Kahn translates: 'Man's character is his fate' (*The Art and Thought of Heraclitus*, Cambridge University, 1979, 81).

79   *BW*, 234/47.

80   Aristotle, *Politics*, 1253a8.

81   I. Kant, *Anthropologie in pragmatischer Hinsicht* (1798/1800), Akademie Ausgabe, Vol. 7, 237/321; see also, 9/127.

82   *BT*, 12.

83   '*Akousai ouk epistamenoi oud' eipein*' (DK, 19; Kahn's translations).

84   '*Ho anax hou to manteion esti to en Delphois oute legei oute kruptei alla sēmainai*' (DK, 93).

85   '*Polla ta deina kouden anthrōpou deinoteron pelei*' (*Antigone*, 333). 'Many are the

wonders, none is more wonderful than what is man' (*Antigone*, University of Chicago, 1991, 174). Once again, Grene's translation is not wrong, but Sophocles writes without being.

[86]   E. Levinas, *Totalité et Infini*, Nijhoff, 1971, 79; my translation and emphasis.

[87]   *Iliad*, Bk. 11.472. See *Odyssey*, 16.99–103 and Aristotle, *Rhetoric*, 1387a35. For an analysis of us as *phōs*, see my forthcoming, *Unity and Aspect*.

[88]   *BW*, 240/53; translation modified.

[89]   *IM*, 9/7; cf., Derrida, *De l'esprit*, 41/68.

[90]   See below; Chapter 5.

[91]   *Identität und Differenz*, Neske, 1957, 35.

[92]   *BW*, 241/53.

[93]   *BW*, 241/54.

In a lofty sense ambiguous

5.1

Now here, in 'The Question Concerning Technology',[1] essence is at stake, the essence of technology, as well as that of human beings. And the task is to differentiate the modern from the ancient. But if the text demonstrates just the opposite, namely that such a distinction is impossible; it may point us elsewhere, to another essence of technology, another technological truth, another truth. In order to make this argument however, it is necessary to examine both the said and the unsaid, at least to the extent this is possible.

Indeed, Heidegger seems to argue that modern technology – as a way of gathering and placing, putting and positing, keeping and maintaining, framing and enframing power in a *Ge-stell* – is characterized by its ability to produce and maintain a standing-reserve, a *Bestand*, a storehouse of capital or information or energy, ready to be called upon, exploited, used by human beings in accordance with our will; hence a fulfilment of Descartes' dream to become the master and possessor of nature. And the essence of modern technology lies in its way of determining that which is given through means/ ends, revealing that which is (the whole of beings), demanding and commanding, challenging it to conform to us, the subject.

Having its own way of producing and reproducing however, determining and revealing, nature takes care of itself; the becoming of beings is not a function of human *technē* – a tree produces wood, not beds. And to the extent that we care for nature, let it take its course, act in accordance with its way of being, its way of revealing itself, treat it as an end in itself, *en heautōi*, autonomous, self-legislative, free, rather than taking it as a means to our ends, finding its end in another, *en allō*, heteronymous, subject to the law of another – to this extent, nature can be that which it is (for us and for itself). Caring for the land then, harvesting that which nature provides, is not mechanized food production; removing wood for heat from a forest where it lies dead is not the same as destroying bio-diversity in order to plant tree rows for the paper industry – while both are ways of acting, particular arts or skills, modes of revealing, they differ with respect to the cause of how they act or do not act, reveal and conceal. Indeed, everything rests not with that, *daß*, *quid facti*, but how, *wie, quid juris*, a given technology functions, the way in which it allows beings to show themselves.

Technology then, is a cause, *aitia* – but causality is not simple instrumentality, not merely a means to an end, and thus never just a function of utility. As Aristotle reminds us: four-fold causality is charged with being responsible for becoming – for *aitia* (both 'cause' and 'charge') means: *hūle, causa materialis*, the matter out of which something is made; *eidos, causa formalis*, the form or shape into which the matter enters; *telos, causa finalis*, the end to which some combination of form and matter is directed; *archē causa efficiens*, the beginning of change. Yet today, the multiplicity of causes are quickly reduced to one: the hegemony of cause *qua* efficient causality. For Heidegger however, the essence of causality lies in that which unifiedly determines how the four ways of owing, of being responsible for becoming, the *Weisen des Verschuldens*, belong together – for each way of being has a cause to which it owes its being; and each kind of change in a thing has a cause to thank, something that is responsible for making it that which it is, letting it show itself or appear. Humans then, are as responsible as nature for making things, for bringing them out of a certain matter into a particular form, for a specific end, from a given source. Making can, therefore, never be reduced to a single cause, such as efficient causality and *poiēsis* means bringing-forth, letting-come-to-presence, letting happen or occur, setting a place free for presencing, for the arrival of beings. But insofar as both nature and humans belong to *physis*, both are unifiedly responsible for the becoming of beings: the flower itself coming into bloom, as well as the sculptor letting the figure emerge from stone, that which is not yet present come forth into presencing, *Anwesen*, come 'out of concealment into unconcealment'.[2] Thus *poiēsis* too is a kind of revealing, *Entbergen*, of truth, *alētheia*.

Modern technology however, as opposed to *poiēsis*, reveals the truth in its own terms: either it treats beings as means to an end in which every end is never at an end, but always only underway to another end, framed and calculable standing-reserve, potentiality ready to be actualized; or as an end in itself, still participating in the economy of means and ends, it fails to safeguard nature from being enframed by us, as well as to protect human beings from being disengaged from nature and set up as ends. But this is not just our fault – for nature is always open to being misconstrued, and the real danger lies in our potential for taking nature exclusively as a standing-reserve, as raw material for us – and that means we may ultimately take ourselves that way as well (a way for which fascism is merely one extreme example). We come to believe that all beings are our constructs, that in confronting nature we are actually always only confronting ourselves, and that we know of nature only that which we put into it. Thus the anthropocentric prejudice of means/ ends thinking and acting, that conceals our place in nature, and our responsibility to and for nature, rather than just to ourselves, is the essential difference between modern technology and ancient *technē*.

Heidegger suggests therefore: we need only apprehend in an unbiased way, open our eyes and ears, unlock our hearts, give ourselves over to that which has always already been given, respond to the call of that which primordially unfolds and comes into unconcealment, act 'as if' all this were possible.[3] For nature is a possibility, a power that has the power to present or reveal itself to us; *physis* lets itself to be taken as means and ends, as *Bestand* – or as self-responsible, self-generative. The Rhine, for example, is revealed in an essentially different way when dammed for a power station, when turning a water-wheel, when offered as a tourist destination, and when serving as the title of a poem. So *poiēsis* too is a possibility, that which allows nature to appear as it is in truth, as a possibility, a possibility of a possibility, the power of nature – and *poiēsis* would be the place 'wherein unconcealment, i.e., truth, itself happens'.[4] But if nature can come forth through *poiēsis*, so too can humans encounter themselves, the essence of their truth.

Even technology then, is not dangerous in itself. And as Heidegger (or Hölderlin) reminds us: 'but where danger is, grows / the saving power also'.[5] The concealment of technology's essence as standing-reserve however, means that, in spite of all critique – or perhaps because of it – technology's power to enframe through means/ends remains intact. And 'the threat to man does not come in the first instance from the potentially lethal machines and apparatus of technology. The actual threat has already afflicted man in his essence.'[6] Insofar as technology is natural however, its power originates with *physis*, as do we humans – so we are also given the power to respond otherwise, to nature, to ourselves, to our technologies, and to our response. There are then at least two ways of responding to nature: with a technology that subsumes the other as a means to end, overlooks and conceals the essence of natural beings in order to enframe them as quantitative standing-reserve; or taking responsibility for our way of framing in order to let it show itself as self-framing, of beings and of us, a way of being that is therefore 'proper' to its essence – to the extent that this is possible – for 'poetically dwells man upon this earth'.[7]

It is essential therefore, to grasp the essence of technology's threat to nature and to see the power of nature itself therein. Essence however, is not merely whatness, *quidditas*, nor a mark that would allow categorization according to genus and species, nor a general concept; it is the way, *Weise*, in which something comes to be and endures, is and continues, *west und währt*. Essence therefore, is not only that which is immortal, *aei on*, in a being, like a Platonic form or *idea*, but that which is permanently given as present to mortal beings; it is that which is continually granted, not what never dies, but that which endures throughout – and it is this that modern technology tends to conceal. As Heidegger insists:

> The essence of technology is in a lofty sense ambiguous. Such ambiguity points to the mystery of all revealing, i.e., of truth. On the one hand, enframing challenges forth into the frenziedness of ordering that blocks

every view into the event of revealing and so fundamentally endangers the relation to the essence of truth. On the other hand, enframing itself happens for its part in the granting that lets humans endure – long inexperienced, but perhaps more experienced in the future – as that which is used for the safekeeping of the essence of truth.[8]

Thus, revealing technology's ambiguous essence, its *zweideutige Wesen*, both the danger and the saving power, is discovering the mystery that lay there all along, the happening of truth – for technology's original essence lies with *technē*, and thinking this ambiguous essence is the 'piety of thought'.[9]

So it seems. But what about this ambiguity? Both the higher sense of ambiguity Heidegger assigns to the essence of technology, and the ambiguity that points to truth? Is this ambiguity itself unambiguous? Can the senses of ambiguity be disambiguated? Or does Heidegger insist upon this ambiguity in order to demonstrate how it remains ambiguous? Is he seeking the ambiguous essence of technology to show that at the moment its essence is found to be ambiguous, it cannot be found? Articulating the possible as a possibility never to be actualized? Or already actual as a power? Is he attempting to apprehend in an unbiased way so as to reveal the bias of the unbiased, the prejudice of those who insist they are above prejudice? Or because such an attempt is impossible? Asking us to open our eyes and ears, unlock our hearts, in order to show that the eye remains shut when open, wide shut, that ears remain deaf, and that the heart stays most locked when unlocked? Is Heidegger arguing that, giving ourselves over to that which has always already been given, we can never do so? Do we respond to the call of that which primordially unfolds and comes into unconcealment so as to accomplish just the reverse, namely, a non-response to the non-call of that which never primordially unfolds and never comes into unconcealment?

If so, Heidegger's piety would be far more impious, a disloyal loyalty; then 'The Question Concerning Technology' would reveal that the question concerning technology can properly be neither answered nor asked. And if questioning is the piety of thought, the height of impiety would not be refusing to question, nor continually failing to question in spite of all attempts, but demonstrating the impossibility of questioning itself – for we couldn't do it even if we tried, and that may be the point. The question concerning technology would then point us away from the question, away from the happening of truth, the mystery, piety, away from *technē* and *poiēsis*, and in another direction for thought, toward another relation to technology.

5.2

To this end, three thinkers introduced by Heidegger react upon 'The Question Concerning Technology' – and the question is no longer simply

'What is the essence of technology?', but rather 'Who asks and who answers the question concerning technology?' 'Who is speaking for what, and for whom?' 'Who is the technician, *technitās*?' Indeed, we must be wary, as Agathon warns in Plato's *Symposium*[10] – for everyone gives pride of place to their own vocation when thinking (about technology), be they doctor or lawyer, physicist or philosopher or poet. Every technician is tainted by the technology they love (or hate), be it atom smasher and electron microscope, or pen and paper – for the love of technology is just as much a technology of love. What then is the effect of Heidegger's introduction of Plato, Aristotle and Heisenberg into 'The Question Concerning Technology'?

First, Plato's *Symposium* is primarily not a discussion of technology, but an attempt (perhaps designed to fail) to speak about love. And Heidegger quotes Diotima's comment to Socrates in order to clarify the essence of *poiēsis* – but this testimony argues that poetry (like love) has no single essence. Indeed the reduction of poetry to a single name, an essentially unified being, would constitute the most superficial of errors. Similarly if every kind of creation is poetic, every artist is a poet, and poetry (like artistic creation) loses all specificity and meaning – if everything is poetic, nothing is poetic. The attempt to reduce technology to *poiēsis* therefore, is doomed to failure. And the attempt itself must point elsewhere, to another truth.

Yet undoubtedly Heidegger knows the context of the quote – the whole dialogue is hearsay, second-hand memories of decade old events that may or may not have happened: Apollodorus is relating to a friend, in the words of Aristodemus, the speeches of others given on love. Everything here is suspect, and Socrates most of all – for he claims that his kind of wisdom is a paltry thing at best, equivocal as a dream, while insisting that love is something he knows.[11] And when it comes time for Socrates to give his own speech, after five others have offered eulogies to love, he resorts to the pretence of recalling the teaching of another (presumably Diotima, but this too seems a pretence, or pretence of a pretence). Indeed, what could it even mean to know and understand *Eros* (or *poiēsis*)? And can we believe Socrates' claim? Or would the 'special Socratic knowledge' of love be precisely that love cannot be an object of knowledge? And is this not Heidegger's print as well?

Regardless, Socrates insists that he prefers not to produce merely beautiful words about love, nor to lay out the truth, but (as he does in the *Republic* with respect to justice)[12] to state the facts, select the most attractive points, display them as beautifully as possible, to do so by saying who and what love is, and then describing its functions.[13] He therefore promises not to eulogize, but (adopting Diotima's method, which is his own as well, of question and answer) to tell the truth about love, with the warning that here, those in the know should not be taken in so easily.[14] Thus we too must be careful not to be taken in by Socrates' (and Heidegger's?) words, even when he proposes that love is lack, *endeia*,[15] even when he proposes that the lover of wisdom is between ignorance and knowledge[16] – for if we possessed wisdom (like the gods), we would not seek it, just as if we had what we loved, we would not want it.

If love then, is not that which we love, but far more a relation to lack, no wonder the lover of wisdom can never possess the wisdom of love (and that Socrates cannot speak the truth about the wisdom he loves). The truth of truth (that we want the truth) is itself not a truth that we ever have, only that which we want. And here love as lack cannot escape lack – for it can never show itself as it is. We know that we do not know because we cannot know – and even at the moment that we know that we do not know, we still don't know. There is no escape from that which always escapes – like our own shadow over which we cannot jump, or those little sileni in the marketplace – and noticing that we do not notice because we cannot notice can itself never be noticed. Knowing that we do not know always leaves an unknown, an infinitely unknown, just as filling the lack of knowledge about love with lack cannot remove lack. Thus even Diotima's attempt to articulate a (systematic) philosophy of love, to grasp the form or *eidos* of lack in a final revelation of eternal loveliness, to possess the essence or being of love (or beauty, or technology), its whatness or *quidditas*, the love of love, is doomed to failure from the start – once lack has been introduced into the discourse of truth, it can never be filled, but nor could it be lacking.

The *Symposium* itself therefore, is the history of an error, or a series of errors, errors built upon errors – and it is Diotima's error that Heidegger introduces into 'The Question Concerning Technology':

> Oh, it's nothing to worry about, she assured me. You see, what we've been doing is to give the name of Love to what is only one single aspect of it; we make just the same mistake, you know, with a lot of other names. For instance...? For instance, poetry. You'll agree that there is more than one kind of poetry in the true sense of the word – that is to say, calling something into existence that was not there before, so that every kind of artistic creation is poetry, and every artist is a poet.[17]

So the reduction of multiplicity to a single essence (of love, beauty, technology) is to be avoided by the lover of wisdom: poetry is not one, but many, even more many than many. And when seeking truth, the synecdochic abbreviation of ambiguity to a unified name must mislead – making cannot be reduced to *poiēsis*; not every calling into existence out of nonbeing is art; every artist is not a poet; just as lack is only one aspect of love, and one that necessarily overlooks love itself.

But it is precisely this mistake that Heidegger makes: overlooking love. The standard *Symposium* translation by Schleirmacher reads:

> Do not let it worry you, she said. For we extract only a particular kind of love, to which we give the name of the whole and name love, and for the

others we need other names. – Like which ones? I said. – Like these, she
said. You surely know that poetry is something quite multiple. For that
which is the cause of something stepping out of nonbeing into being is in
general poetry. Thus poetry also lies at the foundation of the bringing-forth
of all arts, and the masters here are all poets.[18]

But Heidegger translates only the second half of the argument: 'Every
occasion for that which always passes beyond and forward from the
nonpresent into presencing is *poiēsis*, bringing forth.'[19]

Certainly Heidegger may use Plato for his own ends in order to raise the
question concerning technology, but he cannot expect us to ignore its origin.
The introduction of the *Symposium* begs us to reread it in order to access how it
reacts upon 'The Question Concerning Technology'. And if Heidegger
overlooks the synecdoche that Diotima underlines, it is not simply because he
believes it is not an error, but because it is essential, used by Heidegger not
only to point out our failings, but his own as well. The technique of reducing a
multiplicity of causes to a whole is as inevitable as our failure to notice it. If
Heidegger then, treats technology (the word or concept) as unitary, overlooks
that which cannot be seen by a 'philosophy of technology', is it not in order to
demonstrate the failings of essentialist presuppositions? For is the standing-
reserve of the *Ge-stell* – precisely the kind of philological pun against which
Plato warns[20] – not the truth of technology, but only one of its ways of being?
And would the lack of essence in an investigation into the question concerning
technology not be truer if it sought to know that and how it could not know?
To think the non-essence of technology, and that which could never be
known? Is that perhaps the reason why Heidegger asks the question 'about'
technology? The question 'after' or 'towards', *nach* (not just 'of') technology?

Second, Aristotle's discussion of scientific knowledge and art in the
Nicomachean Ethics (Bk. VI) – a discussion that Heidegger introduces and
insists is of special importance[21] – demonstrates not merely that we claim that
making and acting, *poiēsis* and *praxis*, are different, but that every attempt
(including Heidegger's) to fix their difference as pure is sure to fail. As Aristotle
argues, having split the soul into virtues of intellect and character, having
further dirempted those of intellect into rational (scientifically contemplating
the invariable) and irrational (calculating and deliberating on the variable),
and having delineated the powers of soul that control action and truth
(sensation, desire and reason) – the states by which the soul possesses truth are
five-fold: art, scientific knowledge (dependent upon syllogism and induction to
presupposed starting-points, axioms),[22] practical wisdom, philosophic wisdom
and intuitive reason. And when considering things whose original causes are
variable, he maintains: things made and things done are different; making and
acting are not to be confused – 'so that the reasoning state of capacity to act is
different from the reasoning state of capacity to make'.[23] In fact, the distinction
is apparently so important that Aristotle repeats: 'for neither is acting making

nor is making acting'.[24] And *technē* must be kept absolutely separate from *phronesis*, practical wisdom – for although both are concerned with that which can be otherwise (unlike natural science which studies physical laws, the necessary unfolding of nature), making has an end other than itself, but action is its own end.[25] And where error can be intentional and part of its excellence, excellence in art is possible, but not in practical wisdom.

Aristotle's diaeresis of the soul however, like Plato's of the sophist, breaks down at both its outer and inner limit. On the one hand, there is no justification for the five-fold states of soul. If not infinite, why not six or seven states? The external limit of analysis is arbitrary. On the other hand, there is no pure split between art and practical wisdom (just as there is nothing that can mark the absolute difference in kind between art and science). A work of architecture, Aristotle's example,[26] belies the difference he asserts – for a house is both a means to an end (*eneka tinos*, for the sake of something; or *pros ti kai tinos*, for something and someone) and an end in itself, *telos haplos*, an absolute end, both shelter and beautiful. And the difference between making and doing is impossible to fix – not only are they both states of reason, *meta logou*, but making is acting and acting is making, the act of making, making an action, doing art, making good decisions and judgements. At the inner limit, it is impossible to distinguish the two capacities (even via the 'insofar as'), just as it is impossible to claim that things made are not done, or that things done are not made. We may call them by different names, but we are unable to fix their difference: *poiēsis* is a *praxis*, and practice is poetic. Similarly, Aristotle can insist that art and practical wisdom are to be differentiated, but can he tell us wherein their difference lies? Clearly both are necessary in order to build a house, both the skills of a craftsperson and the practical sense for the good, both look to the end, as well as to the means – but is technique not a kind of practical wisdom and is practical wisdom not a kind of technique? So is there really a difference that makes a difference between *technē* and *phronesis*?

The failure of the diaeresis in the *Ethics* however, is not a setback for Aristotle's thought; on the contrary, it points us away from diaeresis as a method (favoured by sophists, and sometimes Plato). In other words, (the failure of) Aristotle's argument shows that we would be mistaken to treat art and practical wisdom as separate, and especially to accept the inherited prejudice of their difference from others. That which is special about the observations in Book VI of the *Ethics*, is that it demonstrates that, in both form and content, a distinction between *technē* and *epistēme* is impossible. And Heidegger therefore insists: 'Both words are names for knowing in the widest sense. They mean knowing-one's-way-around in something, the self-understanding of something. Such knowing gives an opening-up.'[27] But if both *technē* and *epistēme* are names for knowing, how can we maintain their difference? And can the difference between the Rhine as dammed for power, as water-wheel turner, tourist spot and poem title be assured?

In fact, Heidegger's diaeresis suffers from the same problems as Aristotle's:

break down of largest and smallest difference. On the one hand, the Rhine is infinitely multiple in its possible meanings, and we cannot stop it from simultaneously serving as a means of transport, object of a painting, political pawn, environmental disaster. On the other hand, the difference between the Rhine as means and as end can never be split – for who could determine, when ferrying across, that its natural beauty has stopped and its utility for transportation has begun? Who could say that the water-wheel too, or the painter, does not take the river as a means to an end? That Hölderlin does not 'use' the Rhine for his own ends? So just as Aristotle is unable to fix a difference between making and doing, so too Heidegger cannot separate *poiēsis* from *Gestell*. And although the danger of technology is supposed to lie in our ability to take nature exclusively as a means, we cannot erase the Rhine's beauty, even in damming – and it may be that in damming it, we far more reveal its poetic force. Then if human reason is part of nature, if culture is natural, every *Gestell* is *poiēsis* and every *poiēsis* a *Gestell*. The water-wheel takes nature no less as a means to an end than does the dam; using the Rhine as the title for a poem is lyrical exploitation. There is no pure end in itself, no absolute Rhine – every end is a means, every means an end. There is no closed axiomatic system of interpretation that could escape modern technology. no pure language of *poiēsis*, not even for an instant. Indeed, Heidegger's text demonstrates the impossibility of a place where *poiēsis* could reveal itself as the happening of truth. With 'The Question Concerning Technology', the myth of the metaphysics of nature as an end in itself, of humans as pure ends in themselves, is itself – if it wasn't already for the Greeks – at an end.

Third, Heidegger introduces Heisenberg (twice)[28] – and if quantum theory cannot be reconciled with relativity theory, the Uncertainty Principle cannot but react upon 'The Question Concerning Technology'. Certainly, Heisenberg could be seen to support Heidegger's claim that technological enframing dominates both the human and natural sciences. But Heidegger cannot invoke Heisenberg without the essence of technology suddenly becoming uncertain, but so too the essence of its essence.

Heidegger himself therefore, invites a re-reading of technology in the light of Heisenberg. If quantum theory implies that the essence of technology cannot be known with certainty, the attempt to grasp essence may be bound to fail from the start. 'The Question Concerning Technology' then instantiates our inability to ask or answer the question. The thing itself, both 'the question concerning technology' and 'technology as an object of (phenomenological or thoughtful) investigation', would be only ever probably what and where we think, and we are unable to confirm or deny Heidegger's questions and answers. In this way, as Heisenberg insists: we find ourselves shaken 'in the foundations of our Dasein',[29] and for a number of reasons.

First, for quantum theory, we only know of technology that which we put into it: 'Heisenberg played Kant to Bohr's Hume'.[30] The question can no longer ask for the essence of technology itself, in itself, in and for itself, or in space and time; or even for the essence of the question, if as Heidegger insists: 'the content of the question reacts upon the questioning itself'.[31] Just as the instruments of investigation affect that which is investigated, so too the *technē* of thinking that thinks *technē* is itself a *technē*. Heidegger's text is just as much the question concerning *technology*, as the *question* concerning technology, the question of the question – hence the impossibility of questioning the question *per se*. And phenomenology, the *technē* that attempts to go 'To the things themselves!', to allow technology (and its question) to show itself not only as another but as itself, falls prey to its own methodology – for in 'allowing' technology to show its essence, it sets up the conditions under which essence can show itself, namely, phenomenological permission, and the willing submission to showing, to always show, as itself or as another. Similarly, quantum theory means that any thinking (questioning, poetry, art, science) necessarily constitutes that which can be thought, and thinking can be nothing other than pious, nothing less than loyal questioning (just as the atomic physicist can no longer observe the elemental particles as they are, insofar as the very light particles used to see alter that which is seen). As Heisenberg writes: 'the method's means-of-access changes and reformulates its object, so that the method can no longer distance itself from the object. The natural-scientific world-picture thereby stops being actually naturally-scientific.'[32] Similarly, Heidegger's text stages the limits of questioning and thought – for it shows that our relation to technology (itself a *technō*) excludes any pure questioning of technology's essence. Heisenberg insists: 'We are not only audience, but always also co-players in the play of life',[33] not just *Zuschauer*, but *Mitspielende*. And even if we could isolate our means of observation (or bracket out our phenomenological seeing or thought's way of allowing to be seen, questioning, opening our eyes and ears, unlocking our hearts), we would be no better off – for we could observe nothing.[34] So not only do we not know the essence of technology, but we don't even know ourselves as not knowing, albeit clutching to the illusion of knowledge and self-knowledge. Thus Heidegger insists: '*In truth, however, precisely nowhere does man today any longer encounter himself, i.e., his essence*'[35] – not because we don't yet encounter it, or should do so, but because we can't and won't; just as we don't even know that we can't know the essence of technology, or even properly raise the question concerning technology.

Second, if quantum theory demonstrates that the sciences stand between the natural and human world in such a way that they form a part of everything they investigate, the usual distinction between subject and object, inner and outer world, body and soul – like the Cartesian difference between *res extensa* and *res cogitans* that Heidegger 'destructures' in *Being and Time*[36] – cannot be maintained. Our way of questioning technology puts us in touch with it in such a way that we can no longer keep its essence free from our own; we find ourselves caught up in an economy of investigation, interpretation, thought, observation, seeing, showing, questioning from which we cannot extricate ourselves. Then the belief in the objective sciences, like objectively valid truth (like the Platonic world of the ideas), is merely a belief. As Heisenberg writes: 'The claim that often stands at the beginning of the developed creed of our time, namely, that it concerns itself not with belief, but with scientifically grounded knowledge, contains then an inner contradiction and rests on a self-delusion.'[37] So in questioning technology we find ourselves participating in the technology in question, as well as the technology of questioning understood as an encounter between humans and nature. Here there is no outside of questioning; only the recognition that there is no outside – we are caught in our own net, subject to the law, objectively neither objective nor subjective; for 'in the drama of existence we are ourselves both players and spectators'.[38] And in the question concerning technology, we are both questioner and questioned; just as technology is both that which we think, and that which thinks us.

Third, unlike classical physics, quantum theory demonstrates that an essential uncertainty lies at the core of every investigation of the natural and human sciences. Heisenberg writes:

> Let us consider a radium atom, which can emit an α-particle. The time for the emission of the α-particle cannot be predicted. We can only say that in the average the emission will take place in about two thousand years. [Either] a foregoing event as cause for the emission at a given time cannot be found ... [or] we know the forces in the atomic nucleus that are responsible for the emission of the α-particle. But this knowledge contains the uncertainty which is brought about by the interaction between the nucleus and the rest of the world. If we want to know why the α-particle was emitted at that particular time we would have to know the microscopic structure of the whole world including ourselves, and that is impossible.[39]

Indeed, while Einstein shows how time and space shift as we approach the speed of light, for Heisenberg: 'an objective description for events in space and time is possible only when we have to deal with objects or processes on a comparatively large scale, where Planck's constant can be regarded as infinitely small. When our experiments approach the region where the quantum of action becomes essential we get into all those difficulties.'[40] But when are we not 'approaching' the 'universal' constant of the speed of light? And when can Planck's constant be regarded as 'infinitely' small? When are we not 'approaching' the region where the quantum of action becomes essential? In fact, although we would like to ignore the effects of relativity and quantum theory as 'practically infinite',[41] they react upon everything we do, everywhere, all the time. Practical infinity is no infinity at all. And uncertainty is everywhere. The quantum world constantly interferes with phenomena, with things as they show themselves, and as they are thought, with technology itself and with our attempt to raise the question of its essence. And overlooking events on the quantum level is a 'dangerous oversimplification',[42] like splitting the world up into subject and object, us and nature, like forgetting the technology of the question.

Fourth, quantum theory's 'principle of complementarity' implies the 'principle of uncertainty'. The same quantum can appear as a wave and a particle (then as both matter and force); just as the same building can appear as shelter or art, *poiēsis* or *Gestell*. If matter is completely mutable ($E = mc^2$, one substance, energy, Aristotelian *potentia*), if it can show itself in a multiplicity of forms; then at any point a given quantum's identity remains undecided – for observing it in one way or another participates in its identity, and every measurement reintroduces the impossibility of certainty. Each quantum has 'coexistent potentialities'.[43] In other words, prior to its appearance as a wave or particle, the quantum in itself is unknown and unknowable, merely a 'could-be' wave or particle, 'something standing in the middle between the idea of an event and the actual event, a strange kind of physical reality just in the middle between possibility and reality'.[44] And the discontinuity exhibited everywhere (e.g., any scintillation screen or Geiger counter), is an effect of the translation or 'transition from the possible to the actual'.[45] So too, when raising the question concerning technology, we can only hope for probabilities, can only approach essence – a could be *Gestell*, or might be *poiēsis* (or something altogether different?). And between observations or interpretations, as in a world where *esse est percepi*, we may know that something happens, but cannot say what it is without participating in the event itself; nor can we hope to create a concept to describe or explain phenomena – for not only would we need an infinity of other concepts for these concepts,[46] but an explanation in which we participate is a *contradictio in adjecto*. All we have then is systematic coherence and inner consistency (expressed by a mathematical scheme), that is, closed systems of mutually exclusive interpretations that provide an exact (although limited) description of phenomena, each perfect in itself and essentially different from any other – for just as 'the electron possesses both wave-like and particle-like aspects',[47] so too the Rhine shows itself as both power-source-like and inspiration-like. Just as quantum physics insists upon the complementarity of interpretations and the uncertainty of the 'real', each language opens up a new world, creates another 'reality', neither simply better nor worse, but both and neither, participating in each other, translatable and untranslatable.

Does this then mean that the essence of technology is uncertain as well? That Heidegger's interpretation of the question reveals just one complement of that which can essentially never be thought? And does phenomenology and thought – if it is no longer to be simply metaphysics – not fall prey to the same kind of participation in its object, the matter of thought, that taints the results of physics?

5.3

Three thinkers then, introduced by Heidegger into 'The Question Concerning Technology', seem to leave the attempt to differentiate *Gestell* from *poiēsis* in question. The multiplicity of technology cannot be reduced to a unitary essence. The smallest and largest difference between technology as a means-to-an-end and an end-in-itself, between a building as art or shelter, or the Rhine as power-source or source of inspiration, cannot be maintained – nor could it be disregarded for practical purposes as infinitely small. And the question concerning technology cannot even be asked (or answered) with certainty – for phenomenology reframes technology, just as thought participates in thought, and the questioning in the question. The attempt to ask the question concerning technology then, and respond with the *Gestell*'s standing-reserve, is an oversimplification – and it is as impossible to determine its essence as the standing-reserve of *Gestell*, as to think *technē* as *poiēsis*.

Still, even after Plato, Aristotle and Heisenberg participate in this 'symposium' on the question concerning technology, Heidegger seems to remain committed to the piety of thought, and therefore loyal to the question: What is the essence of technology? The *Symposium*, however, serves as a reminder that with the question of 'what', the question of 'who', of who speaks and thinks, or not, is forgotten, repressed, unnoticed, or not even, but far more un-unnoticed – perhaps the most inescapable *alētheia*. But at the moment we attempt to exclude it from technology in order to delineate its essence as *technē*, as *poiēsis* or truth, art or skill, the 'who' comes back to haunt us.

Plato therefore does not (and cannot) contain the effects of the introduction of a certain 'who', a drunken Alcibiades into Agathon's orderly feast – and the question shifts from 'What is love?' to 'Who is Socrates?', to 'Who is this philosopher who speaks about love, this technician of thought?' and 'Who is this seducer of men and lover of wisdom?' Immediately, we are forced not only to notice the technique of questioning, of answering and asking the question of the 'what', but just as much the *technē* of Socrates the philosopher, Agathon the poet, Eryximachus the doctor, Pausanias the lawyer – for each asks and/or answers the question within the limits of their science and their world. Each speaks of love, but only Alcibiades the lover speaks of the person he loves, Socrates his beloved. And although he speaks the truth about Socrates in articulating the 'what' of the 'who', Alcibiades also speaks the 'who of the who', speaks of himself – for his eulogy and retrial of Socrates is just as much an attempt to gain the upper hand in a love triangle: Agathon–Alcibiades–Socrates – truth as strategy (sophistry?).

Who then is Plato's Socrates, the philosophical *technitās*? He is not only the thinker of love as lack, but just as much the Pied Piper of men, impish as the satyr Marsyas and as bewitching as a siren, the turner of souls and dialogical seducer, the lover and friend of wisdom, half-way between knowledge and ignorance. And Socrates is not only the seeker of truth – for no one really knows him – rather as Alcibiades insists thrice over: 'What he reminds me of more than anything is one of those little sileni that you see on the statuaries' stalls; you know the ones I mean – they're modeled with pipes or flutes in their hands, and when you open them down the middle there are little figures of the gods inside.'[48] So not only is Socrates himself an appearance – the resemblance is even more profound – he is a dissembler and appearance of appearance, an appearance of himself, shell of a shell and mask of a mask of his 'true' self, of both that which he is and that which he is not, and no one really knows him.[49] Indeed, he spends his life in play,[50] hiding the hidden, concealing when revealing, pretending to accomplish the impossible in order to demonstrate its impossibility, feigning that he does not know, not because he knows, but because he knows that he does not know, and not because he could know, but because he cannot know – hence the Socratic 'sideways glance'.[51] And as Alcibiades insists – all this holds not only for the man, but also for his words [52]

Who then is Heidegger the questioner? The thinker of the question concerning technology; the one who introduces Plato's Socratic irony, Aristotle's diaeresis and Heisenberg's uncertainty; the one whose task is to reveal the essence of technology as *technē*, or rather as *poiēsis*. In this way, the *technē* and *poiēsis* of thinking and questioning recoils upon the thinker, reacts upon the questioner who participates in the question, upon the one supposed to be concerned with technology. And if the question of the 'what', essence, *quidditas*, *Wesen*, that is, of the question concerning technology, becomes the question of the 'who'; then the question of who is Heidegger the *technitās* demands that we ask the question of technology's essence once again.

5.4

What then is the essence of technology as *technē* for whom? Certainly, it is skill or art, a way or manner of producing, the artist's craft, the pathway of *poiēsis*. But *technē* is not merely a function of the body's dexterity; it is a kind of knowledge or practical wisdom about making and doing: *technē* is technique insofar as it is the knowledge of the rules of an art, and the ability to follow them or not. In this sense, *technē* threads a course between the Scylla and Charybdis of dogmatism and scepticism – for it is grounded in freedom, in the ability to neither slavishly submit to the law as if it was our own, nor to simply reject the rules of art altogether in the name of desire. In other words, *technē* is the power to make or do, to allow truth to happen in the work of art, the knowledge that allows us to treat nature and humans in the right way, and to answer questions of justice not with definitions or calculations, but with the right decision in the right moment (the *praxis* of freedom) – for *technē* is the improvisational, the raft of *poiēsis*.

There is however, yet another sense of *technē*, as Heidegger undoubtedly knows, one that threatens, once again, to participate in everything – for *technē* means not only art, but artifice, the power to deceive, pull a fast one, slip one over, to act not *mit Recht und Fug*, right and justice, but resorting to cunning or calculation, or ruse or sham, *List, Täuschung, Vortäuschen*. *Technē* is therefore, essentially artificial, *künstlich*; appearance as opposed to reality, fake as opposed to real, *Schein* not *Erscheinung*. Indeed a *Gestell* is always some kind of mechanical contrivance, a banausic solution to a perhaps similar problem – low and lowdown – but so too is *poiēsis*. And *technē* is itself no less an act of intellectual prestidigitation – for the meaning participates in the meant, the signified inquinates the signifier, the scheme or schematism reacts upon the schemer, and the lie upon lie, as well as upon the liar, framing the framer, questioning the questioner. Thus *technē* never only indicates an honest skill or craft, never just the way of letting truth and untruth happen, but always also the lie of honesty, truth as lie, the non-event of that truth and untruth that never happens, craftiness of craft – for *technē*, the essence of technology, is essentially the calculated ability to deceive, trick, con, sham.

And modern technology then, like every philosophy of technology, is merely *technē*'s most recent translation. The magic it appears to work is itself a ruse; the beauty with which it inveigles is simply sleight-of-hand. Indeed, the *technē* of modern technology lies in its ability to trick us once again into believing that it's magic. For who isn't charmed by the magician's smile? Seduced by the power and promise of technological control? Or nostalgic for the aura of the artwork, the tactility of the book, the rituals of black magic dressed up in new clothes? In other words, modern technology remains essentially true to the essence of technology, that is, the truly lying artifices of *technē*, of *technē* as artifice. But if *technē* is artifice, the question of the artificer remains. If the essence of technology is artifice, is this not also artifice? And the artifice of thinking the essence of technology, the seriousness of the most serious philosophy – is it any less or more than feigned? And is the question concerning technology not the question of the most artful artificer, the feigning fuggler, cogitating cogger, tricky trickster? And what then?

Notes

1   *QCT*, 293/11.
2   *QCT*, 293/11.
3   *QCT*, 300/18.
4   *GA65*, §§1, 89–94.
5   *QCT*, 309/27; translation modified.
6   *QCT*, 310/28; F. Hölderlin, 'Patmos', *Hölderlin Gedichte*, Insel, 1969, 176; *Friedrich Hölderlin Poems and Fragments*, University of Michigan, 1966, 462–3.

[7] *QCT*, 309/28.

[8] *QCT*, 316/35.

[9] *QCT*, 314/33; translation modified.

[10] *QCT*, 317/36.

[11] Plato, *Symp.*, *The Collected Dialogues of Plato*, Princeton University, 1985, 196d6-e1.

[12] *Symp.*, 175e3; see 177d7-8.

[13] S. Benardete, *Socrates' Second Sailing*, University of Chicago, 1998, 35.

[14] *Symp.*, 198d3-7, and 201e1-2.

[15] *Symp.*, 199a7.

[16] *Symp.*, 200e9.

[17] *Symp.*, 202a5-9, 203e4-204b2.

[18] *Symp.*, 205b4-c2.

[19] ' – *Lass es dich nur nicht wundern, sagte sie. Denn wir nehmen nur eine gewisse Art der Liebe heraus, die wir mit dem Namen des Ganzen belegen und Liebe nennen, für die anderen brauchen wir andere Namen. – Wie doch etwa? Sprach ich. – So etwa, sagte sie. Du weisst doch dass Dichtung etwas gar vielfältiges ist. Denn was nur für irgend etwas Ursache wird aus dem Nichtsein in das Sein zu treten ist insgesammt Dichtung. Daher liegt auch bei den Hervorbringungen aller Künste Dichtung zum Grunde, und die Meister darin sind sämmtlich Dichter'* (F. Schleirmacher, *Platons Werke*, Reimer, 1857, 295; my translation).

[20] *QCT*, 293/11; translation modified.

[21] *Symp.*, 185c4-5.

[22] *QCT*, 295/13; cf. also, Heidegger, *Platon: Sophistes*, Klostermann, 1992; *Plato's Sophist*, Indiana University, 1997, §7.

[23] Aristotle, *An. Post.* 71a1.

[24] Aristotle, *Nic. Eth.*, *Basic Works of Aristotle*, Random House, 1941, 1140a4-5.

[25] *Nic. Eth.*, 1140a6-7.

[26] *Nic. Eth.*, 1140b6-7.

[27] *Nic. Eth.*, 1140a7.

[28] *QCT*, 294–5/12–13; translation modified.

[29] *QCT*, 304/23, 308/27; see also *ZS*, 122.

[30] *NhP*, 45; my translation.

[31] P. Heelen, *Quantum Mechanics and Objectivity*, Nijhoff, 1965, 48.

[32] *IM*, 4/4.

[33] *NhP*, 52.

[34] *NhP*, 40.

[35] *PP*, 25.

[36] *QCT*, 308/27.

[37] *BT*, 89ff.

[38] *NhP*, 51.

[39] *PP*, 25.

[40] *PP*, 49–50.

41 *PP*, 111, for Heidegger's consideration Einstein see, for example, *BT*, 499n4; *ZS*, *122*..
42 *PP*, 110.
43 *PP*, 63.
44 *PP*, 127.
45 *PP*, 11.
46 *PP*, 94.
47 R. Descartes, *Meditations on First Philosophy* II, *Philosophical Writings of Descartes*, Cambridge University, 1984.
48 P. Davies, 'Introduction' to *PP*, xiv.
49 *Symp.*, 215a6-b3; cf., 216d6, 221d5, 222d4.
50 *Symp.*, 216c7-d1.
51 *Symp.*, 216e4; cf. also, 218d.
52 *Symp.*, 221b3-4; see Aristophanes, *Clouds*, 362.
53 *Symp.*, 221d6.

6

Only a god can still save us

6.1

What then? What then. Well, Heidegger dies. But in May 1976, after he is dead, the *Spiegel* publishes an interview – Voice from the grave? Yes, and no, but from ten years earlier, September 1966, an interview that Heidegger insisted should not be published in his lifetime, and that should clear up his case, at least with respect to questions regarding his activities during the Third Reich. Unfortunately or not, the interview does nothing of the sort; on the contrary, it raises more questions than it answers, and not only about fascism, about what Heidegger did or did not do.

What then can be heard in the interview? Can we take it seriously? Is Heidegger answering the questions? Making them questionable? Or is he refusing to participate? Questioning the questioners and the questions? Questioning in answering? What role does he and the *Spiegel* interviewers, R. Augstein and G. Wolff, play in the dialogue? To what extent is the interview choreographed, framed, improvised? Is that the interviewers' technique? Can we find here proof clear enough to condemn or acquit Heidegger? Or does the interview itself, in spite of every effort by Heidegger to control its publication, every wish to direct the dialogue, to clarify who did what to whom, when and where and how, and every attempt to take the matter at hand seriously, does the interview itself get out of hand, out of Heidegger's hands, the *Spiegel*'s, and out of ours?

These are important questions, *wichtige Fragen* – ours as well as those asked by Augstein and Wolff. As Heidegger insists however, at the beginning of the interview: 'These are important questions, but who is to say that I can answer them all?'[1] Indeed, who can say? A question that answers a question, that doesn't answer the question, but far more places questioning in question – this is the kind of interviewee we face, one who will not answer questions, who tampers with the evidence from the start, one who will not bear witness to the events of the past, nor to those of the present interview, nor to the witness. Thus another refusal, after the refusal to publish during his lifetime, thereby avoiding a continual dialogue, a dialogue with the dialogue – the refusal to answer. And who can say that this double-refusal does not react upon everything that follows?

Can Heidegger then answer these important questions? Or will he answer? And if he answers, with an answer or a question, has he answered? Or has he simply shown that questions and answers are interchangeable? That the interviewer is no less questionable than the interviewee? And has he then provided a sign that he seriously would answer the questions, that he will try to give them just consideration? Or that he won't take them seriously? And if not then is it because he can't, insofar as they are not serious questions, or because he refuses to continue the discussion about his activities in Nazi Germany? And this out of fear, or the desire to seriously address other more philosophical issues of thought? Or because speaking is perhaps his way of being silent, or silence a way of speaking, a speaking-silence – Heidegger reminds us – that the press, like the *Spiegel*, practice all the time, as they did in 1934 when he resigned from his post as rector of Freiburg University?[2]

Who can say? On the one hand, no one can say whether Heidegger can or will answer the questions; on the other hand, we assume – rightly or wrongly – that he will seriously attempt to answer the questions. When Heidegger therefore asks, 'Who can say whether I can answer them all?' does he mean that someone can say, or nobody? That he can answer them all or can't? That he will or won't? Or both?

No one can say – and this is the serious situation with which Heidegger begins the interview, begins the interview again – for it has already begun, begun with Heidegger's refusal to publish in life. And even before the question of the possibility or impossibility of answering such important questions, Heidegger has reversed the roles of the interview, changed places, upset the balance of traditional power, as if turning the mirror onto the *Spiegel* – for the interviewers begin with a statement, and the interviewee begins with a question: '*Spiegel*: Herr Professor Heidegger, we have stated time and again that your philosophical work has been somewhat overshadowed by some events in your life which, while they did not last very long, have still never been cleared up. *Heidegger*: You mean thirty-three?' And the interviewers answer: 'Yes, before and after.'[3] So who is interviewing whom? Is the voice from the grave that of Heidegger interviewing the *Spiegel*?

In fact, these confusions haunt the interview throughout, not only with the ghosts of its participants, but with unanswered and perhaps unanswerable questions, questions that call the serious enterprise of the interview into question, that not only question the motivations or intentions of the interview, but the seriousness of any interview whatsoever. And it is these confusions that Heidegger will exploit – As a thinker? – not merely in responding to accusations regarding his behaviour during the Third Reich, but just as much in the event of the interview of 1966, in the event of its publication in 1976, and in the event of its reading, today and tomorrow.

We must turn therefore to the interview itself – for Heidegger finally does begin to answer the *Spiegel*'s questions regarding Nazism, primarily by providing testimony about what he did or did not do, empirical facts of history, by referring to statements in his lectures and published work, admitting human failure, *menschliches Versagen*, and even going so far as to agree that compromises were made, actively and passively, while insisting that some statements he would not write today, and that even in 1934 he no longer said – all in a climate of surveillance and slander, subject to a law that we might claim was no law at all, under the threat of violent death, not just the end of philosophy; but just as much in a time of excessive courage, heroism, resistance and refusal.[4]

But who can say? And who can say what Heidegger means when responding to the *Spiegel*'s reminder that in 1935 he wrote, even if he did not speak – and whether he did or not remains questionable – in the *Introduction to Metaphysics*: 'All this calls itself philosophy. In particular, what is peddled about nowadays as the philosophy of National Socialism, but which has not the least to do with the inner truth and greatness of this movement [namely the encounter between global technology and modern humanity], is fishing in these troubled waters of "values" and "totalities."'[5] Who knows what Heidegger understands to be the 'inner truth and greatness' of National Socialism? Does he see there an opportunity in the new dawn? A chance squandered? The possibility for a response to the unreflective advance of global technology, or to fascism, and on a national scale? One that would uphold the social over and against the desire of the individual? Or is the inner truth and greatness of National Socialism the truth and greatness of the Greeks to which he refers in the Rectoral address, and in which philosophy and science, according to Heidegger, should be rooted? Hence an inner truth and greatness that is denied by the Nazis? Who can say?

In fact, Heidegger thinks he can – thus he insists that he did not read this passage aloud because he was convinced that there were dumb spies in the audience who would understand him as they saw fit, no matter what, as well as those who would have a correct understanding, the *rechten Verständnis*. But how can he be so sure? How can he be certain both that he is understood correctly, and that he could differentiate between the smart ones and the dumb ones? How can he be sure that the *Spiegel* interviewers, and we today, are not the dumb ones? Or that there is a correct understanding of his comment about the 'inner truth and greatness of National Socialism'? And can he separate the response to the enframing or *Ge-stell* of global technology (that may have been possible with the Nazis) from everything else that National Socialism undertook? Or is that merely one of the compromises that he let be? Or is Heidegger perhaps not pointing us in another direction, namely, to the impossibility of differentiating the dumb from the smart? In other words, could Heidegger's statement in the interview not underline the role that desire plays in generating understanding, correct or not, the desire of the audience in 1935, in 1966, in 1976 and today, our desire to understand the other or understand otherwise? Or could he be showing that every attempt, his own included, to separate National Socialism's policy on global technology, real or imagined, actual or potential, from their other national and social activities, is bound to fail? Then would his argument not simultaneously be self-critique, Heidegger's destructuration both of his attempt to separate National Socialism from the Holocaust, and of its inner truth and greatness, wherein he might find a kernel of resistance to the *Ge-stell*, from its outer fascistic shell.

Who can say? Compromises were made – for political or philosophical reasons, in 1933 and in the interview itself. And this demonstrates the problem and power of compromise – or of the question as to how, even before we compromise, we are already compromised. Yet perhaps this is Heidegger's point; then the interview is no less compromised than the political activities – the compromised compromise means not only that we must remain uncertain with respect to outcomes, but that we can never be certain the compromise itself is in earnest. Indeed once the very possibility of compromise, of compromises, is introduced we can no longer know whether they were made in the name of resistance or collaboration, pragmatism or idealism, survival or out of some other motivation. And if compromises were made, it may be in order to show that they are always made, not only possible, but necessary, whether we compromise or not.

6.2

Still for Heidegger, neither National Socialism, nor Communism, nor Americanism, nor Democracy seem to be genuinely able to confront the calculated devastation propagated by global technology – for as half-truths, mere *Halbheiten*, they take technology as a tool over which we have control, failing to see its essence in *technē* and its relation to *poiēsis* (and then failing even more so to see the origin of this origin in improvisation) – so no wonder they are unable to approach the 'inner truth' of human action. It may seem that only thinking and poetizing are the activities that can give us the measure – but Heidegger is careful to avoid assertions; rather we must raise the question, 'whether timeliness is the measure of the "inner truth" of human action, or rather, whether thinking and poetizing are not the activity which gives us the measure'.[6] And these questions do not just answer the question of modern technology, but once again demonstrate the impossibility of an answer – for if thinking and poetizing could give us the measure, what would give us the measure of the measure? Or is it that a measure for measure is no measure at all? That measure and measuring themselves must be overcome or superseded or destructured? And is this the reason why we still have no proper or corresponding way to respond to the essence of technology – not only because we take it as a tool, but just as much because we seek a measured response, rather than the immeasurable? Hence the immeasurable activity of thinking and poetizing?

Regardless, as Heidegger insists: 'everything is functioning'[7] – before, during and after National Socialism. And this is what is so uncanny, so *unheimlich*: not only that the world is being devastated by us, not simply that functionalism remains the measure of all things (and not even Protagoras' 'Man', Protagoras), not merely that philosophy has been unable to effect an immediate transformation of the human condition or the course of history, nor that we are not at home in the world, but uprooted and displaced with respect to our tradition – not only all this, but just as much that everything is still functioning, functioning in spite of, or perhaps because of, in the name of, as a legitimation and continuation of National Socialism; and that it escapes our notice, or that its escape escapes our notice, or if not, then perhaps that our noticing functions precisely by escaping that from which there is no escape.

So then the most thought-provoking thought may be that we are not provoked. And it seems that nothing can save us from the fact that everything is functioning – not philosophy, nor any other merely human thought or endeavour. Heidegger therefore insists: '*Nur noch ein Gott kann uns retten*', 'only a god can still save us',[8] and we can prepare for the appearance or absence of the god in our declining time. Indeed, if we are declining, floundering, it is because the godly is absent – but this is no assurance that a god will or can come into presence, no claim that we will not decline and flounder. On the contrary, if only a god can save us, is it because this god can or cannot appear? Is everything functioning because god is dead? The last god too? Or because the god is living elsewhere, uprooted and displaced – or at home in its displacement, wandering and on the road? Or is it because we have not prepared properly? And if all we can do is prepare for the god's appearance or absence, can we ever do anything more than prepare, and prepare the preparations, an infinite or impossible preparation for a god that will not come because it cannot come?

Perhaps we cannot respond to these questions – because we cannot be certain whether a god can save us and thus we must prepare, or because the god is dead and cannot save us and we must therefore face the god's absence, the necessity of our decline, the failure of our preparations in thinking and poetizing. So either a god can save us and we better get ready; or a god can save us, but unfortunately there are no gods left so we are fated to flounder, or fortunately with the absence of god we are thrown back upon ourselves, liberated from our fallenness amidst beings – and the uncertainty with which we face the interview's comments may even be matched by the uncertainty with which we face the absent god.

Heidegger does, nevertheless, seem to propose a kind of mediate, if not immediate, response to our godless time of functionalism – not the philosophy that has ceded its place to natural science and cybernetics, not the metaphysical tradition that stretches from Platonism to Nietzsche, and can no longer respond to global technology, but the other thinking, *das andere*

Denken.[9] Yet if everything is functioning via metaphysical distinctions such as theory and practice, the task can be neither to unblock the blockage, unpack the package, destructure the structured, unbuild that which we have built up over 2500 years of philosophy, nor to stand in dialogue with the functioning world – for this merely serves functionalist ends (and fascism, however limited, certainly no less than Americanism or Communism or any other politics or philosophy, as each in its own way no doubt attempts to achieve 'an adequate relationship with the essence of technology')[10] – and presumably, the difference between 'those people' and 'these people' (although it remains to be seen whether such a distinction can or cannot be maintained), between those who achieve an adequate relationship to technology through the other thinking, lies neither in a simple clearing or unblocking of the block, nor in a mere pushing aside of philosophy as metaphysics; but in a kind of thinking and speaking in dialogue with poetry (Hölderlin), for which the Germans are presumed to be specially qualified, thanks to the inner relationship, the *innere Verwandtschaft*, between German and Greek, a relationship that Heidegger takes to be so self-evident that even the French confirm it for him: 'When they begin to think, they speak German, being sure that they could not make it with their own language'[11] – although why they don't go directly to Greek remains at least unclear, especially if Heidegger sees 'grave consequences' with the transformation of Greek into Latin, at least insofar as 'one can translate thinking no more satisfactorily than one can translate poetry'.[12] Thus the other thinking seems to be faced with a three-fold blockage: *verbaut* by the metaphysics of theory and practice, *verlegt* by the functionalism that culminates in American pragmatism, *verwehrt* by translation.

Heidegger therefore insists that the path of thinking has reached the point where silence is required. And in this way, he violates his own proposal: speaking of silence, telling the truth about lying, or being serious about irony. But this violation may be the mark of the other thinking, self-violation, not the moralistic preaching and judgement of others, not the teaching of a pre-ordained harmony or disharmony, not the practical instructions of one who would function in a calculating world of winners and losers, of those for and against, nor thinking the unthought or unthinkable, noticing the unnoticed and unnoticeable, but not-thinking and not-noticing, self-contradiction as the ambiguous truth of silence. Indeed, if everything is functioning in the present age, the introduction of the non-functional serves as sabotage; if everyone is speaking, silence may be the most responsible response – just as the immeasurable resists the will to measure, the impossible disrupts the possible and its preconditions, as the question makes everything questionable, even the question itself, just as uncertainty makes us uncertain even about uncertainty.

6.3

At some point however, the interview is at an end – time is up: the thinker must return to his thought, and Heidegger to his grave. But in the end, something strange occurs: the interviewer and interviewee finally, as in the final book of the *Republic*, turn to the question of art. And the thinker trips. Heidegger slips up. Having claimed that there are no authoritative assertions in thinking, he offers an authoritative assertion: modern art is destructive, or at least 'present-day literature, for example, is predominantly destructive'.[13] And Heidegger knows he has slipped-up (thinking too metaphysically?) – for immediately he recants: 'All right, cross that out.'[14]

But what should we cross out? That which is not crossed out? Or that which is crossed out, such that we cannot even notice that it is crossed out? Or that which only can be noticed once it is crossed out? Or that which cannot even be noticed when crossed out? Should we cross out the assertion that modern art is destructive? Or just the word destructive? Or the modern art? Or perhaps the cross itself? And are we seriously asked to cross out that which is not and cannot be crossed out – or is the demand itself far more its own self-crossing out, the crossing of the cross, x of the x, the x that equals x, sign of the sign that signifies both another and itself, that says: Good, cut it? Or is the demand itself far more in question – so that the inclusion of the exclusion demonstrates the impossibility of exclusion? The deed has been done; it cannot be cut – or at least the certainty of the demand must remain uncertain.

Notes

[15] *The Heidegger Controversy*, MIT, 1993, 91; *Der Spiegel*, Nr. 23/1976, 193; translation modified.

[16] *Spiegel*, 201.

[17] *Spiegel*, 193; translation modified.

[18] *Spiegel*, 198–201.

[19] *IM*, 152; *Spiegel*, 204.

[20] *Spiegel*, 206.

[21] *Spiegel*, 206.

[22] *Spiegel*, 209; *GA* 65, 405–17, 508–9. As Derrida notes: 'The meaning I have attached here to the words "utopia" and "aporia" suggest to me, as I reread this, an ironic and somewhat playful interpretation of a particular statement made by Heidegger in the *Der Spiegel* interview ... How could anyone deny that the name "god to come" just might be suitable for an ultimate form of sovereignty that would reconcile absolute justice with absolute law and thus, like all sovereignty and all law, with absolute force, with an absolute saving power? One will always be able to call "god to come" the improbable institution I just invoked above by

speaking of a "faith in the possibility of this impossible thing" ... Of course, such a fanciful interpretation would have shocked Heidegger. This is certainly not what he "meant".' (*Philosophy in a Time of Terror*, University of Chicago, 2003, 190n14).

23 *Spiegel*, 212.
24 *Spiegel*, 214.
25 *Spiegel*, 217, 25, 116.
26 *Spiegel*, 217. The impossibility of translation however, does not seem to be sufficient for maintaining the priority of German over French, or any other language.
27 *Spiegel*, 209.
28 *Spiegel*, 219.

Post-scriptum

Cross that out. Perhaps Heidegger wasn't being ironic. Perhaps his texts shouldn't be read in this way. Maybe it's just perverse. Seriously.

If the task of this book, however, has been to raise the question of seriousness and the threat of irony, with respect to Heidegger and in defence of philosophy, then perhaps we have been somewhat successful. Or at least, if not, maybe we've managed to do so in such a way that the question has become questionable and the threat threatening. It might be then important to recall the following questions, or threats:

Is it still possible to take seriousness seriously, without laughing? Or does the introduction of irony into philosophy not mean that we begin to question both the serious and the ironic? Do we then become uncertain of this difference? And does this uncertainty not become the truth of irony and seriousness alike? That from which there is no escape, *alētheia*?

Is it then still possible to do phenomenology? Or has the attempt to raise the question of the meaning of being, and time, and unity and aspect, insofar as it remains faithful to an economy of showing, become uncertain about that which doesn't show up? And does the introduction of the sham not threaten the difference between showing and non-showing, as well as the possibility of phenomenology itself?

Is it then still possible to defend philosophy against those scientists or sophists, false-friends or fascists, who would take it over for perhaps less than philosophical purposes? Or can we – and should we philosophers – remain certain of the uncertainty of the totality of what is? Must we then perhaps not become uncertain of this totality, this question, of our ability, even of uncertainty itself? Will no one keep us from this? Has the matter already been decided – if it could be? Or could we still fail to do it? And might that not be a spectacular failure?

Is it then possible, turning from philosophy to art, to take the work and thought of art seriously? To differentiate the work of art from non-art, representation from non-representation, in order to think the origin of art in *poiēsis* as the happening of truth? Or must we rather go further, and think the origin of *poiēsis* in improvisation?

Is it then possible to think of ourselves, no longer simply as human or *zōon logon echon*, *animal rationale* or *ens finitum*, substance or even subject, but as shepherds of being? Or is the thought that takes us as dwelling in the opening of divine advent, the lighting in which the other comes to presence – is this a *Sackgasse* or *Holzweg*? Then are we not pointed elsewhere, to a way of thinking without being, and a relation to the other that is more intimate than presence? And is our task then no longer to think ourselves as *anthropos* or *Dasein*, but to illuminate us as phos?

Is it then possible, in seeking to differentiate between modern *Gestell* and ancient *poiēsis*, to question what and who is charged with being responsible for technology's essence? Or if technology is essentially ambiguous, can we not disambiguate it, but think that which cannot escape ambiguity? And then might we be in a position to let the question concerning technology react upon the questioning to the point where we may no longer question without participating in that which we question, without translating everything into the language of the question? So then – going further – would technology's ambiguity not show itself as only possible through uncertainty? Not the certainty of physics or metaphysics with respect to uncertainty – itself a dangerous oversimplification – but the uncertainty of uncertainty? Not knowing that we know or do not know – but not knowing? Or is this just another *technē* of a philosophical *technitās*?

Indeed, is it possible to take philosophy seriously after all these questions? Because of these questions? Or as them?

All right. Cross that out. All the questions. We can't be serious. Or so they say, mockingly. But of course: 'Anyone who gives his life to philosophy is open to such mockery.'[1]

Notes

[1]   Plato, *Thea.*, *Collected Dialogues of Plato*, Princeton University, 1961, 174a; *FD*, 2.

Bibliography

Adorno, T., 'Letter', *Diskus'*, University of Frankfurt student newspaper, January 1963.

Aristotle, *The Basic Works of Aristotle*, New York: Random House, 1941.

Aubenque, P., *Le problème de l'être chez Aristote*, Paris: PUF, 1966.

Augustine, St., *Confessions*, New York: Image Books, 1960.

Beaufret, J., *Questions III et IV*, Paris: Gallimard, 1976.

Benardete, S., *The Being of the Beautiful*, Chicago: University of Chicago, 1984.

Benardete, S., 'Plato *Sophist* 223b1-7', *Phronesis*, 1960.

Benardete, S., *Socrates' Second Sailing*, Chicago: University of Chicago, 1989.

Benjamin, W., *Gesammelte Schriften*, Frankfurt: Suhrkamp, 1972.

Bernasconi, R., 'Habermas and Arendt on the Philosopher's "Error"', *Graduate Faculty Philosophy Journal*, 1991.

Bernasconi, R., *The Question of Language in Heidegger's History of Being*, Atlantic Highlands: Humanities Press, 1985.

Bigelow, P., *The Conning, the Cunning of Being*, Tallahassee: Florida State University Press, 1990.

Bohrer, K. H., *Sprachen der Ironie, Sprachen des Ernstes*, Frankfurt: Suhrkamp, 2000.

Brentano, F., *Von der Mannigfachen Bedeutung des Seienden nach Aristotles* (1862), Hildesheim: G. Olms, 1960.

Brogan, W., *Heidegger and Aristotle*, New York: SUNY, 2005.

Capelle, P., *Philosophie et théologie dans la pensée de Martin Heidegger*, Paris: Editions du Cerf, 1998.

Caputo, A., *Vent'anni di Recezione Heideggerianna (1979–1999)*, Milano: FrancoAngeli, 2001.

Casper, B., 'Martin Heidegger und die theologische Fakultät Freiburg 1909–1923', *Freiburger Diözesan-Archiv*, 1980.

Celan, P., *Gesammelte Werke*, Frankfurt: Suhrkamp, 1983.

Courtine, J.-F., *Heidegger et la phénoménologie*, Paris: Vrin, 1990.

Danto, A., *After the End of Art*, Princeton: Princeton University, 1997.

Danto, A. 'The Artworld', *Journal of Philosophy*, 1964.

Davis, M., *The Autobiography of Philosophy*, Lanham: Rowman and Littlefield, 1999.

Davis, M., *The Poetry of Philosophy: On Aristotle's Poetics*, South Bend: St. Augustine's Press, 1999.

Denker, A., *Historical Dictionary of Heidegger's Philosophy*, Lanham: Scarecrow Press, 2000.

Derrida, J., *De l'esprit: Heidegger et la question*, Paris: Galilée, 1987.

Derrida, J., 'How to Avoid Speaking', *Languages of the Unsayable*, New York: Columbia University Press, 1989.

Derrida, J., *La dissémination*, Paris: Seuil, 1972.

Derrida, J., *La vérité en peinture*, Paris: Flammerion, 1978.

Derrida, J., 'Le temps des adieux: Heidegger (lu par) Hegel (lu par) Malabou', *Revue Philosophique*, 1998.

Derrida, J., *Philosophy in a Time of Terror*, Chicago: University of Chicago, 2003.

Derrida, J., *Psyché*, Paris: Galilée, 1987.

Derrida, J., *Voyous: Deux essais sur la raison*, Paris: Galilée, 2003.

Descartes, R., *Ouvres et lettres*, Paris: Gallimard, 1953.

Dondeyne, A., 'La différence ontologique chez M. Heidegger', *Revue Philosophique de Louvain*, 1958.

Edwards, P., *Heidegger on Death*, La Salle: The Monist, 1979.

Einstein, A., *Über die spezielle und die allgemeine Relativitätstheorie (1917)*, Braunschweig/Wiesbaden: Vieweg, 1988.

Farías, V., *Heidegger and Nazism*, Philadelphia: Temple University, 1989.

Franzen, W., *Martin Heidegger*, Stuttgart: Metzler, 1976.

Gadamer, H.-G., 'Martin Heidegger's One Path', *Reading Heidegger from the Start*, New York: SUNY Press, 1994.

Goethe, J. W. von, *Faust*, Frankfurt: Suhrkamp, 2007.

Guignon, C. (ed.), *The Cambridge Companion to Heidegger*, Cambridge: Cambridge University Press, 1993.

Haar, M. (ed.), *Martin Heidegger*, Paris: L'Herne, 1983.

Haas, A., *Hegel and the Problem of Multiplity*, Evanston: Northwestern University, 2000.

Heelen, P., *Quantum Mechanics and Objectivity*, The Hague: Nijhoff, 1965.

Hegel, G. W. F., *Gesammelte Werke*, Hamburg: Meiner, 1968ff.

Hegel, G. W. F., *Science of Logic*, Atlantic Highlands: Humanities Press, 1969.

Hegel, G. W. F., *Werke in Zwanzig Bänden*, Frankfurt: Suhrkamp, 1986.

Heidegger, M., *Basic Writings*, New York: Harper & Row, 1977.

Heidegger, M., '*Die Selbstbehauptung der deutschen Universität*', Frankfurt: Klostermann, 1983.

Heidegger, M., *Zollikoner Seminare*, Frankfurt: Klostermann, 1987.

Heidegger, M., *Der Begriff der Zeit: Vortrag vor der Marburger Theologenschaft Juli 1924*, Tübingen: Niemeyer, 1989.

Heidegger, M., *Der Ursprung des Kunstwerkes*, Stuttgart: Reclam, 1960.

Heidegger, M., *Die Frage nach dem Ding*, Tübingen: Niemeyer, 1962.

Heidegger, M., *Die Grundprobleme der Phänomenologie*, Frankfurt: Klostermann, 1975.

Heidegger, M., *Die Selbstbehauptung der deutschen Universität und Das Rektorat 1933/34*, Frankfurt: Klostermann, 1983.

Heidegger, M., *Die Technik und die Kehre*, Pfullingen: Neske, 1991.

Heidegger, M., *Einführung in die Metaphysik*, Tübingen: Niemeyer, 1987.

Heidegger, M., 'Europa und die deutsche Philosophie', *Europa und die Philosophie*, Frankfurt: Klostermann, 1993.

Heidegger, M., *Gelassenheit*, Pfullingen: Neske, 1959.

Heidegger, M., *Gesamtausgabe*, Frankfurt: Klostermann, 1978ff.

Heidegger, M., *Hegels Phänomenologie des Geistes*, Frankfurt: Klostermann, 1980.

Heidegger, M. and Fink, E., *Heraclit*, Frankfurt: Klostermann, 1970.

Heidegger, M., *Holzwege*, Frankfurt: Klostermann, 1950.

Heidegger, M., *Identität und Differenz*, Pfullingen: Neske, 1961.

Heidegger, M., *Metaphysische Anfangsgründe der Logik im Ausgang von Leibniz*, Frankfurt: Klostermann, 1978.

Heidegger, M., 'Nur noch ein Gott kann uns retten', *Spiegel*, Nr. 23/1976.

Heidegger, M., *Prolegomena zur Geschichte des Zeitbegriffs*, Frankfurt: Klostermann, 1979.

Heidegger, M., *Questions IV*, translated and assembled by J. Beaufret, F. Fédier, J., Gallimard, 1966.

Hervier, J. Lauxerois, R. Munier, A. Préau and C. Roëls, Paris: Gallimard, 1976.

Heidegger, M., *Sein und Zeit*, Tübingen: Niemeyer, 1993.

Heidegger, M., *Über den Humanismus*, Frankfurt: Klostermann, 1949.

Heidegger, M., *Unterwegs zur Sprache*, Pfullingen: Neske, 1959.

Heidegger, M., *Vorträge und Aufsätze*, Pfullingen: Neske, 1954.

Heidegger, M., *Was Heisst Denken?*, Tübingen: Niemeyer, 1984.

Heidegger, M., *Zur Sache des Denkens*, Tübingen: Niemeyer, 1969.

Heisenberg, W., 'Das Naturbild der heutigen Physik', *Jahrbuch*, Max-Planck-Gesellschaft, 1954.

Heisenberg, W., *Physics and Philosophy*, New York: Harper and Row, 1958.

Hölderlin, F., *Gedichte*, Frankfurt: Insel, 1969.

Homer, *Odyssey*, Books I and II, translated by P. Jones, Warminster: Aris & Phillips, 1991; also translated by R. Fagles, New York: Penguin Books, 1996.

Hume, D., *An Enquiry Concerning Human Understanding*, Buffalo: Prometheus Books, 1988.

Husserl, E., *Essential Husserl*, Bloomington: Indiana University, 1999.

Husserl, E., *Ideen zu einer reinen Phänomenologie und phänomenologischen Philosophie*, Den Haag: Nijhoff, 1976.

Husserl, E., *Die Krisis der europäischen Wissenschaften und die transzendentale Phänomenologie*, Hamburg: Meiner, 1982.

Husserl, E., *Logische Untersuchungen*, Den Haag: Nijhoff, 1984.

Hyppolite, J., *Genèse et structure de la Phénoménologie de l'esprit de Hegel*, Paris: Aubier, 1946.

Hyppolite, J., 'The Structure of Philosophic Language According to the "Preface" to Hegel's *Phenomenology of Mind*', *The Languages of Criticism and the Sciences of Man*, Baltimore: Johns Hopkins, 1970.

Jaeger, W., *Aristoteles: Grundlegung einer Geschichte seiner Entwicklung*, Berlin: Weidmann, 1923.

Janicaud, D., *Heidegger en France*, Paris: Albin Michel, 2001.

Kahn, C., *The Art and Thought of Heraclitus*, Cambridge: Cambridge University, 1979.

Kant, I., *Kritik der reinen Vernunft* (1781/87), Hamburg: Meiner, 1990.

Kant, I., *Opus postumum*, Cambridge: Cambridge University, 1993.

Kant, I., *Werke*, Frankfurt: Suhrkamp, 1958.

King, M., *A Guide to Heidegger's* Being and Time, New York: SUNY, 2001.

Kirk, G. S., Raven, J. E. and Schofield, M., *The Presocratic Philosophers*, Cambridge: Cambridge University, 1991.

Kisiel, T., *The Genesis of Heidegger's Being and Time*, Berkeley: University of California Press, 1995.

Lang, B., *Heidegger's Silence*, Ithaca: Cornell University, 1996.

Laruelle, F., *Nietzsche contre Heidegger*, Paris: Payot, 1977.

Levinas, E., *Totalité et Infini*, The Hague: Nijhoff, 1971.

Levinas, E., *De L'Évasion*, Paris: Fata Morgana, 1982.

Löwith, K., *Nietzsche's Philosophy of the Eternal Recurrence of the Same*, Berkeley: University of California, 1977.

Löwith, K., *Von Hegel zu Nietzsche*, Hamberg: Meiner, 1986.

Malabou, C., *L'avenir de Hegel: Plasticité, Temporalité, Dialectique*, Paris: Vrin, 1996.

Mehring, R., *Heideggers Überlieferungsgeschick. Eine dyonisische Inszenierung*, Würzburg: Königshausen & Neumann, 1992.

Nietzsche, F., *Kritische Gesamtausgabe*, Berlin: de Gruyter, 1967ff.

Nordquist, J. (ed.), *Martin Heidegger: A Bibliography*, Santa Cruz: Reference and Research Services, 1990.

Owens, J., *The Doctrine of Being in the Aristotlean Metaphysics*, Toronto: Pontifical Institute of Mediaeval Studies, 1951.

Philipse, H., *Heidegger's Philosophy of Being*, Princeton: Princeton University, 1998.

Plato, *The Collected Dialogues of Plato*, Princeton: Princeton University, 1961.

Richardson W. J., *Heidegger: Through Phenomenology to Thought*, The Hague: Nijhoff, 1974.

Rorty, R., 'Taking Philosophy Seriously', *New Republic*, 1988.

Rosen, S., *Plato's Sophist*, New Haven: Yale University, 1983.

Rosen, S., *The Mask of Enlightenment*, Cambridge: Cambridge University, 1995.

Rosen, S., *The Question of Being*, New Haven, Yale University, 1993.

Sallis, J. (ed.), *Reading Heidegger*, Bloomington: Indiana University, 1993.

Sartre, J.-P., *L'Existentialisme est un humanisme*, Paris: Gallimard, 1996.

Sass, H.-M., *Martin Heidegger: Bibliography and Glossary*, Bowling Green, Ohio: Bowling Green State University, 1982.

Schapiro, M., 'A Note on Heidegger and van Gogh', *Theory and Philosophy of Art*, New York: Braziller, 1994.

Schleiermacher, F., *Platons Werke*, Berlin: Reimer, 1857.

Schleiermacher, F., *Sämtliche Werke*, Hamburg: Meiner, 1958.

Schmitt, G., *The Concept of Being in Hegel and Heidegger*, Bonn: Bouvier, 1977.

Schürmann, R., *Le Principe d'anarchie: Heidegger et la question de l'agir*, Paris: Seuil, 1982.

Scully, S., 'Interpretive Essay', *Plato's Phaedrus*, Newburyport: Focus Publishing, 2003.

Sheehan, T., 'Heidegger's Lehrjahre', *The Collegium Phaenomenologicum: The first ten years*, Dordrecht: Kluwer, 1988.

Strauss, L., *The City and Man*, Chicago: University of Chicago, 1964.

Strauss, L., *Persecution and the Art of Writing*, Chicago: University of Chicago, 1952.

Taminiaux, J., *Heidegger and the Project of Fundamental Ontology*, New York: SUNY, 1991.

Taminiaux, J., 'The Origin of "The Origin of the Work of Art"', *Reading Heidegger*, Bloomington: Indiana University, 1993.

Thomä, D., *Die Zeit des Selbst und die Zeit danach. Zur Kritik der Textgeschichte Martin Heideggers*, Frankfurt: Suhrkamp, 1990.

Windelband, W., *Lehrbuch der Geschichte der Philosophie* (1892), Tübingen: J.D.B. Mohr (Paul Siebeck), 1993.

Young, J., *Heidegger, Philosophy, Nazism*, Cambridge: Cambridge University, 1997.

Index

Absolute, the 134
Absolute Knowing 125
Absolute Spirit 125
Absolute Subject, Spirit is the 125
acting/action 148–9
action, essence of 106, 107, 109
adventure, element of 106
aesthetics 93–4
  overcoming the concept of 93
Agathon 146, 154
Alcibiades 154, 155
ambiguity 135, 136, 144, 145, 147,
  168
Americanism 162
angst 85
anthropology 135
Apollodorus 146
appearance 31–3, 35, 114–15, 130
  appearance of an 114
  symptoms of illness as 31–2
architecture 82–6, 149
Aristodemus 146
Aristotle 20, 22, 57, 95, 126, 134,
  143, 146, 148, 149, 150, 154
  diaeresis 149–50, 155
  of the soul 149
  discussion of scientific knowledge
    and art in *Nicomachean*
    Ethics 148, 149
art 147, 167
  essentially poetry 91
  great art, what is 81
  modern art 165

  the question of art 165
aspect 27–9
authenticity/inauthenticity 37, 38,
  39, 40, 41, 59
  sham of authenticity 39, 40, 41

Baumgarten 94
Beaufret, Jean 105, 107, 118, 130,
  136
  his letter 105
being 36, 37, 38–9, 129–30, 131,
  135
  arrival of, the 129, 136, 142
  essence of 115, 131–2
  is self-giving 130
  gift of, the 130
  relation of being to humans 107
  shepherds of being 130, 133, 168
  social-historical 134
  to experience being 126
  see also meaning of being
being of beings 74, 113
  becoming of beings 142, 143
Benjamin 2
Bohr's Hume 150
Bohrer, Karl Heinz 2

Cartesian doubt 57
causality, essence of 143
cave, allegory of the *see under* Letter
  on Humanism
Celan 47
Christian thought 119

Communism 162
consciousness 125
  and nature 125
cybernetics 163

death 59, 112, 113, 128
Deductions, A and B 25–6
Democracy 162
Descartes 142
diaeresis, the 8, 10, 19, 149–50
  mechanical 73
Diotima 147, 148
  comment to Socrates 146
divinity, our 135

ecstatic existence 125
education 114
Einstein 152
Eryximachus 154
essence of art 70, 73, 82, 86
essence of truth 88, 89–90, 116, 117
ethics 133
  essence of, the 133
  the question of 133
existentia 121, 123
experience 125, 126–9
  and art 131
  and consciousness 125–6
  and thinking 126
  meaning of, the 125
  metaphysical conception of 125
  metaphysics of 129
  pure presentation of thinking,
    the 126
  to experience being 126
  truth of, the 126
experience, of other beings 121
experience of being 125
experience of experience 129
experience of metaphysics 129
experience of thinking 125, 127–9

face, the 135
formal indication *see* indication

functionalism 163, 164
  the functioning world 164

Gadamer, H.-G. 93, 94
  Introduction to Reclam edition
    of 'The Origin of the Work of
    Art' 93
Gauguin 77, 78
German university, the 48–66
  grounding in science 53
giving 130
  meaning of 130
Glaucon 109, 112, 115, 116
God 116
  appearance or absence of 163
  children of 134
Gödel 132
Good, essence of the idea of
    the 115–16
  and truth 116

Hegel 2, 57, 94, 125–6
  'Concept of Experience' 128
  insistence on two-sided
    thought 125
Heidegger
  abandonment of *Being and
    Time* 15
  activities during the Third
    Reich 159, 160
  diaeresis 149–50
  fascism 47
  his politics 47
  Introduction to Metaphysics 121,
    161
  Nazism 47
  Rector's Address/Rektoratsrede
    47–50, 56–60, 120
  seriousness of, the 2, 3, 167
  Spiegel interview 159–63, 165
Heisenberg 146, 150, 151, 152,
    154, 155
Heraclitus 57, 117, 126, 128, 132,
    133, 134, 135

historical inquiry 21
Hölderlin 104, 144, 150, 164
Holocaust, the 50, 162
Homer 112, 135
human being 119–20, 134–5
  metaphysical conception of,
    the 134
  nature of, the 134
  the essence of 119, 122, 134
  the truth of 135
human reason 23, 29, 150
humanism 105, 108, 117–21, 124,
    132, 133
  as metaphysics 118
  metaphysical 120
  restoring meaning to 105–6
  sense of 133
  the thinking of 107
humanitas of the human, the 122
humans, differentiation from
    animals, plants, rocks 121–3
Hume 127, 150
Husserl 30, 39, 52
Hyppolite 3

identity 136
imagination 25–7
improvisation 95, 96, 167
  auto-improvisation 96
  Odysseus' raft 96
  self-improvisation 96
  what is improvisation 96
inauthenticity *see* authenticity/
    inauthenticity
indication, formal 33, 34
intuition 23–8

Kant 20, 22, 23, 24, 25, 26, 27, 28,
    29, 31, 35, 94, 119, 134, 150
  and imagination 25
  and limits of knowledge 57
  and mathematics 132
  critical phenomenology 29
  theory of knowledge 24

Keats' 'Ode to a Grecian Urn' 135
knowledge 23, 24, 25

Lambert 132
language 121, 122–3, 135–7, 153
  the essence of 118
leadership 21
Letter on Humanism 103, 104,
    105, 106, 108, 109, 117–37
  allegory of the cave, the 109–18
  and Jean Beaufret 105
  three questions 105–6
letting, essence of 107
lighting, the 130–2
love 146, 147

making 143, 147, 148, 149
  and acting 148, 149, 150
Marsyas 154
Marx, humanity and society 134
Marxism 119
meaning of being, the 13–21, 30–1,
    36, 39, 41, 115, 119, 130, 131,
    132, 167
  mystery of being 118–19
meaning of meaning, the 14, 15,
    132
metaphysical humanism 120
metaphysical thinking, essence
    of 121
metaphysics 22, 26, 104, 105, 109,
    117–25, 129, 130–1, 132
  and essentialism 122
  and thought, difference
    between 133
  destruction of metaphysics 133
  destructuring of
    metaphysics 104, 108
  Heidegger's 118
  essence of 104
  experience of 129
  language of 104
  metaphysical tradition, the 163
  of experience 129

metaphysics, *cont.*
  of nature 150
  of theory and practice 164
  reversal of, the 124–5
  Western metaphysics 115–16

National Socialism 161, 162, 163
nationalism 56
natural science 163
nature 142, 143, 144, 150
  technology's threat to 144
  the metaphysics of 150
  two ways of responding to 144
Nietzsche 2, 54, 55, 56, 57, 95, 117,
    122, 131, 163
  impossibility of totality 56
  Nietzsche's God 22
  overcoming of metaphysics 55,
    56
nothing 82–7, 120, 132
  essence of 86

ontology
  and ethics 133
  and the meaning of being 17
  destructuring of 29, 30
  destructuring the history of
    21–2
  fundamental ontology 18, 19,
    22, 26, 32, 35, 36, 121, 122,
    133
  supplemented by ethics 106
  the being of 133
origin of poetry, the 94, 95
origin of work of art 70, 71, 90–5,
    167
  is improvisation 95
Oracle at Delphi, the 31, 33
Other, the 134
otherness 9, 10

Parmenides 57
Pausanias 154
phainomenon 24, 28, 30

phenomena/phenomenon 30–6,
    113, 152, 153
phenomenology 19, 20, 28, 29, 30,
    31, 34, 35, 36, 113, 151, 153,
    154, 167
  empirical 32
phosology 135
Planck's constant 152
Plato 2, 5, 7, 48, 105, 108, 109,
    112–18, 146, 148, 149, 154
  bridge between metaphysics and
    humanism 117–18
  concept of truth 117
    remains true to
      metaphysics 117
  doctrine of truth 113, 114,
    115–17
  Republic 106, 114, 165
  Socratic irony 155
  Sophist 7, 41
  Symposium 146, 147, 148, 154
Platonism 119, 122, 163
Platons Lehre von der Wahrheit
    116–17
poetising 162, 163
poetry 135, 146, 147, 148, 164
  the origin of 94, 95
presence 16, 29, 130, 168
  is meaning of being 115
presentation 76, 129
Protagoras 118, 163

quantum of action 152
quantum theory 150, 151–2
  principle of
    complementarity 153
question, uncertainty of the
    57–8
questioning, the technique of 154

reason 23
relativity theory 150
representation 23, 24, 28, 33, 76,
    111, 115, 117, 129, 167

representative and non-
representative art, difference
between 86–7
resoluteness, uncertainty of 58–60
reversal 124–5
Rhine, the 144, 149, 150, 153, 154
riddle of art, the 71, 80, 93, 94
riddle of Man 123
riddle of the origin of aesthetics 94
riddle of the origin of art, the 80–1

St Augustine 15
Sartre 117
Sartrean existentialism 134
Schapiro, Meyer 77, 78, 79
schema-image, Heidegger's 27
Schiller 104
Schlegel 2
science 53, 54, 55
System of 126
the essence of 53, 54, 56, 58
self-deception 70, 81
shepherds of being *see under* being
shoes, the 74–81
of peasant or farmer 74
van Gogh's painting of
shoes 74–7, 79, 80
Heidegger's reference to de la
Faille's no. 255 77
piece from a self-portrait 77
riddle of 79
self-portrait of the painter 79
sight/seeing 109, 110, 111, 112,
113, 115, 131
metaphor of Western
metaphysics and
phenomenology 115
silence 164
Socrates 7, 57, 109, 110, 111, 112,
113, 146, 154, 155
and sophistry 12
Republic, the 146
sophist, the 7, 8, 9, 10, 11, 12, 19
sophistry 7

Sophocles 135
soul, the 117, 124, 148, 149
speed of light 152
Spiegel interview *see under*
Heidegger
Spinoza 57
Spirit 125–6
standing our ground, uncertainty
of 60
subject and object, unity of 125
sun, the 111–15
symptoms of illness as
appearances 31–2
System of Science 126

technology 142–55, 162, 164, 168
ambiguous essence, its 145
differentiating the modern from
the ancient 142
essence of, the 142, 144, 146,
150–1, 153, 154, 155, 156,
162, 164, 167
global technology 161, 162, 163
modern technology 142, 143,
144, 156, 162
multiplicity of, the 154
our relation to 151
technological enframing 150
threat to nature 144
truth of, the 148
temple at Paestum, the 81–7
four-folds, the 87, 88, 89
'The Origin of the Work of
Art' 70–7, 78–83, 86, 88–94
'The Question Concerning
Technology' 142, 145, 146,
147, 150, 154
'The Self-Assertion of the German
University' 47, 52, 62, 65, 66
thing, a/the 71, 72, 73, 76, 87
equipment- and artwork-things,
division between 73
the being of a thing 72
what is a thing 71

thinking 127, 128, 129, 131, 132, 136, 151, 162, 163
  and experience 126
  experience of, the 127, 128
  the other thinking 163–4
thought 118, 119–20, 128, 131, 132, 135, 136, 153
  and metaphysics, difference between 132
  experience of 127
   testimony and reality, connection between 127
  testimony of the thinker 127
throwness 133
  the throw of being 133
time 22, 26–8, 29
  and being 15–16, 29
  homogeneity of 27
  meaning of 30, 167
totalitarianism 55
totality, uncertainty of 57
totality of beings, the 54, 55, 56, 119
transcendence 23, 26
transcendens 16–17, 130

transcendental imagination 25, 26, 27
transcendental philosophy 23
translation 72, 164
truth, the 'abyssal middle' 89
truth, the becoming of 91
truth and being 91
truth as un-truth 91
truth of a work of art, the 81
truth of beings/being, the 94, 105, 106, 119, 120, 130–1, 132
truth of truth 88, 89, 90, 147

uncertainty 57–62, 164, 167, 168
  of uncertainty 61, 168
Uncertainty Principle, the 150

von Möllendorf, Wilhelm 48–9

wisdom 146
  lover of 146, 147
  practical wisdom 149

Zarathustra's teaching 55
Zeno's paradox 131